J . J .

ESSAYS IN CANON LAW

ESSAYS
IN
CANON LAW

A Study of the Law of the Church in Wales

Edited by

NORMAN DOE

CARDIFF
UNIVERSITY OF WALES PRESS
1992

British Library Cataloguing in Publication Data

A catalogue record for this book is available from the British Library.

ISBN 0-7083-1147-4

Typeset by DSC Corporation Ltd., Falmouth, Cornwall
Printed by Hartnolls Ltd., Bodmin, Cornwall

To mark the centenary of

Saint Michael's
Theological College
Llandaff

1892–1992

Contents

Foreword

THE REVEREND CANON J. H. L. ROWLANDS, WARDEN OF ST
MICHAEL'S COLLEGE, LLANDAFF

It is a great privilege to write this foreword to *Essays in Canon Law*:
A Study of the Law of the Church in Wales. The centenary of the
College has been marked by many events, and the publication of this
excellent volume of essays edited by Dr Norman Doe only adds to
the dignity of the celebrations. I am delighted to commend this
scholarly yet accessible collection as a rich source for all who wish
to deepen their understanding of systems of canon law, for it is in
this precise medium that so much of the life and thought of the
Church is expressed. Dr Norman Doe is eminently well qualified to
edit the volume, as he is both a trained lawyer and a theologian. I
owe him an immense debt of gratitude for the idea. I believe that all
who read this volume of essays will be convinced of the importance
of canon law not only as an academic subject but also of its relevance
to contemporary society.

The Feast of Saint Mary Magdalene, 1991

Acknowledgements

Editing this series of essays on the canon law of the Church in Wales has been both interesting and pleasurable, due not least to the enthusiasm of all those involved in the book's production. I am most grateful to each of the contributors for being so receptive to the ideas for each essay which I originally suggested to them, for their patience and forbearance with these suggestions, and above all for writing what I hope will prove to be essays useful to the Church in Wales and an appropriate celebration of the centenary of St Michael's College Llandaff. I should also like to express my thanks to the Reverend Canon John Rowlands, Warden of St Michael's, for his keen support of the project, and to Mr Antony R. Mansell, a member of my own church, St Edward's, Roath, Cardiff, for reading through the essays in the early stages, commenting on the text and suggesting improvements from the lay person's perspective and from a practical point of view.

Generous financial help to cover the cost of publication has come from the Isla Johnston Trust, managed by the Representative Body of the Church in Wales, from the Representative Body itself, and (through Mr Richard Morgan) from the Catherine and Lady Grace James Foundation, Aberystwyth. To these bodies we are most grateful, as we are for the advance purchases of the subscribers listed at the end of the volume, and for the individual gifts towards the cost of publication of Sir Cennydd Traherne, His Honour Judge Bruce Griffiths, His Honour Judge Norman Francis, the Reverend Lindsey Ford, and Mr Michael Preece. Thanks are also due to Mr John Rees, Bursar at St Michael's, for managing the contributions, and to the staff of the University of Wales Press for their assistance, hard work, patience with the typescript, and good cheer: most especially, Mr John Rhys, former Director, with whom I first aired the idea for the book, his successor Mr Ned Thomas, Mrs Susan Jenkins, Senior Editor, Mr Richard Houdmont, Commercial Manager, Ms Liz Powell, Editor, and the external reader. Finally, I thank my family and friends for their encouragement and support throughout.

Norman Doe
Cardiff, 2 April 1992

Notes on Contributors

ROGER LEE BROWN is Vicar of Tongwynlais and an Examining Chaplain to the Bishop of Llandaff. His original area of research was clandestine marriage, for which he was awarded the MA degree of the University of London, but subsequently he has become involved in the history of the nineteenth-century Church in Wales. A joint editor of the *Journal of Welsh Ecclesiastical History,* and convenor of a working party on the nature and incidents of establishment for the Ecclesiastical Law Society, he has contributed papers to a number of journals and symposia and is author of *The Welsh Evangelicals* (1986).

ROY T. DAVIES, educated at Llanelli Boys' Grammar School and St David's College, Lampeter (BA), was a Meyricke Graduate Scholar at Jesus College, Oxford, where he obtained a B.Litt. for a thesis on medieval Welsh religious poetry. After training at St Stephen's House, Oxford, and ordination in 1959 he served in the Diocese of St David's (where he was Chaplain to Anglican students at UWC Aberystwyth), later becoming Secretary of the Church in Wales Provincial Council for Mission and Unity and of the Advisory Commission on Church and Society. He has represented the Church in Wales at the World Council of Churches Assembly at Nairobi (1975) and at several international Anglican gatherings. He became Vicar at St David's, Carmarthen in 1979, Archdeacon of Carmarthen in 1982, Clerical Secretary of the Governing Body in 1983, and Bishop of Llandaff in 1985.

NORMAN DOE was educated at the Rhondda County Grammar School for Boys, Porth, Howardian High School, Cardiff, University College, Cardiff, and Magdalene College, Cambridge. He has an LL. M. and M.Th. (studied through St Michael's College, Llandaff) of the University of Wales, is a barrister of the Middle Temple, London, and has a Ph. D. of the University of Cambridge. After tutoring part-time at Cambridge, he lectured at the University of Essex, and was a visiting lecturer at the University of Nantes in 1990. He has published articles in constitutional law and legal history: his book, *Fundamental Authority in Late Medieval English Law,* was published in 1990. He is now Course Director for the LL. M. in Canon Law at the Cardiff Law School.

ARTHUR JOHN EDWARDS was educated at Pont-y-waun Grammar School, Rhisga, London University, where he obtained a BA in History and M.Phil. (for a work on the administration of Archbishop Cranmer), and St Michael's College, Llandaff. Ordained deacon (1968) and priest (1969) in the Diocese of Monmouth, he has been Chaplain at St Woolos Cathedral (1968–71), Vicar of Llantarnam, Cwmbrân (1971–4), Chaplain and Head of RE at the Bishop of Llandaff High School, Cardiff (1974–8), Vicar of Griffithstown (1978–86), and Rector of Cwmbrân and Diocesan Director of Education since 1986. An Honorary Canon in 1988, Arthur Edwards was made a Canon of Monmouth in 1991. His publications include biographies of Herefordshire MPs in *History of Parliament, 1485–1558,* edited by S.T. Bindoff, *Archbishop Green* (1986), and 'God and Caesar' in *Living Authority,* edited by A.R. Willie (1990).

JEFFREY GAINER was born at Blaenllechau in the Rhondda and educated at Bablake School, Coventry, and Jesus College, Oxford, where he took degrees in Modern History and Theology. Training at Wycliffe Hall, Oxford, he was made deacon in 1977 and has served as assistant curate at Baglan, Vicar of Cwm-bach (1981–5) and Vicar of Tonyrefail. Since 1987 he has been Director of Pastoral Studies and New Testament Studies at St Michael's College, Llandaff. Jeffrey Gainer has written a short history of St Mary Magdalene's Church, Cwm-bach, and an article on Welsh identity for *Discovering Welshness,* edited by O. Davies.

JOHN A. GRIFFITHS, OGS, B.Sc. (Wales), M.Sc. (South Africa), C.Psychol., AFBPs.S, was trained at St Michael's College, Llandaff, and is currently assistant curate in the parish of Neath with Llantwit in the Diocese of Llandaff. Previously, he was Clinical Psychologist with the British Steel Corporation, with the South Glamorgan Health Authority, and lecturer in psychiatry at the Universities of Natal, Capetown and Zimbabwe. His research interests and publications have been principally in the areas of transcultural psychiatry and family therapy, and more recently in issues relating to sacramental theology.

DAVID LAMBERT, LL.B. (Wales), Solicitor and Notary Public, is Legal Adviser at the Welsh Office, Registrar of the Diocese of Llandaff, and Deputy Chapter Clerk, Llandaff Cathedral. David Lambert is a tutor in Constitutional and Administrative Law at the Law School, University of Wales College of Cardiff, and is a consultant on the *Encyclopedia of Education Law*.

ANTONY T. LEWIS was educated at Eton College and the University of Wales. He is a barrister, holds the degree of LL. M., and was formerly a lecturer at University College, Cardiff (1977–89). Antony Lewis is a member of the Representative and Governing Bodies of the Church in Wales, and chairman of the Board of Mission Sector for Ecumenical Affairs. Also, he is co-director of The Skreen, a retreat and study centre, and chairman of the Powys Family Health Services Authority.

ENID PIERCE ROBERTS, MA, D.Litt., was Senior Lecturer in Welsh Language and Literature, University College of North Wales, Bangor, and retired in 1978. She has published (mostly in Welsh) books, booklets and numerous articles on the period of The Poets of the Nobility (*c*. 1350–*c*. 1650), including an edition of the works of the Elizabethan poet Siôn Tudur (2 volumes), and also on the early Welsh Church and its saints.

THOMAS GLYN WATKIN is a Senior Lecturer at the Cardiff Law School and Legal Assistant to the Governing Body of the Church in Wales. He was educated at the Rhondda County Grammar School for Boys, Porth, and Pembroke College, Oxford. He holds the degrees of BCL and MA from the University of Oxford and is a barrister of the Middle Temple, London. A Visiting Professor of English Law at the University of Parma, Italy, Thomas Watkin's publications include *The Nature of Law* (1980) and *Legal Record and Historical Reality* (1989), together with numerous articles on legal history, trusts and Roman Law.

Table of Biblical References

Table of Church in Wales Rules

References are to the two Volumes of the present *Constitution of the Church in Wales.*

Volume I (references to Chapters and their Sections):

Table of Church of England Canons and Measures

Canons Ecclesiastical, 1603:		Canons Ecclesiastical, 1964–70:	
9	128 n.50	A3	126 n.44
10	128 n.50	A4	126 n.44
11	128 n.50	A5	126 n.44
27	128 n.50	B1(d)	126 n.45
30	120	B2	126 n.45
60	129 n.54	B3	126 n.45
95	8	B15A	129

Measures:

Benefices (Exercise of Rights of Presentation) Measure 1931   11 n.14
Church of England (Worship and Doctrine) Measure 1974   149 n.56
Clergy (Ordination and Miscellaneous Provisions) Measure 1964   149 n.56
Clergy (Ordination) Measure 1990   149 n.56
Ecclesiastical Jurisdiction Measure (No.1) 1963   187 n.62
Ecclesiastical Jurisdiction (Amendment) Measure (No.2) 1974   187 n.62
Pastoral Measure (No.1) 1968   88 n.48
Pastoral Measure (No.1) 1983   88 n.48
Sharing of Church Buildings Measure (No.2) 1970   88 n.48
Synodical Government Measure (No.2) 1969   187 n.62

Table of Canons from the Roman Catholic Code of Canon Law

Table of Statutes

Table of Cases

Editor's Introduction

NORMAN DOE

The role of canon law in the life of the Church has proved frequently to be something of a problematic subject. The controversy has centred around the simple idea that, in the life of a body governed by the Holy Spirit and whose members live under grace, there is no real place for law. However, in recent years there has been a renewal of interest in canon law. The Code of Canon Law of the Roman Catholic Church was revised in 1983, and appears now for the first time as an accessible document, having been translated into English. In the Church of England the Ecclesiastical Law Society was formed recently, in 1987, with its own journal and a membership of some four hundred, many of whom are prominent in the life of the Church in Wales. Yet, within the Church in Wales, since the appearance of Archbishop Green's *Setting of the Constitution of the Church in Wales* (1937), canon law and its scholarship have been neglected as subjects otherwise deserving of serious study.

This book is an attempt to contribute to the current and general renaissance of interest in canon law, from a Welsh perspective. As such, it is something of an experiment. The book is the first of its kind, taking the law of the Church in Wales as an example of a system of canon law of a provincial Church within the Anglican Communion. It is an attempt, in part at least, to catch up, so to speak, with other Churches in offering a systematic, but not exhaustive analysis of Welsh canon law. To this end, the book is intended to provide a study of the canon law of the Church in Wales from several stand-points.

First, the book has an historical dimension, with essays and sections of essays devoted to the development of aspects of canon law. The first three essays specifically deal with canon law, and ideas about canon law, by examining problems endemic to the established

Church in Wales, the legal effects of disestablishment and the
contribution to the development of Welsh canon law by Archbishop
Green. Secondly, it is offered as a legal study, a study and explanation
of legal rules, their purpose and justification, and their place within
the context of civil law, which is dealt with in the chapter on the
status of the rules of the Church in Wales. To this end, a general
theme in the book is criticism – the merits of the legal rules of the
Church and their defects and inconsistencies. These themes are
central to the essays on renewal of Welsh canon law, the Welsh
language and canon law and the bishop's *jus liturgicum*.

Thirdly, it has a comparative dimension. It is an attempt to set the
law of the Church in Wales in the context of other systems of canon
law. A feature of the book is the effort made to describe points of
contact with and differences from other systems of canon law,
particularly the law of the Church of England and Roman Catholic
canon law. This is a significant part of the essays on canon law and
forgiveness, canon law and the Church's mission and canon law and
the mentally handicapped.

It is not enough, however, to rely on the influence of external
doctrines or ideas of canon law. It is hoped that this book will convey
to members of the Church the importance of canon law and the need
for an objective analysis of it as a central function of the Church.
Indeed, it is hoped that the discussion will lead to a more general
debate about the place and substance of canon law and to the
development of a specifically Welsh conception of canon law.

In a living and developing society, it is essential to provide
criticism of the Church's law. Canon law as a function of the life of
the Church is not a static thing. The book attempts to treat canon
law as a dynamic function of the Church. Above all, therefore, the
book seeks to view canon law from the perspectives of theology and
pastoral need. For it is only by stressing the theological and pastoral
basis of canon law that its place in the life of the Church can be
understood. In this regard, it hardly needs to be stressed that one of
the fundamental tasks of the canonist is to subject the rules of canon
law to a rigorous examination against the basic Christian theological
doctrines. And it is only by conveying or communicating the theological roots of canon law that it becomes acceptable, and legitimate,
in the minds of the members of the Church, to whom it is directly
addressed.

Indeed, in so far as canon law can be viewed from so many angles,
as an academic discipline the study of canon law is a rich one,

standing, as it does, at the intersection of law, theology and practical church life. This richness and diversity of thought and approach is also something which easily serves to open so many doors to the varied and enormous literature produced by members of other Churches with a strong canonical tradition, not only within the Anglican Communion, but also the Roman Catholic Church and the Orthodox Church. And the fact that so many Churches share a canonical tradition is of considerable importance in the context of common heritages and goals.

The role of canon law in the life of the Church is one of the most convenient ways in which to obtain a glimpse of how the Church sees and organizes itself. The studies in this volume aim toward this. To a greater or lesser extent, each Church has an idea about itself: about its nature, its own identity, about its plan or programme. Each Church has a vision of its contribution to the work of Christ, about its organization, its government and institutional arrangements, about the distribution of responsibilities amongst its members, about its freedom. And this applies as much to the Church in Wales as to any other. When a Church makes an effort to formalize a view about itself, whatever that view may be, this is the canon law of a Church. Canon law is an attempt by the Church to express in a concrete way the Church's view of itself. The canon law is a record, or presentation, of the ideas that a Church has about itself, its work, nature, corporate and individual responsibilities and organization.

Consequently, the canon law is one of the ways in which a Church makes itself visible to society in general and to other Churches. The canon law is, in a sense, a picture painted by a Church of itself. It is one of the means by which a Church communicates its characteristics, qualities and programme to the outside world. It is the product, a record, of the way in which the Church tries to see itself and to manage its life. But it is not only this. A Church must also communicate the theological basis of its canon law. What has been described as a juridical view of scripture has now firmly made its mark in modern theology. God makes demands upon the Church and its members – the demands of the divine law have been revealed and communicated in Christ. The Church identifies those elements of the divine law which it is obliged to obey, and presents those demands for public view – this also is the canon law. The Church ascertains (and there are important questions here for the problem of authority) and accumulates those demands to which it must be obedient if it is to function as Christ intended – the canon law presents those demands in a systematic way and helps to make them immediate for the faithful. For the Church, canon law is a dynamic material or resource.

However, like other institutions within society, the Church has a relationship with the secular State. Thus, the State makes law for Churches: canon law is in part derived from State law – sometimes called the ecclesiastical law. As such, canon law is also the way in which the secular government, the State, sees and treats the Church. In short, canon law is about those rules created for the Church by God, by the Church itself and by the State.

Though the canon law is *descriptive* of the Church's view of itself and its work, the form by which it expresses these ideas is *prescriptive*. Organization is effected by means of rules. Responsibilities are farmed out by rules. Conditions of membership are expressed in terms of rules. The legitimate use and administration of the sacraments are expressed by rules. The powers of those who have legislative or executive power in the Church are distributed by means of rules. Relationships between church institutions are fixed and regulated by rules. In point of fact, there are countless aspects of church life, and the life of individual members, that are directly affected by canon law – institutional, sacramental, pastoral, liturgical and doctrinal – from rights of admission to the sacraments to voting in parochial church councils.

Accordingly, a method by which the Church asserts its ideas about itself is juridical in form – the Church has chosen for itself rules as one way of organizing its life and effecting its programme in society as the body of Christ. The expression of the Church's ideas of itself and its work in a legal framework, the use of rules to effect organization – that is all that canon law is. And when members of the Church do things – preach the Word, proclaim or read the Word, organize church finances – it is the canon law which authorizes and guides in these things.

The use of rules by the Church to express and organize ideas about itself is merely an attempt to present and define its programme and self-view as precisely and clearly as possible. The effect of this is that not only do members function, in discharge of their responsibilities, with at least some degree of certainty, but the Church is made visible to the outside world. Furthermore, each Church is enabled, by looking to the canon law of other Churches, to identify the nature of that other Church and the ideas that it holds about itself. This is why an understanding of systems of canon law is so important for ecumenical purposes. It is, in part at least, by understanding and respecting, reconciling and trying to synthesize dissonant systems of canon law, or their elements, that unity between Churches might be realized. Churches are kept apart by conflict, essentially, between views of themselves as expressed in their systems of canon law.

Of course, we must accept the point that, by explaining canon law as a method by which the Church expresses its ideas about itself, there is great difficulty in determining or identifying precisely the mind of the Church. This may be, after all, in virtue of the diversity of opinions held by members of Churches, nothing more than a fiction. But it is important and practical to concede this. We can only say that canon law expresses the mind of a Church in terms simply of official statements (contained in canon law) by its institutions (themselves creatures of the canon law). It is only when these institutions, which create canon law, are in some sense representative of the general membership of a Church, the faithful, that any rule created by the Church can be said to express the mind of the Church. Nevertheless, in the following chapters, it is hoped that at least some light will be shed on the way the Church in Wales organizes aspects of its life.

It must be emphasized, finally, that the views expressed on the materials examined in the chapters are personal to each writer (and some of the writers differ considerably in emphasis and argument) – they do not represent the official teaching of the Church in Wales.

1

Pastoral Problems and Legal Solutions in the Established Church in Wales

REVEREND ROGER L. BROWN

Fundamental to canon law is the proposition that the law of the Church must be sensitive to the needs of the members of the Church. One of the difficulties besetting the Welsh Church before disestablishment was its regulation by an ecclesiastical law which was not the direct creation of people in Wales whom it affected immediately. Many aspects of the ecclesiastical law which applied in Wales were out of touch with the needs of the Church's members in Wales. It was felt by many Welsh people at the time that the ecclesiastical law was created by those not directly familiar with the real problems and issues of the Church of England in Wales. The problem of patronage is a particularly vivid example – the appointment of clerics to Welsh-speaking parishes whose knowledge of Welsh was either non–existent or so rudimentary that it was worthless for all practical purposes. When Edward Copleston, Bishop of Llandaff, said in 1836, '[t]he patron is at fault who makes such a nomination, the clergyman is at fault who accepts it. The diocesan is at fault who knowingly permits the abuse', he expressed his feelings on a most difficult and emotive problem.[1] It is proposed here to sketch its perception by the established Church as a legal problem, and to describe the difficulties experienced in trying to resolve what was a crucial pastoral problem – that of effective communication between pastor and the faithful – by means of law. The following essay is

1 E. Copleston, *A Charge Delivered to the Clergy of the Diocese of Llandaff* (1836), 19.

a study in the need for the Church, in the creation of law, to be
sensitive to the claims of pastoral need.[2]

Welsh Patronage in a Legal Context: General Principles

The appointment of non-Welsh-speaking English incumbents to
Welsh-speaking parishes was bitterly resented, causing great offence
and the withdrawal of many from the Church into dissenting congregations. From an early stage, this essentially pastoral problem was
set conceptually within a legal framework. There were, it seemed,
general legal principles against these appointments. By Article 24 of
the Thirty-nine Articles it was repugnant to the Word of God and
the custom of the primitive Church that public prayer and the
sacraments should be conducted in language not understood by the
people. But this principle was rarely invoked.[3] An English incumbent
could claim that his appointment of a Welsh-speaking curate could
offset this requirement so far as he was concerned. Similarly, Canon
95 of the Canons Ecclesiastical 1603 permitted bishops twenty-eight
days to inquire into 'the sufficiency and qualities of every minister'
presented by a patron for induction; an appeal lay to the archbishop
if the bishop refused to institute. Yet it was unclear whether sufficiency or its twin, lack of learning, could be interpreted to cover
linguistic competence.

Some suggested it could, including the celebrated English canonist
Edmund Gibson. He argued that 'the lack of language, mainly of the
Welsh', came under the head of 'lack of learning', and was sufficient
cause for a bishop to refuse to institute. Gibson cites the case of
Albany v. *Bishop of St Asaph* (1588) as authority for the proposition
that it did not 'avail to allege, that the language might be learnt, or
that the part of the Cure he was uncapable of, might be discharged
by a Curate'.[4] In the case Bishop Hughes refused to institute John
Bagshaw as Rector of Whittington on the grounds of non-sufficiency
in Welsh. Bagshaw was presented to the parish by William Albany

2 For a contemporary look at the problem see Erasmus Saunders, *View of the
State of Religion in the Diocese of St David's 1721* (Cardiff, 1949).
3 Noted by R. Burn, *Ecclesiastical Law* (4th edn., London, 1781), III, 230, as
an impediment, but so rarely cited – not even in *Albany's Case* (see below, n. 5)
– that E. Gibson, *Codex Juris Ecclesiastici Anglicani* (London, 1713), I, 365, and
G. Burnet, *An Exposition of the Thirty-nine Articles* (4th edn., London, 1738),
262–5, make no reference to this article's validity regarding the Welsh language.
4 E. Gibson, *Codex*, II, 850f.

of London who argued in the Court of Common Pleas that ignorance of Welsh was not a disability when Bagshaw 'had the more excellent languages' – the classics – at his command; he also argued that in any case many of the Welsh bishops were English, that Welsh could be easily learnt, and that the parish might be served by a Welsh-speaking curate. Although these arguments failed to convince the court, Albany won on a technicality that the bishop had neglected to give sufficient notice of his refusal to the patron. Bagshaw remained as rector until 1604.[5] Similarly, in a tract of 1766 (revised in 1768) John Jones, Fellow of the Queen's College, Oxford, argued that the Act of Uniformity 1662 s.27 required all 'ministers and curates' in dioceses where Welsh was common to use the Welsh *Book of Common Prayer* – for this incumbents had to speak Welsh.[6]

The legal issues raised by this pastoral problem were considered by the Court of the Arches in the case of *The Churchwardens of Trefdraeth* v. *Thomas Bowles* (1770–3).[7] Bishop Egerton of Bangor presented a seventy-year-old former schoolmaster to the living of Trefdraeth (one of the most valuable in the diocese) who was unable to speak Welsh. Only five of his 500 parishioners understood English. There was, however, a Welsh-speaking curate. Interestingly (and unusually) the proceedings were instituted by the parishioners, not the bishop. They had the financial support of the London Welsh society, the Cymmrodorion, and the intellectual support of John

5 Sir George Croke, *Reports of King's Bench and Common Pleas* (London, 1689), 119 (Cro Eliz 119); William Leonard, *Report of Cases of Law in the Times of the Late Queen Elizabeth* (London, 1658), 31–3.

6 J. Jones, *Considerations on the Illegality and Impropriety of Preferring Clergymen who are Unacquainted with the Welsh Language to Benefices in Wales* (London, 1768), 28; for other arguments in Jones see ibid., 41, 64, 66, 68. Jones notes that Leonard wrongly assumed that the Act 5 Eliz c.28, requiring the translation of the Bible and the Book of Common Prayer into Welsh, was a private act, and thus could not overrule the 1558 Act of Uniformity requiring the English Prayer Book to be used in all parish churches in England and Wales. The Act of Uniformity 1662 also provided that those who understood both Welsh and English may 'read and peruse them and those who understood only Welsh may, by conferring both tongues together, the sooner attain to the knowledge of the English language'.

7 For the case generally, see Anon., *Depositions and Arguments in the Case of the Churchwardens of Trefdraeth against Dr Bowles* (London, 1773). For the rarity of this method of initiating such a case, see *Encyclopedia of the Laws of England* (2nd edn., London, 1909), XIV, 553, quoted by Helen Ramage, *Portraits of an Island* (Llangefni, 1987), 187. The London Welsh society covered the costs of the case: R.T. Jenkins and H.M. Ramage, *A History of the Honourable Society of Cymmrodorion* (London, 1951), 84f. For a recent study of the case see G. H. Jenkins, ' "Horrid Unintelligible Jargon": The case of Dr. Thomas Bowles', *Welsh History Review*, 15(1991), 494–521.

Jones who, in his tract of 1766, supplied the legal and moral arguments.

The case was adjourned in 1770 by the Court of the Arches (the Provincial Court of Canterbury) in London and heard in 1773 at Llangefni, Anglesey. Bowles's advocates maintained that it was unfair to turn a cleric off his living after several years' service, having maintained a Welsh curate, and declared that as Wales was a conquered country it was proper to introduce the English language into the principality and for the Anglo-Welsh bishops to promote English incumbents into Welsh parishes. In reply the churchwardens argued from Jones's tract, the Act of Uniformity and the *Albany* case – it was not sufficient to plead that the Welsh duty was undertaken by a curate.[8] The Dean of the Arches accepted this principle. Ecclesiastical law required that Welsh-speaking incumbents should be appointed to Welsh-speaking parishes: 'want of knowledge of Welsh is a good cause of refusal in the bishop, and he ought to refuse him if he be incompetent'. The Dean continued: '[t]he inhabitants of Wales have great reason to complain of such presentations. And it is much to the honour of the bishops that they have not had reason to complain before this time'.[9]

The Dean accepted the principle but also considered that, on the evidence, the principle had not been violated. Bowles had been duly inducted and this meant that he had been found sufficient for the cure by both bishop and archdeacon. Indeed, the Dean wondered if Bowles could be deprived lawfully as proceedings were allowed only before induction. The Dean suggested three methods by which such nominations could be stopped: the bishop might decline the presentation; the archdeacon could refuse induction; or the parishioners might enter a *caveat* before induction or institution.[10] In any event, incidentally, Bowles was refused costs: he had perjured himself in the forgery of a certificate confirming his competence in Welsh. The Cymmrodorion published the case and advised the bishops in Wales to take note.

The Legal Arrangements in Perspective

Bowles and the existing legal arrangements were clearly unsatisfactory. The following defects might be noted. First, the time-limits

8 Anon., *Depositions and Arguments*, 53–7.
9 Ibid., 62f.
10 Ibid., 62f; J. Jones, *Considerations*, 68.

were restrictive – twenty-eight days were given to complain after the patron nominated, and legal proceedings had to begin before institution. Secondly, the standard of Welsh was never specified. Thirdly, the Dean's guidance in *Bowles* on stopping such appointments was vague and unrealistic. Certainly the bishop could refuse the presentation – but if he was in London (where they stayed for nine months of the year on parliamentary business) he might well be unaware that a Welsh-speaker was required or that a nominee was linguistically unsuitable for a particular parish, or simply not have time to act or be disinterested.[11] Again, some bishops were advised that a Welsh-speaking curate would suffice – this attracted much criticism at the time.[12] Certainly, as the Dean said, an archdeacon could refuse to institute. But archdeacons in Wales existed in name only, and in North Wales some archdeaconries had become attached *in commendam* to the bishoprics to provide them with a little more revenue. Moreover, an archdeacon was able by ecclesiastical law to delegate his power of induction – though a lesser official or local incumbent was hardly going to risk his prospects by raising inconvenient questions. Certainly, there was the parishioners' right to present a *caveat*. But at common law this amounted simply to a caution for the information of the court – induction performed in defiance of it was still valid.[13] In practical terms there were few in the locality who understood these procedures or were bold and wealthy enough to use them. Nor did parishioners have a right of consultation about nominations.[14]

However, *Bowles* did serve to attract publicity and clearly reinforced the moral pressure against unsuitable appointments. C.W. Wynn in a Commons debate on the Established Church in Wales in 1833 believed 'this great abuse' had been 'for some years past,

11 See also E. Copleston, *Charge* (1836), 19: 'it is wrong to press a doubtful case upon a bishop's acceptance, as if his want of vigilance or of local information could justify an appointment improper in itself '.

12 J. Jones, *Considerations*, 39, 58f. Copleston generally allowed this in those cases where 'hard rules' were inappropriate, Copleston to J.M. Traherne, 6 April 1844, *Copleston Correspondence* (CC), Llandaff Cathedral Archives, used by courtesy of the Dean and Chapter.

13 For the archdeacon's power of delegation and the status of a *caveat* see R. Burn, *Ecclesiastical Law* (4th edn., London, 1781), I, 155f, 264.

14 This was so until the Benefices (Exercise of Rights of Presentation) Measure 1931 (21 & 22 George V no.3) which gave limited powers of representation by the Parochial Church Council to the patron: Halsbury, *Laws of England*, vol.14, *Ecclesiastical Law* (4th edn., London, 1975), para. 818; Burn in his *Ecclesiastical Law* has no title 'Parishioner'.

materially lessened, in consequence of the resistance which had
been made on the part of a parish to such appointment, as
illegal'.[15] Rice Hughes wrote that Bishop Warren of Bangor
(1783–1800) had never conferred a parochial benefice on a cleric
who was not a master of the Welsh language.[16] Bishop Burgess of
St David's (1803–25) took a similar view, having been advised by
the lawyer J.A. Park that ignorance of Welsh was a sufficient
reason to reject a presentation and that it was no answer that
Welsh could be learnt or a Welsh-speaking curate employed.[17]

Indeed, as a result of *Bowles*, numerous presentations of non-
Welsh speaking clerics were withdrawn or redirected. For instance, the presentation of an English-speaker to Aber near
Bangor was withdrawn and that to Defynnog in Breconshire in
1774 exchanged with a Welsh-speaking incumbent in Hereford.[18]
The decision in *Bowles* had another effect. Because of the practical
difficulties of employing the legal methods of preventing unsuitable appointments, it is questionable whether the principle requiring Welsh-speaking incumbents was applied in practice. This
stimulated the adoption of a compromise: appointees must agree
to learn Welsh.[19] The compromise was widespread – but it is
difficult to know whether these clerics actually learnt Welsh,
though there is evidence that some did. For example, in 1817
the Bishop of Chester appointed John William Trevor to
Llanbeblig with Caernarfon. A protest to the bishop, Sumner,
was made by the parishioners who reminded him of his recent
Charge that a cleric should hold 'frequent communion with his
parishioners' – how could Trevor do this without the language
of his 8,000 monoglot Welsh parishioners? Rather than simply
employ a Welsh-speaking curate, Trevor was to learn Welsh.

15 *Hansard* (4 March 1833), 108: this might have applied to Caernarfon in
1817, however.
16 R. Hughes, *A Defence of the Right Reverend the Lord Bishop of Bangor with
Remarks on a most Extraordinary Trial* (London, 1796), 15.
17 National Library of Wales, Aberystwyth, Church in Wales Records,
SD/MISC/1085.
18 Jenkins and Ramage, *Cymmrodorion*, 85. In 1783 in that same parish of
Defynnog Bishop Smallwell of St David's was cautioned against a new incumbent
on grounds of his linguistic incapacity: Church in Wales Records, SD/MISC/70–
1, quoted by M.G.R. Morris, 'Bishop Richard Lewis: his life before Llandaff',
Journal of Welsh Ecclesiastical History, 4 (1987), 69.
19 See for example E.T. Davies, 'The Church in the Industrial Revolution', in
D. Walker (ed.), *A History of the Church in Wales* (Penarth, Church in Wales
Publications, 1976, re-issued 1990).

He did so.[20]

Some bishops clearly felt a responsibility towards this problem. In point of fact, Sir Thomas Phillips suggests that Copleston, Bishop of Llandaff (1828–49) never appointed to a Welsh-speaking benefice a person incapable of ministering to its people in their native tongue (but this was an idealized portrait written at a time of controversy about his appointments).[21] In his 1836 *Charge*, Copleston expressed disappointment at a number of his clergy who had failed to fulfil their promise to learn Welsh (which had been made a condition of their appointment). Privately, though, he accepted that the learning of Welsh 'by book' without a colloquial use of the language, was useless for pastoral purposes.[22] (It must be remembered, of course, that as many parishes in his diocese had changed their linguistic composition during his episcopate the issue of language was not clear-cut.)

The Pluralities Act 1838: Inquiries by Commission

Clearly, the ability of clergy to discharge their liturgical and pastoral duties towards parishioners, and the right of parishioners to pastoral guidance from their clergy, were severely disrupted by lack of a common language. It was natural to continue the attempt to resolve the problem by means of rules. With the Pluralities Act 1838 a legal arrangement markedly more sensitive to pastoral needs was formulated.

Under the Ecclesiastical Commissioners Act 1836, a commission was established to promote reform of the Church and make it fit for the evangelization of the nation. By section 11 the commissioners were to prepare a scheme to prevent the appointment of a non-Welsh-speaking incumbent to a parish in Wales where the majority did not understand English. (Incidentally, a clause in the original bill requiring all four bishops in Wales to be conversant in Welsh had been struck out in the Lords – and a motion in the House of

20 W.D. Leathert, *Origins and Progress of the Gweyneddigion Society of London* (London, 1831), 51f; *Report of the Association of Welsh Clergy in the West Riding of Yorkshire* (1854), 10–11.
21 *Substance of Speeches Delivered at Bridgend and Newport* [in support of the Llandaff Diocesan Church Extension Fund] (London, 1850), 29.
22 As to his private thoughts see *Copleston Correspondence*, Copleston to J.M. Traherne, 16 July 1832, and to Bruce Knight, 5 August 1832. For the promise to learn, see Copleston, *Charge* (1836), 22. Earlier he had declined to accept such a promise to learn Welsh as a qualification for office: letter to Bruce Knight, 31 December 1833 (CC).

Commons to reintroduce the clause lost by six votes.)[23] The commissioners' recommendations led to the enactment of the Pluralities Act 1838, which was intended in part to prevent the appointment of linguistically inadequate clergy to Welsh-speaking parishes. It provided that the bishops of the four Welsh dioceses could refuse institution 'to any spiritual person who after due examination and enquiry shall be found unable to preach, administer the sacraments, perform other pastoral duties and converse in the Welsh language'. It reiterated the right of parishioners to enter a *caveat* and allowed appeal from the bishop's examination to the Archbishop of Canterbury. It also empowered a bishop to appoint a Welsh-speaking curate to parishes where he believed that the ecclesiastical duties were not being satisfactorily performed, 'by reason of the insufficient instruction in the Welsh language' of the incumbent.

This was evidently a step in the right direction, but the legislation had its defects. A clause in the original bill empowering commissioners to enforce the measures had been rejected by the House of Lords: it was left to the bishops to implement it. As stated at the time (and subsequently), it was hard to believe that a bishop would inquire into an appointment made under his own patronage (the North Wales bishops especially had a substantial part of the patronage of their dioceses in their own hands). Again, the bishops were required to inquire and examine the linguistic credentials of nominated clergy, but the means and methods of that inquiry were not spelt out. Appeal to the archbishop was allowed but (as we shall see) no procedures were devised. The same problems as before faced parishioners entering a *caveat*. H.W. Cripps comments that the legislation gave to a bishop the same power which he possessed before: it had 'no other effect than to render it doubtful how far he may possess that [same power] in cases not particularly specified'.[24] Nevertheless, clear guidelines had been given as to the meanings of effectiveness and competence in Welsh. These included the ability to read a Welsh service and the capacity to converse in colloquial Welsh: essentials for the proper discharging of pastoral duties.

One of the central difficulties was the discretion it afforded

23 *Hansard* (3 March 1833), 108f; (12 July 1836), 150–7; (11 August 1836), 1137–41. Also, A.J. Johnes, *A Letter to Lord John Russell on the Operation of the Established Church Bill with reference to the Interests of the Principality of Wales* (London, 1836), 8–12.
24 H.W. Cripps, *A Practical Treatise on the Law relating to the Church and Clergy* (5th edn., London, 1869), 568.

surrounding the method of examination and inquiry. Bishop Jenkinson of St David's appointed commissioners in November 1839 to examine clerics charging them 'on no account to grant a certificate [of competence] to any person who is not able to speak or converse in the Welch language with as much fluency as a native of the Principality who has been accustomed to speak it from his infancy'.[25] The linguistic situation in Llandaff was a little different. There it seems to have been agreed to decide first whether the vacant benefice needed a Welsh-speaking incumbent or not. A commission would make inquiries on the spot, taking evidence from interested parties.[26] Bishop Copleston, says H.A. Bruce, used a commission of two or three clerics but inevitably accepted their report – such as at Penmarc in 1844 and Llantwit Major in 1845 (both in the patronage of the Dean and Chapter of Gloucester). For St Athan and St Brides in 1843 it was accepted that a Welsh-speaker was required – the nominee was instituted after approval by Dean Bruce Knight as a good Welsh scholar.[27]

These procedures were followed over the years. But there were complaints. Four of the five commissioners at Llan-ffwyst parish (Gwent) in 1850 could not speak Welsh – an Englishman was appointed. An Ewenni inquiry discovered twelve people who did not know English – an English incumbent was instituted on condition he appointed a Welsh-speaking curate.[28] The same compromise was reached at St Fagans, near Cardiff, in 1897 when C.A.H. Green was a commissioner. Welsh was hardly used in the parish, save at Llanilltern, where an occasional sermon was preached and hymns sung in Welsh. The Earl of Plymouth's nomination of an Englishman was thus allowed, on the understanding that neighbouring Welsh-speaking clergy would take any Welsh services if the need arose.[29] At Rhisga (Gwent), where no Welsh services were then held, it was

25 *Ecclesiastical Gazette* (December 1839), 115.
26 This was borrowed from Queen Anne's Bounty in its procedures for the augmentation of parishes.
27 *Cardiff and Merthyr Guardian* (CMG) (12 January 1850), 3: the letter of Thomas Williams, ibid. (26 January 1850), 4: W.J. Copleston, *Memoir of Edward Copleston* (London, 1851), 264.
28 For Llan-ffwyst, see *Report* (1852), 35 (vide n. 20). For Ewenni, see *Llandaff Diocesan Memoranda Books*, 12 September and 27 November, 1855 (National Library of Wales, Glyn Simon Deposit, December 1968, Box 1). Other inquiries were conducted in the parishes of Colwinston 1854, Marcross 1870, Pant-teg and St Nicholas 1871. Ollivant also rejected the Lord Chancellor's nomination to St Andrews in 1850 on linguistic grounds (*Haul*, 1885, 129).
29 National Library of Wales, Archbishop Green's Papers, and *Western Mail* (29 September 1897).

decided that the incumbent must have a knowledge of Welsh for pastoral purposes.[30]

The only contemporary account of a commission in action is of one held at Merthyr Dyfan as late as 1902. The commissioners assembled in the parish room after public notice of their meeting and of the terms of their inquiry. They heard evidence from sixteen witnesses. While there were many Welsh-speakers in the parish, all understood English and it was more fitting for a Welsh-speaking curate to be appointed rather than a bilingual incumbent.[31]

Episcopal Examination under the Statute

The Pluralities Act also provided for examination by the bishop before appointment. Therefore, where it was agreed that a vacancy required a Welsh-speaking incumbent, the bishop, if he had reason to suspect the nominee was deficient in this respect, would require examination. Alfred Jenner, presented by his family to the living of Wenvoe, though he failed his examination, was nevertheless eventually instituted.[32] In 1872 W. Ware Harris, nominated by the Earl of Dunraven to Coety, was examined in portions of the church service and required to translate some pages of an English sermon. He failed. The appointment lapsed to the bishop. Ollivant renominated Harris and allowed him three months to prepare for re-examination provided his examiners agreed. One of these, Canon Evans of Rhymni, refused (and told the bishop 'a truth or so').[33] Harris threatened to appeal to the archbishop. Ollivant recorded that he would have been glad to see an appeal to be relieved of responsibility for the matter.[34] In the following year F.W. Edmondes, a Welsh-speaker, was appointed. Bishop Copleston too had been threatened with litigation by disgruntled patrons.[35]

The first legal challenge to these now time-honoured arrange-

---

30 *Cardiff Times* (14 October 1871), 5; (21 October 1871), 5.

31 Church in Wales Records, LL/MISC/1390. In 1848 the prayers were in Welsh and the sermons alternated between the two languages (LL/QA/35).

32 *Diocesan Memoranda Books* for 29 June and 3 September 1851. Copleston had allowed a non-Welsh-speaking incumbent to appoint a Welsh curate in this parish, arguing that in such parishes 'no hard rules were possible': letters to J.M. Traherne, 18 August 1832, and to Bruce Knight, 6 August 1832, 27 June 1834, and 16 March 1843 (CC).

33 John Davies to John Griffith, 16 December 1872, South Glamorgan Library, Cardiff, MS 3508.

34 See also, *Diocesan Memoranda Books*, 14 November 1872.

35 Copleston, *Memoir*, 261.

ments came in *Marquis of Abergavenny* v. *Bishop of Llandaff* (1888). The marquis sued *quare impedit* in Queen's Bench over Bishop Lewis of Llandaff's refusal to institute his nominee Robert Wilkes Gosse, to the parish of Goetre. The case became a *cause célèbre*, with Bishop Lewis threatening to resign if the decision went against him. After the bishop had received representations that the parish was Welsh-speaking, the commission's inquiry found that about forty to fifty people needed Welsh services. Gosse refused to be examined and the bishop refused institution. The marquis claimed the commission had not allowed either him or his nominee to be present or represented at the inquiry – which he said exercised a judicial function – or to produce evidence which showed that few if any of the parishioners were unable to speak English. The archdeacon as chairman of the inquiry argued that this action had been taken because the commission wished to preserve the informal nature of its proceedings. Gosse appealed to the archbishop, who declined to act for lack of jurisdiction: he was competent only to decide on Gosse's linguistic ability, not on the nature of the parish or the proceedings of the inquiry. However, the court held that the 1838 statute applied to inquiry and examination into the nominee's knowledge of Welsh, rather than examination into the requirements of the parish concerned. Moreover, as the statute allowed the bishop discretion as to how to ascertain the needs of the parish, then the manner in which the inquiry was held did not invalidate the bishop's refusal to institute.[36]

Appeal to the Archbishop

Though some aspects of the Pluralities Act were commendable, as we have seen, the rules providing for appeal to the Archbishop of Canterbury led to considerable confusion and further offence to pastoral principles. No procedures were actually laid down for this appeal. What is more, the various archbishops, far removed from the scene, were at the mercy of their own advisers, who were often equally ignorant of the issues involved. Two cases are noteworthy. The first is from 1851.

Michaelston-y-Vedw was a Welsh-speaking parish in Gwent. The

36 [1888] 20 QBD 460; Lambeth Palace Library, Benson MS 58 fos. 211–2 containing extracts from *The Times* (22 and 23 February 1888); *Cymru Fydd*, 1 (1888), 228–30; E.T. Davies, 'Two disputes over advowsons', *Journal of the Historical Society of the Church in Wales*, 27 (1990), 73–6.

bishop sent William Jenkins to Chancellor Williams for examination and he was found incompetent under the statute of 1838. Jenkins appealed to the archbishop, who then sent him to be examined by Dr Lewellin, Principal of St David's College, Lampeter. Lewellin passed Jenkins as competent – but Lewellin's Welsh itself was reputed to be 'proverbially small'. Even Ollivant was outraged, noting that the archbishop had given no directions to Jenkins regarding the need for Welsh in the parish.[37] The second case was more celebrated. In the same year Bishop Thirlwall of St David's nominated Richard Lewis (later to become Bishop of Llandaff) as Rector of Lampeter Velfrey in Pembrokeshire. The bishop would not institute until Lewis acquired a sufficient conversational ability in Welsh (as required by the Pluralities Act). A commission failed him: his conversational Welsh would not be understood by the parishioners. Lewis appealed, arguing not only that his examiners required a higher standard than was needed but also that Lampeter Velfrey had only a minority of its population who would prefer (but did not need) Welsh services. Lewis also submitted himself to the rigours of a crash course in the language. Thirlwall warned the archbishop that if Lewis was appointed as 'a result of such misrepresentations and shallow and frivolous pretences. . .it will inflict a grievous injury on the interests of the Church and will go far to reduce the wise provisions of the statute in respect of the Welsh language'. The archbishop allowed re-examination by Thomas Thomas (Vicar of Caernarfon) who declared that Lewis satisfied the requirements of the statute. Lewis was later instituted but few could claim that he ever had a command of conversational Welsh.[38]

The Association of Welsh Clergy in the West Riding of Yorkshire noted as a result of these appeals that 'any English clergyman may pick up a few Celtic words, and get another who knows nearly as little of Welsh as himself to sign his certificate as a competent Welsh scholar'. Indeed, the Association sent a petition in 1852 to the archbishop to establish a board of examiners to inquire into the Welsh qualifications of those who appealed to the archbishop. Though the petition was not successful, such protests were not in vain. No further appeals to the archbishop appear to have been made.[39]

37 *Report* (1852), 8,33. *Diocesan Memorandum Book* for 22 December 1851.
38 Morris, 'Bishop Richard Lewis', 68f.; *Report* (1852), 8f., 28; F. Jones, 'A Victorian Bishop of Llandaff', *National Library of Wales Journal*, 19 (1975), 33–7.
39 *Report* (1852), 8. For the petition, see ibid., 42–3, and J. Morgan, *The Reverend David James of Panteg* (Pontypool, 1925), 65–7.

Cathedral Chapters and the Case of Sparling

The legislation which we have examined so far was an intentional attempt to resolve the problem of appointing non-Welsh-speaking clerics. However, the creation of the Ecclesiastical Duties and Revenue Act 1841 unintentionally produced a further obstacle to the resolution of this basic pastoral problem. This made provision for appointments to patronage in the gift of cathedral chapters. Section 44 of the statute required any benefice in the patronage of a cathedral chapter to be filled by a member of that chapter, or a person who had served as a minor canon, lecturer or master of a school in connection with that chapter. Failing these the bishop of the diocese had the right to nominate a person who had served within his diocese as an incumbent or curate for five years. Now, the Dean and Chapter of Gloucester had the patronage of a number of Welsh-speaking parishes in the diocese of Llandaff. Conflict was inevitable. It could hardly be expected that the diocese of Gloucester had many Welsh-speaking clergy willing to move into another diocese as the vacancies occurred.

This did not, however, become a problem until the 1880s when the Dean and Chapter of Gloucester devised a scheme of patronage in accordance with the statute, it coming into effect on the death of the last surviving member of the 1840 chapter.[40] The chapter felt, though, that there was some ambiguity in the statutory provisions. It was uncertain which diocese was meant to make the nomination when the field was opened up to diocesan clergy of five years' standing, after the cathedral chapter and its associated clergy had all declined the nomination. Did it mean the diocese in which the cathedral was the mother church (here, Gloucester), or the diocese in which the vacant parish was situated (here, Llandaff)? In 1881 the chapter sought advice from other chapters, most of which (including St David's) understood that an appointment had to be made from within their own diocese – the Canterbury chapter indicated that it had taken this decision having received 'high legal' advice. Yet, the Hereford chapter believed it referred to the diocese of the vacant parish.

The query was put to the test in *Sparling's Case* (1883). It is

---

40 For this and the 1862 proposal of Gloucester to transfer some of its Glamorgan patronage to the Bishop of Llandaff in exchange for some of his patronage in North Wales, see Gloucester Record Office, Records of the Dean and Chapter of Gloucester Cathedral, D936 C/3.

worthwhile spending a little time on the case. In June 1883 Thomas
Edmondes resigned the living of Llanblethian with Cowbridge, a
parish which was partly Welsh-speaking (as late as the 1901 census
64 per cent of those sixty-five years old or over, in the borough, spoke
Welsh).[41] Philip William Sparling, who had been for five years
headmaster of the Gloucester Cathedral School, applied for the
vacant benefice. Sparling was nominated by the Gloucester chapter
to the Bishop of Llandaff. The reply he received from the bishop's
secretary, to his request for a date to be fixed for his induction,
startled both him and the chapter. It indicated that the bishop
believed the bilingual nature of the parish required a Welsh incumbent. He could not proceed unless he was satisfied that Welsh was
not required in the parish or that Sparling could prove he could
officiate in Welsh. Sparling replied that he knew no Welsh, adding
(naively): 'it is my intention however to study that language and as
a schoolmaster accustomed to teach languages I hope to find no
difficulty in it'. Meanwhile, he would insist that his curate spoke
Welsh.

The Bishop of Llandaff, Richard Lewis, had, of course, first-hand
experience of the difficulty of acquiring conversational Welsh. Lewis
made it clear that he would not institute any incumbent to a benefice
'where a knowledge of Welsh is requisite for the due performance of
his ministerial duties without being first satisfied myself that he is
possessed of such a knowledge of that language as will enable him
personally to perform them'. Sparling replied in a personal letter
expressing his disappointment. This was the first living he had ever
been offered, and he felt the bishop's action would lessen any further
chances. He would not be idle in the parish – he would do the English
work and his curate the Welsh. As every parishioner understood
English he would, after all, be ministering in a language all could
comprehend. Surely, he concluded, did not the patron and its nominee have some rights in this matter as well? The Bishop of Gloucester
was also nonplussed. Writing to his dean (Henry Law) he grieved at
the obstinacy of his episcopal colleague in these circumstances. The
Bishop of Gloucester tried to find a more suitable candidate from his
own or former clergy but without success. As news of these difficulties spread, a considerable number of Welsh-speaking clerics wrote
offering their services.

41 B.Ll. James and D.J. Francis, *Cowbridge and Llanblethian* (Barry, 1979),
85,133; see also B.Ll. James, 'The Welsh language in the Vale of Glamorgan',
Morgannwg, 16 (1972), 30.   .

Bishop Lewis now exploited the existing legal arrangements to his advantage. Claiming that Sparling had not appealed to the archbishop within the month allowed by statute, and that the dean and chapter as an ecclesiastical patron could not without his consent either revoke or alter their first presentation, he argued that after six months the living would lapse to him as bishop.[42] This he declined to give. The chapter appealed to the archbishop, suspecting the bishop's motives, and took advice from the well-known ecclesiastical lawyer F.H. Jeune. The Gloucester chapter was forced to concede that the strength of law lay with the Bishop of Llandaff. Lewis then appointed J.H. Protheroe, a Welsh-speaker, to the living in May 1884.[43]

As the controversy over Llanblethian boiled, J. Powell Jones, the doughty evangelical vicar at Llantrisant, died in December 1883.[44] The members of the Gloucester chapter must have wrung their hands in horror at this vacancy in a Welsh-speaking parish within its patronage – especially as they were once again swamped by letters from Welsh clerics offering their services. The same sequence of events followed. The chapter found itself once more unable to present a cleric who was eligible in terms of its own patronage scheme and capable of satisfying the Bishop of Llandaff. Consequently, the living fell by lapse to Bishop Lewis who appointed Joshua Pritchard Hughes.[45] Within eighteen months, the chapter took stock and decided to transfer the patronage of both Llanblethian and Llantrisant to the Bishop of Llandaff. In this case, a clear-minded bishop had employed the framework provided by the Pluralities Act to the pastoral advantage of parishioners in his own diocese.

---

42   The appeal had to be made to the archbishop within one month of refusal by 1 & 2 Vict., c.106, s.104. For the bishop's right of refusal of presentation see Cripps, *Law relating to the Church and Clergy*, 569, and Gibson, *Codex*, II, 836; for lapse see Cripps, op. cit., 593–7.
43   See Benson, Papers 2, fo. 331, and note, fo. 326, Bishop Lewis to Benson, 26 November 1883; Records of the Dean and Chapter, *Vicarage of Llanblethian: Counsel's Opinion*; see also Church in Wales Records, LL/P/1753. See also *Guardian* (12 and 17 September and 10 October 1883).
44   Jones had been appointed by Dean Law, who used his own option to secure a Welsh–speaking incumbent, as he had done earlier for St John's Church, Cardiff, in 1864 (CMG, 30 December 1864, 5).
45   Church in Wales Records, LL/P/880.

Conclusion

This protracted legal activity, in the four basic areas described here, to ensure that Welsh-speaking incumbents were appointed to Welsh-speaking parishes, took place against a backcloth of general decline in the use of Welsh, especially in rural south-east Wales. Here the mass defection to the chapels of Welsh-speaking farmers and trades-people left the Church even more vulnerable to the influence of the Anglicized gentry and gentlemen farmers than might otherwise have been the case.[46] It was these who endeavoured to extend their influence still further by appointing, or forwarding the appointment of, clergy of their own background and culture. It is noteworthy that many of the recorded commissions of inquiry were held for parishes in the patronage of Glamorgan county families.[47] Far too often the fact that many preferred to worship in the language of their birth and hearth was ignored.

One clear lesson is that the ecclesiastical authorities, in creating and applying Church law (enacted, after all, by the State) failed to understand this need – many in authority having themselves been born and bred in an entirely different milieu. Too often the result of the 1838 Pluralities Act was a compromise. Copleston recognized the difficulty of making a fair assessment between rival claims of two languages. In many cases he allowed a nomination to proceed on condition that a Welsh curate was employed (though he accepted that this might equally be unjust to the Welsh-speaking clergy).[48] In other cases he felt unjustified in refusing a particular nomination, as that to Llantwit Major in 1845, though he wished to impress on patrons the need for bilingual appointments in other parishes in their gift.[49] It was still widely believed that a cleric could learn sufficient Welsh. It was commented of Ollivant that he considered his Welsh to be such that people came to hear him speak as they would 'go to see a conjuror or a wild beast'; neither he nor Thirlwall ever acquired a ready facility in the language.[50] A local newspaper of the time purported to state the normal reaction: 'we understand even less of their Welsh than we do of their English'.[51]

The development of the ecclesiastical law is fairly clear, centring

46 James, 'The Welsh language', 28.
47 As noted in an editorial of the *Record* (6 May 1859), 2.
48 Copleston, *Memoir*, 267.
49 Ibid., 264.
50 *Guardian* (10 October 1883).
51 CMG (2 February 1850), 4, letter of Gorbonian.

on the idea that the law existed to serve pastoral and liturgical purposes based on an actual ability in the clergy to communicate with effect. The principle was expressed in various forms – the sufficiency rule, the Welsh-speaking curate rule, the learning rule. The procedural rules too, establishing commissions and inquiries, examination and rights of objection, had their place – though with intrinsic flaws. The problem lay, ultimately, with the application of these legal arrangements and their operation by means of wide discretionary powers (vested in the bishops) unfettered by clear and detailed duties. The earlier nineteenth-century bishops were often forced to compromise, but Copleston clearly endeavoured to err on the side of the parish rather than of the patron. His successors faced a different situation caused by the alterations in the linguistic boundaries of the later part of the century. They were forced to be realists regarding the erosion of these bilingual communities. Though there was no lack of concern on their part, the hope that Welsh-speaking bishops would be more successful in preventing such appointments was thus never fully realized. An indication of the new realism appears in the Pluralities Acts Amendment Act 1885. This allowed bishops to refuse to institute if they believed the nominee was unfit for the discharge of his duty. It provided for such ministrations in Welsh as the bishops might direct so that not more than one Welsh service would be required each Sunday; and provision was to be made for the needs of English-speakers.[52] Bishop Campbell promoted the bill but claimed that this rule restricting the number of Welsh services and the requirement for English services had been included without his knowledge.[53] The statute effectively enabled one English family in an otherwise monoglot Welsh parish to demand an exclusive service for themselves. But by this time the number of exclusively monoglot parishes had diminished considerably. The main objective of these arrangements of ecclesiastical law (and the desire of the bishops) was to provide some degree of fairness between the competing claims of Welsh-speakers and English-speakers. These cases remain clear testimony to the difficulties which establishment brought to the Church in Wales. The ecclesiastical law which addressed the pastoral and liturgical problems posed by language was not, after all, a direct creation of the people of the Church in Wales – it

52 J.H. Hunt, *The Book of Church Law* (8th edn., London, 1899), 234f. The provision was incorporated into s.2 of the Benefices Act 1898.
53 J.C. Campbell, *Tenth Visitation Charge* (1887), 31ff. His hope for an amending bill did not materialize.

was a State law which many Welsh people felt was created by those who were not familiar with the real problems and issues of the Church of England in Wales.

2

Disestablishment, Self-determination and the Constitutional Development of the Church in Wales

THOMAS GLYN WATKIN

When St Michael's College was founded in the closing decade of the nineteenth century, the diocese of Llandaff was one of four Welsh dioceses, all of which were located within the province of Canterbury. The other three were St Davids, St Asaph and Bangor. It was these four dioceses which were disestablished in 1920 under the provisions of the Welsh Church Act 1914 and the Welsh Church (Temporalities) Act 1919, the dioceses of Monmouth and Swansea and Brecon being created after disestablishment in 1921 and 1923 respectively. The fact that it was dioceses which were disestablished and not a province distinguishes what was visited upon the Welsh Church from what had occurred in Ireland. There, the Church of Ireland was created out of the pre-existing provinces of Armagh and Dublin. The four Welsh dioceses, however, had no provincial structure and were left at disestablishment to provide their own structure or none in whatsoever manner they wished. They were, in law, no longer the concern of the established Church of England, of which they had previously been part.

The history of the disestablishment movement within Wales – the motives of those who promoted it, the worries of those who opposed and sought to prevent it, the manner and method of its execution and the response of the Welsh Church to it – is a story that has been told elsewhere in several authoritative accounts.[1] It is not the purpose of this essay to retell it. Instead, it is proposed to inquire into what disestablishment meant and continues to mean to the Church in Wales, to consider what opportunities for constitutional development the Church in Wales has enjoyed as a result of being disestablished, and to assess the extent to which the Constitution of the Church in Wales has helped or hindered the exploitation of those opportunities.

The Meaning of Disestablishment

One fact is undeniable: disestablishment was imposed upon Anglicans in Wales against their will. It was resentment at the privileges and wealth of the established Church which drove the Nonconformist majority to seek the disestablishment and disendowment of what it perceived to be an alien Church, the Church of England in Wales. By severing the Anglican Church in Wales from its English neighbour, it was intended to destroy its privileged status as against the Nonconformist denominations, and by confiscating the endowments of the Church, it was intended to impoverish it. It can readily be believed that the intention of those who sought disestablishment may well have been to drive Anglicanism out of Wales, in the belief that Wales was and should be seen to be a radical and Nonconformist nation. Disestablishment was meant to be a punitive act, severing the Welsh dioceses from their parent province in the hope that that separation would weaken them and possibly wound them fatally.

There is a strange parallel in this which deserves mention. The parallel is with an institution of the ancient law of Rome, which law was to enjoy a new lease of life during the medieval period, influencing the nascent legal systems of continental Europe and most notably the developing canon law of the Western Church. The institution in question is that of emancipation, by which a Roman father as head of his household and family, as *paterfamilias*, could release his sons

1 See Owain W. Jones, 'The Welsh Church in the nineteenth century' and David Walker, 'Disestablishment and independence' in David Walker (ed.), *A History of the Church in Wales* (Penarth, 1976; re-issued 1990), and the relevant sections of the Suggestions for Further Reading contained therein. See also Kenneth O. Morgan, *Rebirth of a Nation: Wales 1880–1980* (Oxford, 1981; 2nd edn., 1982), and C. A. H. Green, *The Setting of the Constitution of the Church in Wales* (London, 1937).

from his power, his *potestas*.[2] Almost without doubt, emancipation in early Roman law was seen as a way in which a disobedient or troublesome child could be disinherited, a method by which the father could terminate his liability for the wrongs perpetrated by a delinquent son. In other words, its effects were punitive. However, by the end of the Republic and during the classical age of Roman law, emancipation was seen as a method by which a son could achieve independence of paternal control before his father's death, which was the moment according to the law of Rome at which a child became independent. Ambitious sons would deliberately seek emancipation so as to run their own lives, and indulgent fathers would arrange this and often give such a son a portion of the family property with which to make a start in life. The parable of the prodigal son in St Luke's Gospel bears witness to this state of affairs in contemporary society. What had originally been a punitive act, cutting the son off without a penny, had become a liberating act, freeing the son from the control of his father, freeing him to make his own way in the world. Doubtless, there was a period in the course of this development when unemancipated sons noticed that their punitively emancipated contemporaries were succeeding in their new condition, and came to desire that condition for themselves, thus changing the perspective from which emancipations were viewed.

With the benefit of seventy years' hindsight, a similar double perspective can be achieved with regard to the disestablishment of the Church in Wales. At the time, it seemed a disaster to the churchmen who suffered it, and who strove in the years separating the passing of the Welsh Church Act 1914 from its implementation in 1920 to prevent its ever coming into force and effect. However, to a generation which did not live through those events, or which lived through them as young children rather than as adults, disestablishment can appear in retrospect to have been emancipation, a freeing from the control of the parent Church of England, a freeing to enjoy an independent development within the growing family of churches which forms the Anglican Communion.[3] It is pertinent, therefore, to ask, firstly, from what the Church in Wales was freed

2 See, e.g., J. A. C. Thomas, *Textbook of Roman Law* (Amsterdam, 1976), 443–4; W. W. Buckland, *A Textbook of Roman Law*, ed. P. G. Stein (3rd edn, Cambridge, 1963), 131–3.
3 See Sir Isaiah Berlin, 'Two concepts of liberty' (Oxford, 1958), 6–19 for the exposition of this analysis of freedom as 'freedom from' and 'freedom to'. This lecture has been reprinted in Anthony Quinton (ed.), *Political Philosophy* (Oxford, 1967), and in Sir Isaiah Berlin, *Four Essays on Liberty* (Oxford, 1969).

in 1920, and, secondly, what was the Church in Wales free to do after 1920 which it could not have done before as part of the Church of England.

The established Church of England was the creature of the sixteenth century, when it had broken free of the control of the Church of Rome. As a sixteenth-century creation, it embodied the assumptions of that time, social, political and legal, as well as theological. The newly established Church of England was a Church in the sense of 'the people of God', the *laos*, of England, and that was, in effect, during the sixteenth century, virtually the whole population. As had been the case during the Middle Ages, not to be numbered among the people of God was to be marginalized if not alienated by the social order of the day. Society was Christian, and not to be a Christian placed one beyond the pale of social life. Non-Christians, such as Jews, were tolerated by society but suffered serious legal as well as social disabilities. Nor was there a choice among Christian denominations available to the believer. Prior to the Henrician Reformation, the only acceptable form of Christian belief in England was medieval Catholicism, and after Henry's reforms, the only acceptable form was allegiance to the Church of which the king and not the pope was now by Act of Parliament the head. The social and religious reforms of the 1530s saw the people of England emerge with a clear national identity, and this was the case in matters of faith as well as in matters of state. Indeed, the two things were not really distinguished. The people of England were a Christian people, the people of God in England. On matters of faith, therefore, they spoke through the same organs as on all other matters, namely through their representatives in Parliament. This was the method by which they were governed in relation to both the sacred and the secular, and the king was their leader in both spheres.

It is this view of the inseparability of the religious element from the other components of national life that is witnessed in Article 37 of the Thirty-nine Articles of Religion, that which treats 'Of the Civil Magistrate':

> The King's Majesty hath the chief power in this Realm of England, and other his Dominions, unto whom the chief Government of all Estates of this Realm, whether they be Ecclesiastical or Civil, in all causes doth appertain, and is not, nor ought to be, subject to any foreign Jurisdiction.
>
> Where we attribute to the King's Majesty the chief government,

by which Titles we understand the minds of some slanderous folks to be offended; we give not to our Princes the ministering either of God's Word, or of the Sacraments, the which thing the Injunctions also lately set forth by *Elizabeth* our Queen do most plainly testify; but only that prerogative, which we see to have been given always to all godly Princes in holy Scriptures by God himself; that is, that they should rule all estates and degrees committed to their charge by God, whether they be Ecclesiastical or Temporal, and restrain with the civil sword the stubborn and evil-doers.

The idea that the realm of the sacred should be separated from that of the secular was one of the results of that intellectual movement which reached its zenith during the eighteenth century, namely the Enlightenment. The theme of the Enlightenment was the cultivation of Reason as the highest goal of man, and from this there stemmed an individualistic concept of freedom, which sought to allow each individual the freedom to use his own capacity to reason so as to reach his own conclusions as to the truth or falsity of competing ideas concerning matters such as politics or religion. From such a viewpoint, it was not acceptable that 'the civil magistrate' should decide the form or content of his subjects' religion nor that his subjects should suffer disabilities as a consequence of dissenting from the religious beliefs of their ruler. Gradually, during the nineteenth century, the consequences of this change of perspective were worked out in the areas of English law dealing with religious disabilities. The universities were opened for the first time to students who were not adherents of the Church of England, and by the end of the century laymen of any or no religious persuasion were admitted to teach within them.[4] It also became possible for dissenters to represent the people in Parliament.[5] As it was now permissible to hold any or no religious opinion, the people of God in the Britain of 1900 were not the whole population of the land. The baptized were, in effect, a sub-group within the larger group constituting the population, and however substantial a sub-group they might be in numerical terms, they were not synonymous with that larger group. Moreover, the political orthodoxy of the age would not have countenanced the interference with personal liberty that an attempt to reinstate such an equation would have entailed.

4 Universities Tests Act 1871.
5 Parliamentary Oaths Act 1866.

Moreover, with the removal of the disabilities inflicted upon Nonconformists and Roman Catholics, the people of God itself now numbered many who were not adherents of the Church of England. Anglicans were now a sub-group within a sub-group, albeit that their Church remained that established by law, enjoying a privileged position within the life of the nation inherited from a time when it was the religion of virtually the whole people. However, this privileged position was a doubtful privilege, in that as a result of the assumptions of the age from which the privileged position had been inherited, the people of God within the Church of England found themselves governed in matters ecclesiastical by the representatives of the people of the United Kingdom as a whole, the same representatives who governed them in matters temporal. In effect, from being a dominant group within the population by virtue of their religion, Anglicans now found themselves dominated in matters concerning their faith by the representatives of that population. The members of the Church of England, for in reality that is what Anglicans had become, had lost the ability to control their own religious development as a group. In a very real sense, the disestablishment of the Church in Wales reflects that state of affairs, in that it was forced upon unwilling Anglicans in Wales by a Parliament in which the vast majority of Welsh members represented the liberal, Nonconformist element which accounted for the greater part of the population. Disestablishment in Wales was forced upon the Church by dissenters.

Herein, perhaps, lies the clue to a distinction which has been much discussed by those concerned with the laws governing the Church of England, and to a lesser extent the norms of government of the Church in Wales, that between canon law and ecclesiastical law. At times, the terms appear to be used synonymously, while at others there is an implied distinction. From what has been said above, it is submitted that both views are correct, but correct only while certain conditions prevail. Canon law is the law of the Church, made by the people of God for the people of God. While the people of God in England were, therefore, synonymous with the people of England, their canon law was the law made for them in matters ecclesiastical by their governors. However, once the people of God became a distinct sub-group of the population, the laws made for the sub-group by their governors in matters ecclesiastical as well as temporal were no longer laws made by the people of God for the people of God, but rather were laws imposed upon the people of God by the State. By virtue of this change which ended the coincidence of Church and State, ecclesiastical law ceased to be a law made for the Church by the Church, and became a law made for the Church by the State. One is very near here to the distinction as it is applied in many continental countries, such as Italy, where canon law is the law by which the Church governs its internal affairs, while ecclesiastical law is that part of the public law of the State by which it governs its relationship with the Church. In England, however, that point has not been reached, for, while the State has freed itself from the Church of England, it has not freed the Church of England from its dependence on the State. The ecclesiastical law made by the State for the Church therefore contains the canon law as well, leaving the Church dependent upon the good offices of its secular governors with regard to its canonical progress.

Disestablishment for the Church in Wales was in effect a freeing from the bonds of this situation. The Church in Wales by virtue of its disestablishment was freed from the control of governors who were no longer representative of the Church. In a sense, the Welsh dioceses were returned to the position which had obtained centuries earlier when the members of the Church governed themselves. The difference at disestablishment was that membership of the Church was no longer the same thing as being a member of the populace; it had become instead membership of a sub-group. Nevertheless, the populace had restored to the Church in Wales the right to govern itself in matters ecclesiastical. Henceforward, the Church in Wales would be governed by norms of its own creation; it would have its own canon law distinct from the ecclesiastical law of the Church of England in that, even if there was considerable identity of content, the source of the binding authority of the canon law of the Church in Wales would be the Church itself and not the State. The Church in Wales was to be governed again by the people of God who were its members; it was to be governed by those whose right to govern was based upon their status as baptized communicants who were within the full sacramental life of the Church.

The Possibilities of Self-determination

The first three sections of the Welsh Church Act 1914 effected this release. Section 1 provided that 'the Church of England, so far as it extends to and exists in Wales and Monmouthshire. . .shall cease to be established by law' and terminated patronage by the Crown and other private patrons to ecclesiastical offices in the Church in Wales.

Section 2 dissolved 'every cathedral and ecclesiastical corporation in the Church in Wales, whether sole or aggregate', thus ending the rights of such ecclesiastical bodies to be treated as persons under the law of the land. The same section ended the rights of bishops from the Welsh dioceses to sit in the House of Lords and removed the legal disabilities of clergymen of the Church in Wales which prevented them from being elected members of the House of Commons. Section 3 terminated the jurisdiction of all ecclesiastical courts and persons in Wales and Monmouthshire and provided that from the date of disestablishment 'the ecclesiastical law of the Church in Wales shall cease to exist as law'. It then went on to provide that the then existing ecclesiastical law, together with the then existing articles, doctrines, rites, rules, discipline, and ordinances of the Church of England should for the future be binding upon the members of the Church in Wales as if those members had agreed amongst themselves to be so bound. In other words, the members of the newly disestablished Church were subjected by the statute to a contract, the terms of which were in effect observance of the ecclesiastical law of the Church of England as at the date of disestablishment. However, in future, this corpus of law would be binding upon the members of the Church in Wales 'subject to such modification or alteration, if any, as after the passing of this Act may be duly made therein, according to the constitution and regulations for the time being of the Church in Wales'. The Constitution and regulations were specifically enabled to provide for the setting up of ecclesiastical courts for the newly disestablished Church, and the power to alter and modify the inherited ecclesiastical law was specifically stated to include the power of altering and modifying such law as contained in Acts of Parliament.

It can be seen from these provisions that disestablishment meant forced abdication by the Church of England of all responsibility for the Church in Wales. Although it was clear that, for the future, the State would not appoint bishops, deans or archdeacons for the Welsh dioceses, nor prefer any clerics to livings within the same, nothing was said as to how such appointments should be made. Likewise, although the jurisdiction of the existing ecclesiastical courts was terminated, there was no obligation upon the emergent disestablished Church to create replacements. In the same manner, nothing was said regarding how the power to alter and modify the inherited ecclesiastical law was to be exercised, although the right of the bishops, clergy and laity to hold synods, elect representatives thereto, and frame constitutions and regulations for the general management and good government of the Church 'in such manner as they think fit' was specifically protected by Section 13(1). The four Welsh dioceses were, as far as the law was concerned, left to their own devices to sink or swim.

The greater part of the Act was concerned with the confiscation of the property of the Welsh Church. The entirety of its property was to be taken into the hands of a corporation, officially designated The Commissioners of Church Temporalities in Wales, but more usually called the Welsh Commissioners.[6] These ultimately were charged with redistributing the property.[7] Ecclesiastical buildings and residences, funds for the upkeep of the same, and certain other items of property were to be returned to the Church, by being transferred to persons appointed to represent the bishops, clergy and laity of the disestablished Church and hold property for their uses and purposes, which representatives might be incorporated as the representative body of the Church in Wales.[8] The residue of the property, however, was to be distributed among various secular bodies, such as local authorities, the National Library of Wales, the University of Wales and its constituent colleges. This property in effect was lost to the Church for ever. It was again left entirely to the Church in Wales as to whether and, if so, how, it should appoint the above-mentioned representatives to hold its property.

Today, sections of the Welsh Church Act tend to be referred to as sources for the powers of the various institutions of the disestablished Church. The statute is not usually treated as a whole, other than perhaps by historians. Read as an entity, it is still a chilling document. By virtue of its enactment and execution, the Church in Wales was left to all intents and purposes in a legal and constitutional vacuum.

The original intent of the legislature was complete disestablishment, with every vestige of the Church's once privileged position under the law removed. However, this was not to be. In two areas, the legislature was forced to back-pedal. These two areas were marriage and burial.

As a result of its position as an established Church, the Church of England continues to enjoy special privileges with regard to the solemnization of Holy Matrimony. Whereas other religious denominations are permitted to have weddings solemnized in their places

6 Welsh Church Act 1914, ss.4, 10.
7 Ibid, s.8.
8 Ibid, s.13(2).

of worship, in the eyes of the law, such weddings are civil ceremonies which take place outside the normal place for such ceremonies, namely the Register Office. The place of worship to the law is 'a registered building' and, if the services of the civil registrar are not required, this is because the officiating minister or the person who will complete the register is an 'authorized person'. A Church of England wedding is, however, a different matter. Such a ceremony follows the publication of banns, an ecclesiastical not a civil formality, and in the eyes of the law, this is not a civil ceremony in a registered religious building, but an ecclesiastical ceremony of equal validity. Indeed, the ecclesiastical ceremony is the older of the two institutions, the civil ceremony having been introduced during the nineteenth century as one of the concessions to dissent mentioned earlier.[9] That the ecclesiastical ceremony was the original norm was a relic of the notion that Church and State were synonymous, although this was not really the case by the time that Lord Hardwicke's Marriage Act was passed in 1753 making the ecclesiastical ceremony essential for the contracting of a valid marriage. In so far as an ecclesiastical ceremony had once been necessary for the solemnization of a valid marriage, it followed that there was a duty upon the established Church to solemnize the marriages of all subjects of the State, regardless of their religious persuasion or lack of one. Not long after the passing of Lord Hardwicke's Act, it was held in the courts that a clergyman who refused to solemnize the marriage of a duly qualified person committed an ecclesiastical offence, although he was not liable to an action for damages, nor as was later determined to a criminal prosecution.[10] It does not appear to have been decided whether the clergyman's obligation to marry a duly qualified parishioner could be enforced in the civil courts by a prerogative order of mandamus, although, as this is a discretionary remedy and a civil marriage ceremony is now available, it appears unlikely that the courts would seek to overrule a reasonable refusal based on canonical principle, for instance on the basis that the parties were unbaptized.

The intention of the framers of the Welsh Church Act was to bring to a close the recognition of ecclesiastical marriage in the Church in Wales, and to place the disestablished Church on an equal footing

9 Marriage Act 1836.
10 *Argar* v. *Holdsworth* (1758) 2 Lee 515; *Davis* v. *Black* (1841) 1 QB 900; *R* v. *James* (1850) 3 Car. & Kir. 167.

with other denominations. Section 23 of the 1914 Act provided that from disestablishment:

> [t]he law relating to marriages in churches of the Church of England (including any law conferring any right to be married in such a church) shall cease to be in force in Wales and Monmouthshire, and the provisions of the Marriage Acts, 1811 to 1898, relating to marriages in registered buildings, shall apply to marriages in churches of the Church in Wales.

If this provision had actually been carried into effect, marriage by banns, common licence or special licence would have ceased to be possible in Wales from the date of disestablishment.

However, it was not carried into effect, for section 23 was repealed before disestablishment by virtue of section 6 of the Welsh Church (Temporalities) Act 1919. This section provided that nothing in the Welsh Church Act 1914 or the 1919 Act itself should affect the law with respect to marriages in Wales and Monmouthshire. Thus the 1919 Act retained for the Church in Wales a privileged position with regard to the solemnization of Holy Matrimony. Marriage following banns and common licences, the ecclesiastical formalities, remained valid in Wales, as also did the Archbishop of Canterbury's powers with regard to the issue of special licences.[11] Thus, despite having been disestablished, the Church in Wales continues to enjoy a privileged position with regard to the solemnizing of marriages and remains subject to the powers of the Archbishop of Canterbury with regard to the issue of special licences.

This raises the vexed question of the extent to which the disestablished Church in Wales remains obligated to perform marriage ceremonies for parishioners who are not communicants of the Church, and especially with regard to the unbaptized. As with the Church of England, the clergy of the Church in Wales enjoy a statutory right to refuse to marry divorcees in their churches,[12] but no such protection is afforded with regard to the unbaptized. As indicated above, refusal to marry a duly qualified person is an

---

11 See Walker, 'Disestablishment and independence', 167–8, for an account of the passing of the 1919 Act. It should be noted with regard to the retention of the Archbishop of Canterbury's power to issue special licences that he enjoys this power throughout England, in the Province of York as well Canterbury, and that the Archbishop of York has no such right. In addition, there was no Archbishop of Wales at the time of disestablishment, to whom the power could have been transferred.

12 Matrimonial Causes Act, 1965, s.8(2).

ecclesiastical offence.[13] However, an ecclesiastical offence is an offence under the ecclesiastical law and, by section 3 of the 1914 Act, the ecclesiastical law of the Church in Wales has ceased to exist as law and has become merely the terms of the contract which binds the members of the Church together as members of an unincorporated association. Thus, any offence is committed against the terms of that contract not against the law of the land, and the only persons who can complain of that contract being broken are parties to it, that is members of the Church. It would appear, therefore, that unless the unbaptized person can find a willing Church member who is prepared to support the complaint, the Church in Wales cleric is safe in his refusal to marry the unbaptized. He is certainly not liable to criminal prosecution or to an action for damages, and, as has been said, a reasonable refusal is unlikely to meet with the issue of a prerogative writ of mandamus ordering the cleric to solemnize the wedding.

The other vestige of establishment which continues to cling to the Church in Wales relates to burials. The extent of the confiscations which the Welsh Church Act sought to inflict upon the Church in Wales can hardly be evidenced better than by the elaborate provisions for taking from the Church the very churchyards surrounding its churches, together with any other church burial grounds. While allowing existing incumbents to enjoy their rights to the freehold in all such burial grounds, including churchyards, the Welsh Commissioners were thereafter to transfer the burial grounds into the hands of the appropriate secular authority.[14] The inconvenience of this proposal is nowhere better attested than in the Act itself, where provision had to be made for allowing the church authorities a right of way across the churchyard to get to the church, to prevent funerals being held so as to interfere with church services, to compel the maintenance of paths leading across the churchyard to the church and to allow extensions to the church to encroach upon the churchyard land.[15] The manifest inconvenience of this proposal to virtually all concerned is apparent on the face of the Act, and the provisions are a monument to the disaffection existing between the established

---

13 *Argar v. Holdsworth* (1758) 2 Lee 515. However, this is a case concerning marriage by common licence, and it is unclear from the report whether the ecclesiastical offence was refusal to marry or contempt of the directions of the diocesan bishop. The decision also dates from the time when only Church of England ceremonies constituted valid legal marriages.

14 Welsh Church Act 1914, s.8(1)(b)

15 Ibid, s.24(3)

Church and the Nonconformist population. However, the inconveniences were so great that in 1945 the policy was reversed.

The Welsh Church (Burial Grounds) Act, 1945 repealed section 8(1) (b) of the 1914 Act, and provided that the Welsh Commissioners, while continuing to honour the freehold of any surviving predisestablishment incumbents, should transfer burial grounds not to the secular authorities but to the Representative Body of the Church in Wales.[16] Moreover, the 1945 Act provided that in the case of burial grounds that had already been handed over to the secular authorities, the Representative Body should be allowed to negotiate their retransfer to the Church.[17] Thus churchyards and burial grounds came to be retained by the disestablished Church. However, in this there remained a problem. While the Church was established, its law was part of the law of the land and, as such, non-members had control over its provisions through the secular government. With regard to such matters as burial, this was important, as that part of the ecclesiastical law dealing with burial fees, fees for the erection of monuments and indeed the right of burial itself, could clearly affect non-members. Once such burial grounds were in the hands of the disestablished Church, such control was lost, for, as has been shown, from disestablishment ecclesiastical law ceased to be law in Wales and became merely the terms of a contract binding the members of the Church, and only those members. The members alone could alter or modify the content of the contract and thus could severely prejudice the position of non-members whose interests could still be affected in matters such as burial rights. In this regard, therefore, the Church in Wales is still subject to the control of the law of the land. With regard to such matters as rights of burial and burial fees, the Church in Wales is not free to do as it wishes. Under the provisions of the Welsh Church (Burial Grounds) Act, 1945, the Church, through the Representative Body, may make rules relating to these matters, but to be valid the rules have to be approved by the Secretary of State. This system recognizes that persons other than members of the Church have an interest here, and the Church therefore is not free to do as it wishes. The Secretary of State in effect approves the rules on behalf of the population as a whole, including the non-members whose legitimate interests are affected. The Church retains, therefore, certain public duties in this area, for non-members continue to enjoy rights of burial, and it is likely that

16   Welsh Church (Burial Grounds) Act, 1945, s.1.
17   Ibid, s.2.

the courts would enforce the public duties involved with prerogative orders of mandamus.

The Uses of Self-determination

These last points in relation to marriages and burials represent remnants of the established order which passed in Wales in March 1920. With its passing, the Church in Wales faced the necessity of providing for itself many of the things which had previously been provided for the Welsh dioceses by the establishment. Gone were the methods by which bishops and other members of the higher clergy had been appointed under Crown patronage; gone was the method by which clergy were preferred to certain livings by being presented by a private patron, and gone was the corporate status of the Welsh cathedrals. Gone also were the jurisdictions of the ecclesiastical courts in Wales, together with the enforcement of ecclesiastical law in the civil courts. The Church in Wales also found itself in need of representatives to hold the assets left to it after disestablishment, as well as governmental structures at all levels including an organ of provincial government capable of providing a constitution and regulations for what the 1914 Act had termed 'the general management and good government of the Church in Wales'. The Welsh dioceses found themselves at disestablishment outside any ecclesiastical province and therefore outside the metropolitical jurisdiction of any archbishop.

The gap between the passing of the Welsh Church Act in 1914 and its being brought into force in 1920 allowed the Church in Wales, and particularly the bishops, to remedy these deficiencies. By the time that disestablishment actually occurred on 31 March 1920, the Church in Wales had a Constitution ready for its government. It was this Constitution which was to fill the vacuum left by the withdrawal of English ecclesiastical law.

The withdrawal of Crown patronage regarding the appointment of bishops meant that the Church in Wales had to provide its own method for ensuring its episcopal succession. This it did in what is now chapter VIII of the Constitution.[18] The method adopted for the election of bishops for the Church in Wales was that of an electoral college. The college would be summoned upon

18   All references to the Constitution of the Church in Wales are to the Constitution as it stands at the date of publication of this volume.

a see becoming vacant, and would consist of the diocesan bishops together with six clerical and six lay representatives from the vacant diocese and three clerical and three lay representatives from each of the other Welsh dioceses. The representatives would be appointed by their dioceses through the respective Diocesan Conferences, and the lay representatives would all be communicant members of the Church in Wales. The college then meets in the cathedral church of the vacant diocese on an appointed day, and its deliberations may continue for up to three consecutive days. If, after that time, it is unable to reach a decision as to whom to appoint, the appointment passes to the Archbishop of Canterbury. The election is by ballot, and a two-thirds majority is required before a bishop-elect shall be deemed to have been chosen. The bishops of the Church in Wales then meet as the ancient Sacred Synod of the province and, if satisfied as to the fitness of the bishop-elect, they approve his election.

This method of choosing bishops for the Church in Wales can be seen to involve representatives of the whole people of God in Wales, clergy and laity, and is a radical departure from Crown patronage. It is important to stress that the electoral college does not regard its choice as reflecting the wishes of the electors or of the dioceses from which they come. It regards itself as reaching its decision by guidance of the Holy Spirit. To that end, its meetings are bound by the Constitution to begin with a celebration of the Holy Communion, and are throughout punctuated by prayer. Those attending the college, the deliberations of which are strictly confidential, are often surprised at the spirituality of the occasion.

The disestablished Welsh dioceses had determined by the date of disestablishment that they would form a new province within the Anglican Communion. This therefore required that an archbishop be appointed to act as metropolitan of the new province. The method of choosing an archbishop for the Church in Wales is also by electoral college and is broadly similar to that for the election of bishops. However, there is no double membership for any diocese and the college is restricted to choosing an archbishop from among the diocesan bishops of the Church in Wales. The approval of the Sacred Synod is not required.[19]

With regard to other ecclesiastical offices within the Church in Wales, appointments to these are now governed by chapter VII of the

19 Constitution, IX.

Constitution. Deans, archdeacons and cathedral canons are appointed by the bishop of the diocese, while preferments to benefices within Wales are now subject to a system of patronage entirely within the control of the Church. Basically, the bishop, the Diocesan Patronage Board and the Provincial Patronage Board take turns to present to each benefice. The turns of patronage follow a fourfold cycle – bishop; diocese; province; diocese. The patronage boards consist entirely of clerics and communicant members of the Church. Again, as with the appointment of bishops and the archbishop, patronage within the Church in Wales has been restored to the control of the people of God. With the abolition of ecclesiastical corporations, the organization of the Welsh cathedrals is now governed by a series of Cathedral Schemes, being regulations made by the Church in Wales using the powers given it by the 1914 Act. As the wholesale confiscation of property and disendowment of the Church at disestablishment left little to support the clergy, clerical stipends are now paid by the Representative Body in accordance with further regulations known as the Maintenance of the Ministry Scheme.

The Church in Wales took full advantage of the powers given it by the Welsh Church Act to set up a system of courts to replace the ecclesiastical courts lost at disestablishment. Chapter XI of the Constitution provides for these, and there are now Welsh Church courts at archdeaconry, diocesan and provincial level. The Constitution provides for the appointment of judges to serve in these courts as well as for registrars. The jurisdiction of each tier is laid down in chapter XI, which also contains provisions for a Special Provincial Court and a Supreme Court for the Church in Wales. The procedure of these courts, and forms and precedents for use in matters within their jurisdiction, is provided in detailed rules framed by the Rule Committee. These rules continue amongst other things a faculty procedure for the regulation of additions and alterations to church buildings. The jurisdiction of the courts is, of course, limited to the membership of the Church in Wales, jurisdiction in effect being accepted as one of the terms of that contract which from disestablishment has bound the membership of the Church in Wales into an association.

The Church in Wales also took advantage of the opportunity to incorporate the representatives who were to hold its property on trust for its uses and purposes. Chapter III of the Constitution provides for the membership of this Representative Body. The diocesan bishops are members, together with representatives of each of the dioceses. There are also opportunities to co-opt and nominate further members, who are usually chosen in order to make use of their particular knowledge, skills or business acumen. The members form the Representative Body of the Church in Wales, which was duly incorporated by royal charter. It is a charitable trustee and, as such, answerable in the civil courts for the discharge of its obligations. Its duty is to hold the property vested in it on trust for the purposes of the archbishop, bishops, clergy and laity of the Church in Wales. Subject to its statutory duties, it is by charter required to perform its functions in accordance with the wishes of the Governing Body of the Church in Wales. The Governing Body, as will be seen, is the highest policy-making and legislative organ of the Welsh Church, so that the Representative Body is in effect controlled by the people of God who make up the Church in Wales. It cannot, however, do anything which conflicts with its civil law duties as a charitable trustee corporation.

The Representative Body holds the legal title to the churches and parsonages which the Church in Wales acquired from the Welsh Commissioners at disestablishment. The continuance of a faculty procedure to protect churches from the introduction of inappropriate ornaments and from possibly harmful alterations has already been mentioned. The Church has also provided regulations governing the proper maintenance and insurance of churches (the Church Fabric Regulations), regulations relating to the procedure for declaring a church redundant, and regulations governing what is to be done with the proceeds of sale of churches and church sites. As church-yards and other burial grounds are now vested in the Representative Body, there are also regulations for the administration of those churchyards and governing the removal of gravestones within them. The regulations relating to the administration and upkeep of the stock of parsonages vested in the Representative Body are to be found in chapter X of the Constitution and in the Supplementary Regulations thereto. The Representative Body also provides resources to support the ministry: for those in training through the Regulations to provide resources for training; for those in service through the Maintenance of the Ministry Scheme; and for those who have retired through the Clergy and Deaconesses' Pension Scheme contained in chapter XII of the Constitution.

The powers to frame constitutions and regulations given by the Welsh Church Act have also been put to good use by the Church in

Wales so as to provide organs of Church government at all levels, from the parish to the province. Parochial administration is provided for in chapter VI of the Constitution, the work of the Ruridecanal Conference in chapter V and that of the Diocesan Conference in chapter IV. The highest governmental and legislative organ of the Church in Wales, however, is the Governing Body, and the composition, functions and procedures of this body are dealt with in chapter II of the Constitution.

Section 13(2) of the Welsh Church Act provided that:

> Nothing in any Act, law or custom shall prevent the bishops, clergy and laity of the Church in Wales from holding synods or electing representatives thereto, or from framing, either by themselves or by their representatives elected in such manner as they think fit, constitutions and regulations for the general management and good government of the Church in Wales and the property and affairs thereof, whether as a whole or according to dioceses, and the future representation of members thereof in a general synod or in diocesan synods, or otherwise.

In the period leading to disestablishment following the enactment of this provision, the decision was taken that the general management and good government of the Church required the existence of a provincial body charged with the accomplishment of those tasks. The Governing Body is the result. It consists of three orders: the order of bishops, which consists of the diocesan bishops of the Church in Wales; the order of clergy, which consists of all assistant bishops, deans and archdeacons together with representatives of the clergy in each diocese; and the order of laity, which again consists of representatives of the laity elected on a diocesan basis. The holders of certain key positions in the government of the Church enjoy *ex officio* membership, and the Governing Body can co-opt further members. All members, however, whether *ex officio*, elected or co-opted, belong to one of the three orders outlined above.

The Governing Body has the plenitude of power to frame constitutions and regulations for the government of the Church in Wales. Its powers are very wide, in that it can and has amended the ecclesiastical law which the Church in Wales inherited from the Church of England at disestablishment. It has full power to amend the existing articles, doctrines, rites, rules, discipline and ordinances of the Church, and similar powers over ceremonies, formularies and even the faith of the Church. Its powers indicate better than anything the freedom to control its own destiny which the Church in Wales enjoys as a result of disestablishment.

The Limits of Self-determination

It is in this freedom that danger lies. The powers of the Governing Body are sufficiently wide to allow it to add to, alter, amend or abrogate matters relating to the faith, discipline, ceremonies, articles, doctrinal statements, rites and formularies of the Church in Wales in such a way as to risk or cause schism between it and the other provinces of the Anglican Communion. Schism, it is submitted, is caused when the Church in one province is not able to remain in full communion with a sister Church in another province, full communion being understood to entail each Church being prepared to admit members of the other to its sacraments and being prepared to allow ministers of the other to administer its sacraments.[20] The manner in which the Anglican Communion has developed during the last century and a half has created the serious possibility of such schism occurring, as has been forcibly argued by Bishop Eric Kemp in a lecture to the Ecclesiastical Law Society of the Church of England.[21] The fact that the Governing Body of the Church in Wales enjoys such wide powers has sometimes been interpreted to mean that it is the legal sovereign of the Church in Wales, to use the jargon beloved of late nineteenth- and early twentieth-century constitutional lawyers and legal theorists.[22] Indeed, such notions clearly affected one of the earliest commentators on the Constitution of the Church in Wales, Archbishop Green.[23]

However, such notions are fundamentally erroneous. They are based upon an approach to the Constitution and canon law of the Church in Wales which is not only legal, but legal in an exclusively

20 See the various canons relating to full communion with other churches in the Canons of the Church in Wales to be found Vol. II of the Constitution. Full communion is different from intercommunion in that the latter concept allows members of each church to receive the sacraments of the other but does not allow interchange of ministers. This, it is submitted, is the correct distinction, although regrettably the terms 'full communion' and 'intercommunion' have become confused even within the canons themselves.

21 Right Reverend Eric Kemp, 'Legal implications of Lambeth', *Ecclesiastical Law Journal*, 1(5) (1989), 15–23.

22 See particularly, John Austin, *The Province of Jurisprudence Determined* (London, 1832) and A. V. Dicey, *An Introduction to the Study of the Law of the Constitution* (London, 1885).

23 Green's *Setting* is clearly so affected; see T. G. Watkin, 'Authority within the Church in Wales', in A. R. Willie (ed.), *Living Authority : Essays in Memory of Archbishop Derrick Childs* (Penarth, 1990), 165–178.

secular sense. This secular sense relegates canon law to an uncertain but definitely subordinate existence within the larger and more manageable concept of ecclesiastical law, which in turn is part of the public law of the State. In other words, this approach is founded entirely on an understanding of canon law obtained from its place, or lack of a place, in the English legal system immediately prior to disestablishment. To discover the true risk of schism arising from the activities of the Governing Body, one must examine the workings of that body according to its own implicit assumptions. It is there that one will find the constitutional principles of the canon law of the Church in Wales.

To begin with, it is worth noting that for most matters which come before the Governing Body, a resolution of that body can be obtained by a simple majority of the members. No vote by orders is required. However, on any issue, it is open to any ten members or any one diocesan bishop to demand a vote by orders. If such a request is made, a vote by orders must be taken, and the motion will then become a resolution only if it obtains a majority in each of the three orders. In other words, a majority of the bishops could prevent a motion being passed even if all the other members of the Governing Body were in favour. This power of veto entrusted to the episcopal order is even more apparent when one considers those matters which the Constitution deems so important as to require resolution by bill procedure. Attempts to alter, amend or abrogate matters relating to the faith, discipline, ceremonies, articles, doctrinal statements, rites and formularies of the Church in Wales can be made only by the enacting of a canon, and this requires bill procedure. A bill has to be presented to the Governing Body, have three readings before that body and finally receive a two-thirds majority in each of the three orders voting separately before it becomes a canon and part of the law of the Church in Wales. Again, therefore, the order of bishops has an effective power of veto. As any two Governing Body members may introduce a bill for consideration, the episcopal veto means that no change can be forced upon the Church without episcopal assent. Further, with regard to articles, doctrinal statements, rites, ceremonies and formularies, no bill may be considered by the Governing Body unless it has been backed and introduced by a majority of the order of bishops. Any attempt to institute change in those areas is the prerogative of the bishops, but they cannot themselves secure such changes without the assent of the orders of clergy and laity.[24]

24 Constitution, II, 34–43; Watkin, 'Authority', 167–70

The implicit assumption in these constitutional provisions is that no change to the received tradition of the Church in Wales should be made without the approval of its episcopate, and no change should be made which does not command the support of clergy and laity as well. The Church should move as one body, not in division but in unity. The bishops act within this structure as guardians of the received tradition of the Church, and it is their responsibility to see that the powers of the Governing Body are not exercised so as to destroy the unity of the Church in Wales or the unity which the Church in Wales enjoys with its sister Churches in the Anglican Communion and possibly with other Trinitarian Churches as well. It is in this function of the episcopate that the guarantee against schism lies. Likewise, no person may be admitted to the episcopate in Wales without the approval of the existing bishops in Sacred Synod.[25] The bishops are the guarantors of the orthodoxy of canonical development within the Church in Wales. In this role, they ensure that the Church remains true to the tradition it has received from Apostolic times. Theirs is the heavy responsibility of ensuring that contemporary developments do not offend against the essentials of the received tradition, and it is for them to assess such developments against that background before signifying their approval and allowing the development to proceed.

This desire for unity within the Church on the basis of the tradition received and developed from Apostolic times is expressed clearly in one of the collects used at the start of each session of the Governing Body:

> O Almighty God, who hast built thy Church upon the foundation of the Apostles and Prophets, Jesus Christ himself being the head cornerstone: Grant us so to be joined together in unity of spirit by their doctrine, that we may be an holy temple acceptable unto thee. . .

The aspirations of this prayer are the foundations of the principles which underlie the constitutional workings of the Governing Body. The role of the bishops within that body is a manifestation of their duty to be a centre of unity; it illustrates what is meant in the Catechism when it states that the 'ministry of a bishop is . . . to guard the Faith'.

It may be felt at this point that the discussion has moved away from the legal into the realm of the theological. This is indeed so and

25 See above, pp. 38–9, and Watkin, 'Authority', 173–4.

stands in no need of apology as it should be so where the legal system being described is that of the Church. The Constitution of the Church in Wales is a part of the post-disestablishment canon law of that Church, replacing the ecclesiastical law which it lost at disestablishment. As has recently been insisted by the Roman Catholic canon law scholar, Father Robert Ombres OP, there is a theology of canon law and a theology in canon law.[26] What has been written above relates to the latter concept, the theology within the Constitution of the Church in Wales. It accepts that the Church is the people of God, a body instituted by Christ and constituted by the Holy Spirit.[27] As such, it seeks to develop in the unity of that spirit so that it may be acceptable to God. Talk of legal or political sovereignty is out of place; it is a relic of the pre-disestablishment situation in which the Church was not free from the control of the State, not free – or at least not as free – to follow where the Spirit willed.

It could be argued that the Holy Spirit can work as effectively through secular institutions which control the Church as through ecclesiastical institutions, and doubtless a theology of such a situation could be supplied. The important point for this discussion is that the theology within the canon law and the Constitution of the disestablished Church in Wales cannot be unaffected by disestablishment. Once one accepts that disestablishment gave the Church in Wales freedom from secular control and freedom to respond to the Spirit, one is faced with the question of the extent to which its Constitution and canon law have risen to the challenge of the opportunities afforded. Regrettably, it would be misleading to pretend that the Church perceives its Constitution as a theological document; more convincingly it might be said to perceive it as a necessary but unwelcome legal guest. This in part no doubt reflects its genesis in an ecclesiastical law which was not of the Church's own making, but, as has been shown, the law of the Church in Wales has changed a great deal since then. In part, the defect may lie in the fact that the Constitution and canon law are not sufficiently studied, criticized and appreciated from a theological standpoint. Roman Catholic ordinands, for example, receive a whole year's tuition in canon law as a compulsory part of their theological training.

26 Robert Ombres, 'Faith, doctrine and Roman Catholic canon law', *Ecclesiastical Law Journal*, 1(4) (1989), 33–41.
27 See John D. Zizioulas, *Being as Communion* (London, 1985), 140, quoted and developed in Tom Smail, *The Giving Gift: The Holy Spirit in Person* (London, 1988), 191–7.

There are, it is true, many facets of the Constitution of the Church in Wales which remain marked by its emergence from the ecclesiastical law of the established Church of England. Many Welsh Anglicans despair, for instance, over the technicalities of bill procedure, particularly in dealing with such issues as liturgical revision. However, the principle at the root of bill procedure is hardly objectionable, namely that important changes should be carefully considered on more than one occasion before being carried into effect. Although in its Governing Body form, it clearly owes much to parliamentary procedure, its beginnings are believed to have been in the ancient world, where a change to the customs of some societies had to be considered on three successive market days; once to alert people to the proposed change, once to debate the principle embodied in the change and once to approve the actual change in detail.

Perhaps, however, the Church in Wales should consider whether its legislative procedures are suitable for an ecclesiastical body. Debates at the Governing Body follow what can be described as a well-behaved parliamentary model. The model is, nevertheless, adversarial, motions being formally proposed and then opposed. One wonders whether an inquisitorial model, based on the procedures of some of the continental legislatures, might not be more appropriate, particularly as there have been some interesting experiments at Governing Body meetings in recent years with such an open forum approach. The difficulty is that such a system is foreign to those brought up amid the institutions of the United Kingdom.

However, the continued use of those institutions as the model for Church government reflects the legacy of establishment. Traditionally, the models for the institutions of the canon law were those of the civil law derived from ancient Rome and revived by the societies of continental Europe during the Middle Ages. *Ecclesia vivit lege romana:* the Church lives by Roman law, and this was as true of the Church of England before the Reformation as of the Church on the Continent. Indeed, civilian practice continued to be the model for the ecclesiastical courts of the Church of England until the middle years of the nineteenth century. It was therefore less than a century before disestablishment that the adversarial model replaced the traditional inquisitorial approach in the Church courts, and it was parliamentary control that introduced it into Church government.

Conclusion

The Church in Wales since disestablishment has enjoyed freedom from subservience to secular authority and freedom to respond to the promptings of the Holy Spirit. It has been able to develop a Constitution which has a theological as well as a legal integrity. It has the opportunity to revive a proper appreciation of the place of canon law in the whole life of the people of God in Wales. Such an appreciation can inform theological discussion within the Church as much as a knowledge of the history, doctrine and moral teaching with which it is inextricably linked. Due regard for the canon law of the Church can only serve to deepen understanding of the Christian tradition within which it stands.

3

Building a Canon Law : The Contribution of Archbishop Green

REVEREND CANON ARTHUR J. EDWARDS

In St David's Cathedral there is a stone statue of St David with a dove on his right shoulder. Thousands of children and adults probably think of St David in terms of this statue although it was placed there only at the beginning of this century. With St David dressed like a medieval bishop, the statue is an anachronism. When Charles Green (1864–1944) was a choirboy, living at St David's, he could not have seen this statue. Had he done so, he would probably have liked it. What other paradigm could one possibly have for a bishop?

St David's was the place of Charles Green's earliest childhood memories and where he received his primary education from his own father, master of the Cathedral Grammar School. It was the traditional education of an English cathedral school, though Green's father had learned Welsh and could teach it to the boys 'if there was no objection to it'.[1] From an educational background of Classics, Mathematics, English and Divinity, Green went on to Charterhouse, leaving there to take up a scholarship in Classics at Keble College, Oxford in 1883. He read Greats but never looked like getting a First – he spent too much time at the Oxford Union of which he became president. Keble confirmed Green's character. He became articulate, Anglican and anti-disestablishment – a Tractarian, a Tory, and a toff.

In contrast to Green's immediate heredity and environment, the real establishment in Wales at the time was essentially Nonconform-

<hr />

1 D.W. James, *St David's and Dewisland: A Social History* (Cardiff, 1981), 140–5.

ist and Liberal. Green's approach to ecclesiastical law and order was both a reaction to the social and political conditions in Wales in the second half of the last century, and a response to Tractarian theology and the ecclesiastical polity that he inherited through his education. This essay is an attempt to reconstruct, in outline, the central elements of Green's conception of canon law – its nature, its objects and its place in the life of the Church – as presented in his *Setting of the Constitution of the Church in Wales* (1937), and to trace his part in the formulation of the canon law of the Church in Wales at disestablishment.

Ecclesiastical Law and the Orders

The Catholic party in the Anglican Church believed that bishops were of the *esse* of the Church. Had not Cyprian declared *ubi episcopus, ibi ecclesia* and *extra ecclesiam nulla salus est*? It followed, therefore, that a bishop was necessary for salvation. He was not simply a convenient ecclesiastical official for whom enough work had to be found to keep him busy – as some in the Elizabethan Church had thought. The Catholic principle of episcopacy was dearest of all the Catholic principles of the Church of England for Anglo-Catholics at the time of Green.

In 1898 A.J. Mason, an Anglo-Catholic, wrote a biography of Archbishop Thomas Cranmer which would have met with Green's approval as a Catholic biography of an enigmatic archbishop.[2] Neither Green nor Mason would have liked the verdict of Professor Patrick Collinson that the 'apologists of the Elizabethan church could not have regarded episcopacy as a catholic principle, properly so called, or as an essential attribute of the Church of England'. Nor would they have cared for Collinson's assertion that the 'English reformers. . .were inclined to regard the division between bishops and inferior clergy as a distinction of rank rather than of order, an indifferent, political matter rather than a point of doctrine'.[3]

Certainly, from the earliest centuries, there was in Catholic theology an understanding of ministry that was essentially twofold rather than threefold – suggesting an order of bishops–presbyters above an order of deacons.[4] Thus the statement (in the preface to

2 A.J. Mason, *Thomas Cranmer* (London, 1898).
3 G.J. Cuming (ed.), *Studies in Church History* (Ecclesiastical History Society, London, 1965), III, 93–4.
4 S. Sykes and J. Booty (eds.), *The Study of Anglicanism* (London, 1988), 148.

the *Ordinal* of 1550) that, from the Apostles' time, there have been these orders of ministers in Christ's Church – bishops, priests and deacons – is not to assert that there have always been three strictly separate orders of ministry in Christ's Church. Charles Green would have been shocked by such an assertion and it is largely because of his work that many in the Church in Wales today, equally, would be shocked.

Green's notion of episcopacy for the Church in Wales was based on a monarchical model of the bishop, constitutionally limited. He wrote that:

> [T]he Constitution of the Church in Wales neither confers, nor is meant to confer, any authority or power upon the Bishops which did not already belong to them, by Divine Command. The Church is a Theocracy, not a Democracy. . .The totality of the Christian Ministry stands in the Bishop alone: he sums up all subordinate ministries in his own.

He adds, 'the Constitution of the Church in Wales recognizes the Diocesan Bishop alone as actually and ordinarily possessed of full Apostolic Authority'. However, Green conceded that '[i]n the exercise of his Ministry, the Bishop is regulated by the Ecclesiastical Law'. There had to be a separate order of bishops – but for voting purposes at the Governing Body only diocesan bishops belonged to the House of Bishops since 'they alone constitute the Sacred Synod of the Province' (thus, assistant bishops belonged to the House of Clergy).[5] Indeed, it also seems that, at first, the model of Green's bishop is the focus of unity and guarantor of the valid Eucharist – like the idea of a bishop in Ignatius of Antioch (d. *c.* 110). Yet, as Green's thought unfolds it is clear that the medieval prelate is envisaged so that 'all ministrations, clerical or lay in the Church derive their validity from the Bishop, in whom is vested the plenitude of Apostolic authority and power'.[6]

Green's is a very high doctrine of episcopacy carried into the official thinking of the Church in Wales because its principal exponent was an Anglo-Catholic. Green shared with the Tractarians an abhorrence of the utilitarian view, which saw episcopacy as nothing

5 C.A.H. Green, *The Setting of the Constitution of the Church in Wales* (London, 1937), 13,14,21,22. For a succinct discussion of bishops in the Church in Wales and the problem of authority, see T.G. Watkin, 'Authority within the Church in Wales', in A.R. Willie (ed.), *Living Authority: Essays in Memory of Archbishop Derrick Childs* (Penarth, 1990), 165.
6 *Setting*, 15.

more than a convenient system of government.[7] Green's theology was reinforced by the political situation in Wales which had contributed so greatly to disestablishment. Bishops, then, held authority by divine commission, not by popular permission. In the established Church, their styles, or titles, according to Green, did not refer to their membership of the House of Lords – 'Lord Bishop' was 'the natural address to a Monarchical Bishop'.[8] Green's model is preserved in spite of disestablishment.

In his first chapter of the *Setting*, Green wrote: 'When we speak of the Historic Episcopate we mean the Episcopate such as it had been in fact during the long history of the Church'. Green goes on to say that the 'Historic Episcopate thus stands in contrast with all Bishops devised for mere convenience in modern times, who in reality are nought but presidents or inspectors'.[9]

Green and the Stubbs–Maitland Controversy

The medieval bishop, of course, owed allegiance to the pope and derived authority from Rome. Anglo-Catholics have always lived with the tension created by this. The Anglo-Catholic view of the development of papal authority in the Middle Ages was this: the pope's powers of appointing bishops in England and Wales without reference to the king increased in the thirteenth century. From the historical and legal writings of their champion, Bishop William Stubbs, Anglo-Catholics concluded that the Church here had been guided by laws passed independently of the pope under the protection of the king. There was, therefore, a body of English canon law operating independently of the papacy. The *ecclesia anglicana* of the twelfth century and the Church of England of the early Tudor State were essentially the same creature governed independently of the pope.[10] As Kemp puts it, 'Stubbs believed that the Roman canon law, as contained particularly in the *Corpus Juris Canonici* and proceeding in the main from the popes, did not or was not regarded as possessing any inherent authority in England, other than as a useful

7 See generally, A.J. Mason, *The Church of England and Episcopacy* (London, 1914).
8 *Setting*, 11.
9 Ibid., 12.
10 W. Stubbs, *Seventeen Lectures on the Study of Medieval and Modern History and Kindred Subjects* (3rd edn., Oxford, 1900), 351, 354–5. See also, R. Phillimore, *The Ecclesiastical Law of the Church of England* (London, 1895), 14.

and scientific guide'.[11] The text of the Report of the Commission on the Ecclesiastical Courts (1882) sums it up: '[t]he canon law of Rome, though always regarded as of great authority in England, was not held to be binding on the courts'.[12]

This was challenged, in a celebrated controversy, by Frederic William Maitland in the 1890s. For Maitland, writing of pre-Reformation arrangements, '[t]he archbishop may make for his province statutes which are merely declaratory of the *ius commune* of the church. . .[h]e may supplement the papal legislation; but he has no power to derogate from, to say nothing of abrogating, the laws made by his superior'.[13] Though R.H. Helmholz has recently expressed the view that Maitland overstated his attack against Stubbs, since this controversy, Maitland's thesis has won general acceptance.[14] Maitland's stance was reinforced by Professor Z.N. Brooke's study, in the 1930s, of early collections of canons and decretals. For Brooke, in short, '[t]he English Church recognized the same law as the rest of the Church; it possessed and used the same collections of Church law that were employed in the rest of the Church. There is no shred of evidence to show that the English Church in the eleventh and twelfth centuries was governed by laws selected by itself'.[15]

Green's outlook was wholly at odds with the new learning. Green turned to the English canonist William Lyndwood's *Provinciale* (1430). Green asked whether the Church of England had after 1234 its own insular canon law. He concedes, citing Maitland, that '[a] negative answer is generally given by eminent modern students'. However, he questions: why was it necessary for Lyndwood to write *Provinciale*, in which he codified and annotated the canons and constitutions made in English ecclesiastical councils, if the common ecclesiastical code of Christendom (the Roman canon law) 'covered the whole ground'? He also asks why the Convocation of York in 1463 accepted the Canterbury provincial constitutions (codified by Lyndwood in his *Provinciale*) to be incorporated into the provincial

11 E.W. Kemp, *An Introduction to Canon Law in the Church of England* (London, 1957), 13.
12 *Report of the Commissioners Appointed to Inquire into the Constitution and Working of the Ecclesiastical Courts* (London, 1883), I, xviii.
13 F.W. Maitland, *Roman Canon Law in the Church of England* (London, 1898), 19; see also ibid., 15.
14 R.H. Helmholz, *Roman Canon Law in Reformation England* (Cambridge, 1990), 4–12.
15 Z.N. Brooke, *The English Church and the Papacy from the Conquest to the Reign of John* (Cambridge, 1931), 113; see also ibid., 100.

law of York and to be 'observed as law'? Maitland's answer had been, in short, that provincial constitutions were mere glosses upon that Roman canon law which was absolutely binding in *ecclesia anglicana* (which, as the Roman Catholic Professor Charles Duggan said, was 'not designed or understood to imply a separateness from the *ecclesia romana*', but used 'to safeguard the right of the Church against the encroachments of secular rulers').[16] Moreover, as Maitland pointed out, Lyndwood himself, at the height of the conciliar controversy, did not incline to the populist thesis of canon law: Lyndwood implies rather that the pope was above the general council and that papal law was valid and of the highest authority without the council's consent.[17] The Maitland stance was, of course, employed by the liberationists at the time of the Welsh Church Disestablishment Bill in 1912.[18]

Green was not alone, however, in his sympathy towards Stubbs's view. Canon A. Ogle too opposed the Maitland thesis in 1912, but without real conviction. The conclusion of the historical argument was well summarized by Duggan in 1965: 'Maitland and Zachary Brooke established two conclusions regarding the medieval English Church which have never subsequently been seriously challenged.'[19] The motive for Ogle's attempt, as Green knew, was precisely the use to which Welsh Nonconformists turned Maitland's evidence in 1912. By 1890 Stubbs himself had acknowledged the correctness of Maitland's study. And he realized how much his own views of the medieval period had been shaped by the ecclesiastical law of his time – and particularly by the ecclesiastical jurisdiction of the Judicial Committee of the Privy Council in liturgical affairs.[20]

The Stubbs–Maitland controversy is important in our understanding of Charles Green's view of canon law. It is very revealing that the Report of the Archbishops' Commission on the Canon Law of the Church of England in 1947 accepted the Maitland line, and argued that the non-enforcement of parts of papal law in the

16 See C.H. Lawrence (ed.), *The English Church and the Papacy in the Middle Ages* (London, 1965), 108.
17 Maitland, *Roman Canon Law*, 15, n.3, 16. See also N. Doe, 'Fifteenth-century concepts of law: Fortescue and Pecock', *History of Political Thought*, 10 (1989), 257 at 262–4.
18 Cuming, *Studies in Church History*, III, 52: it was not Maitland's intention to be used in this way.
19 Lawrence, *The English Church*, 107. For A. Ogle, see his *Canon Law in Medieval England* (London, 1912).
20 Cuming, *Studies in Church History*, III, 51.

ecclesiastical courts was 'not because Churchmen denied the legislative powers of the papacy but because they were forbidden and restrained from doing so by the civil power, and were forced to acquiesce in this prohibition'.[21] The Church of England had known nothing of the bitter divisions of a disestablishment campaign. The pressures for disestablishment, and the attendant propaganda, did more damage than the deed itself to the Church in Wales. When Green reviewed the setting of the Constitution of the Church in Wales ten years before the Report on Canon Law in England, he was still much more influenced by the activities in Wales in the two decades before 1920, when the Church in Wales became a separate disestablished province of the Anglican Communion. Consequently, Green took a very different view (the Stubbs view) from the Commission (the Maitland line) on the possible canonical autonomy of *ecclesia anglicana* before the Reformation.

Green used the Anglo-Catholic (Stubbs) stance in his paper against disendowment presented at the Llandaff Diocesan Conference at Cardiff in October 1912. In Green's opinion Roman Catholics could never have a better claim to the land and property that the Church held in Wales before 1234, because the Reformation merely abolished 'the late medieval system of papal jurisdiction which had grown up after the *ecclesia anglicana* had become established'. Since the faith and discipline of Roman Catholics had changed so much since the Reformation, 'it was preposterous for politicians to advance Roman Catholic claims to be the Church that received the ancient titles originally'.[22]

For Green (as for Stubbs and Phillimore) the Church of England was most truly herself when she was regarded as a national Church. Accordingly, there had been a short time before the Reformation when a temporary aberration had interfered with this autonomy – but the ancient Church was an autonomous province (or two) of the universal Church. So it was also for the Church in Wales. For Green the province of Wales is an autonomous province of the universal Church now rightly restored, through disestablishment by the State, to the ancient status that had been hers before the Norman conquest. So, according to chapter II, section 2 of the present Constitution, the 'Order of Bishops. . .sit and act as representing the ancient Provincial

21 *The Canon Law of the Church of England: The Report of the Archbishops' Commission* (London, 1947), 38.
22 A.J. Edwards, *Archbishop Green: His Life and Opinions* (Llandysul, 1986), 35–6.

Synod, and shall, subject to the Constitution of the Church in Wales, retain and exercise all the authority and powers of and belonging from of old to a Provincial Synod'. As Green told the clergy of the Rural Deanery of Aberdare in 1902, 'behind our Chapter to-day. . .there lies a history of nearly one thousand years'.[23]

Green's Concept of Ecclesiastical Law

Chapter 5 of Green's *Setting* contains a summary of the development of ecclesiastical law from Apostolic times (there is even a reference to Amos). There is more detail than a modern reader would require, and Green employed many varying sources for his discussion, which is largely derivative – including Van Espen, Fournier and Le Bras (*Histoire des Collections Canoniques*), Vinogradoff, Maitland, Brooke, Reichel and Harnack (whose *Constitution and the Law of the Church in the First Two Centuries* was given as a Christmas present from Green's wife in 1910).

Using the Roman Catholic Reichel's definition, according to Green 'the Ecclesiastical Law is a System of Rules, for soul and body, which governs the relation of member to member, and of all the members to the entire Church, which is the Holy People of God'.[24] He argues that '[a]part from alliance with the State, breaches of this Law are punishable, spiritually, by the dread of the Divine Displeasure arising from disobedience, temporally, by varying degrees of exclusion from the common life of the Christian Community'. Writing more generally, and drawing on Van Espen, Green explains that '[t]he *Jus Ecclesiasticum Universum* includes all those beliefs, doctrines, customs, edicts, judgments, canons and statutes "which have been generally accepted by the Church as binding her members for the purposes for which she exists"'.[25] Green turns to Harnack to identify the basic function of canon law: 'The conviction that it (the Church) was the Messianic Community of the latter days also led to legislative enactments, for as such it was bound to keep itself pure and holy, which in the last resort could be accomplished only by punishment and excommunication'. And 'it was bound to develop new rules of life, i.e., legislative enactments, because it claimed

---

23 Ibid., 32.
24 *Setting*, 80; O.J. Reichel, *The Canon Law of Church Institutions* (London, SPCK, 1922).
25 *Setting*, 80,81; Z.B. Van Espen, *Jus Ecclesiasticum Universum*, 5 Vols (Louvain, 1753), I, xi.

jurisdiction over the whole of the life and thought of its members, as well as their social relations to one another'.[26] Green offered no critique of these ideas.

Green reviewed the development of canon law through the *ius antiquum* until Gratian's *Decretum* (*c.*1140), to the *ius novum*, the various collections of canon law, culminating, he said, in 1582 with 'the five collections, prefaced by the *Decretum* of Gratian, [which] were published in one work by the command of Gregory XIII, under the title *Corpus Iuris Canonici*'.[27] In Green's opinion, the ecclesiastical law 'which the Church in Wales took over' at disestablishment included 'many Acts of Parliament. . .together with the Canon Law and the Common Law of the Realm, as composing that System of Ecclesiastical Law existing on the 30th of March, 1920'. He added, of course: 'The Church in Wales is not irrevocably tied to that Legal System, as it existed then; it can be revised, altered and enlarged'.[28]

Having spent almost fifteen pages tracing ecclesiastical law up to the Reformation, Green spent only four pages on its development to his time. Moreover Green failed to indicate the identity of, or provide examples of, those statutes and judicial decisions which survived disestablishment as rules applicable in the Church in Wales. Indeed, Green had a negative view of the place of nineteenth-century ecclesiastical legislation. His message for the Welsh Church was that '[s]ince the date of Disestablishment new Ecclesiastical Legislation is passed in the Provincial Assembly, known as the Governing Body, wherein the Laity and Clergy share with the Provincial Synod of Bishops the duty of forming and enacting Ecclesiastical Canons and Laws'.[29] Though he seems also to have scorned the general use of a populist theory of government: after all, the Church for Green was a theocracy not a democracy. Indeed, he seems to have been particularly disturbed that '[i]n the nineteenth century the Church of England found herself on the verge of Democephalism, so far had

26 *Setting*, 82; A. Harnack, *The Constitution and Law of the Church in the First Two Centuries*, English Translation by F.L. Pogson (London, 1910), 20, 21, 22.
27 *Setting*, 82–93.
28 Ibid., 97, 98; Welsh Church Act 1914 s.3(2) and (4). Indeed, Green adds that as 'every fresh Canon of the Church in Wales, promulgated since March 30th, 1920, is "a law of the Church in Wales and binding on all the members thereof". . .some notion of the meaning of "Ecclesiastical Law" is necessary for the intellectual outfit of every member of the Church in Wales' (ibid., 80).
29 *Setting*, 98. Green also regretted the disappearance of Doctors' Commons (an association of ecclesiastical lawyers which was dissolved in 1857). See Edwards, *Archbishop Green*, 97.

she departed from the Discipline of the Primitive Church' – he defined *democephalism* as 'making the Populace the Head of the Church'.[30]

Church and State in Green

For Green 'there is a fundamental dissonance between the Christian Church and the State, for their aims and processes differ'.[31] But, in the final chapter of the *Setting*, Green acknowledged the advantages allowed to the Church in Wales by the State – the power to employ its own courts 'for the settlement of disputes'; by granting the applicability of pre-1920 rules of English canon law, the State had saved the need for the Welsh Church to formulate there and then an ecclesiastical law for itself; and the State allowed the Church to create its own canon law. Above all the State protected in the disestablishment legislation 'the inherent right of the Bishops to hold Synods'. Some pre-1920 English statutes, listed in chapter 2, section 97 of the Constitution (1936), were now expressly excluded from the categories of applicable sources. These included the notorious Public Worship Regulation Act of 1874. As we have seen in chapter 2, the disestablishment legislation had a distinctly liberating effect, and Green recognized this.

In his first Ordination Service in Monmouth Parish Church in September 1922, Green invested the deacon and priest with a dalmatic and chasuble respectively. This prompted correspondence in *The Times* with Bishop Hensley Henson. Green reminded Henson that it was part of the law of the Church in Wales that 'the courts of the Church in Wales would not be bound by any decision of the English Courts or of the Judicial Committee of the Privy Council in relation to matters of faith, discipline and ceremonial' – this was embodied in XI,36 of the Constitution.[32] Indeed, the Public Worship Regulation Act had been disliked in England – allowing the imprisonment of clerics caused more scandal than the liturgical offences they committed. English bishops frequently used their veto to prevent proceedings under the statute. In short, for Green, disestablishment removed from lay interference the liturgical practices of the Welsh bishops: 'the Statute of 1914 has secured the Spiritual

---

30 *Setting*, 97.
31 Ibid., 297; Green cites here I John, 4:4-6.
32 *Setting*, 302.

liberty of the Church in Wales'.[33]

An important part of Green's discussion was also the positive way in which law created directly for the Church by the State may function to benefit the Church. There are several statutes, he maintains, 'which give protection and security to the Church in Wales'. The Brawling Act 1553 provides that 'any person disturbing licensed preachers in their sermons, or disturbing a Priest performing Mass or other such Divine Service, or abusing or mishandling the Blessed Sacrament of the Altar, may be arrested by constables and imprisoned by order of the Justices of the Peace'. Similarly Green pointed out that a statute of 1860, whilst reserving clerics charged with brawling to trial in the ecclesiastical courts, provided that:

> any person who shall be guilty of riotous, violent or indecent behaviour. . .in any Cathedral Church, Parish or District Church or Chapel of the Church of England. . .during the celebration of Divine Service. . .[or] disturb. . .any preacher duly authorized to preach therein, or any clergyman in Holy Orders ministering or celebrating any Sacrament. . .[shall] be liable to a Penalty.

Green identifies numerous examples when '[t]he State has by many Acts of Parliament secured and protected' the Church, such as in the area of property or those privileges which the common law allows the clergy (such as exemption from jury service). However, he also identifies actual conflict between State law and Church law: in the area of marriage, for example, Green saw a dissonance between two competing legal systems – 'the State dissolves what the Church declares to be indissoluble, and allows what the Church forbids'.[34]

Green on Ecclesiastical Law and Discipline

Section 31 of chapter II of the original Constitution gave power to the Governing Body 'to make any scheme for the observance and maintenance by the Archbishop, Bishops, Clergy and Laity of the Church in Wales of discipline, faith and ceremonial'. Now, for Green Church discipline was of the highest importance. 'The Standard of conduct set before the Church is high.' The ecclesiastical law concerned 'the conservation and development of that Common or Mutual Faith which animates the Body of Christ'.

---

33 Ibid.
34 Ibid., 311.

Green appeals to Paul's condemnation of 'the works of the flesh' (Gal. 5:17,19, 20, 21) as 'the justification of all External or Public Discipline'. As Green explained:

> The Scheme provided for the trial of 'any member' of the Church in Wales for (a) having been convicted on indictment of treason, felony, or of a misdemeanour, and sentenced to imprisonment; (b) having been adjudged father of a bastard child; (c) having been found in a matrimonial cause to have committed adultery.

It also provided for charges against any clergyman of the Church in Wales for 'immorality, or conduct giving just cause for scandal or offence' (XI,27 of the 1936 Constitution).

Green's treatment in the *Setting* which deals with this scheme of discipline, applicable, of course, to both lay and clerical members of the Church in Wales, is as follows: 'The Scheme is defective', declared Green:

> . . .in that it does not include among the charges to be determined by the Provincial Court the case of a person found guilty of Drunkenness, or found guilty of oppression or extortion, and other notorious sins, which weaken the hands of the Church in her perennial warfare against wickedness .[35]

A modern reader might instinctively feel that Green's regret that the provincial court could not deal with the discipline of lay people in this way is a measure of the extent to which Britain has changed in the last seventy years. But there are still parts of the Anglican Communion where the acceptance of such lay discipline is not questioned.[36] Green's awareness of the need for personal discipline among the laity and the clergy in the life of the Church was sensible but the solution he proposed was manifestly absurd. Indeed, the Register of the Provincial Court of the Church in Wales records no case ever having been brought against a lay person in the area of discipline. We shall discuss later cases brought during Green's lifetime against clerics.

---

35 Ibid., 285. However, he concedes that 'even as it stands, the Scheme is a witness to the Standard which is expected of all the Members of the Christian Church, whose Faith commits them to live "under law to Christ", because "he that was called, being free, is Christ's bondservant"' - I Cor. 9:2 (Green asks his reader, however, to compare I Pet. 2:16 - but he does not add any comment).
36 The Anglican diocese of Sabah in Malaysia provides one specific example. Contrast with this the Lambeth Conference Report, 1988, 35(26).

Practice and Green's Theory

Though Green was critical of elements of the actual canon law of the Church in Wales, it could not be said that there was a dissonance between Green's theoretical analysis of canon law in the *Setting* and the actual Constitution itself. The correspondence between Green's theoretical outlook and the actual canon law of the Welsh Church is in part a tribute to the influence that he exercised upon the framing of that canon law, and his part in the political and theological debate in the Church in Wales during the First World War.

While the principal protagonists of Church defence, Bishops Edwards and Owen, were still trying to win the arguments against disestablishment and softening the disendowment proposals, Archdeacon Green (as he then was) seems to have been the only Welsh Church leader to understand the full significance of disestablishment for the catholic order of the four dioceses which would thus become disestablished. Their representatives would not be able to continue as members of the Convocation of Canterbury. There could not be a separate Church Assembly in Wales acting independently of the Provincial Synod of the Welsh Bishops. There would have to be a separate Governing Body for Wales in which the bishops sat as the Provincial Synod. The Bishop of Bangor had already opposed the setting up of a separate Welsh province, and Bishop Owen opposed the immediate institution of the Governing Body – he represented those who still hoped in 1917 that the disestablishment legislation would be repealed after the war.[37]

As early as September 1914, Owen had described Green as 'a very able and level-headed man'. In explaining Green's role in the meeting of the Cardiff Convention in 1917, Owen said that 'the Archdeacon put the whole matter in its historical setting', a verdict that could have applied to the whole of Green's book. When Owen wrote to Archbishop Davidson in September 1918, he said that 'Archdeacon Green, who is a weighty authority on Canon Law, was exceedingly valuable to us'.[38] Green's principal contribution to that meeting had been to safeguard the spiritual rights of the bishops in the matters of institutions to benefices and the deprivation of clergy from office.

While Lloyd George (tired by this time of disestablishment) thought that he had finished with the Established Church in Wales, and the old champions of Church defence vainly hoped to turn back

37 E.E Owen, *The Later Life of Bishop Owen* (Llandysul, 1961), 265, 275.
38 Ibid., 367.

the tide, Green was intent on the preservation of *catholic order* within the new province. To this extent he was forward-looking and creative in his administrative proposals both for the new province and, later, for the new diocese of Monmouth. Two architects of the nascent constitution, Mr Justice Sankey and Mr Frank Morgan, acknowledged separately Green's unique grasp of the legal and theological issues that lay behind the new constitutional arrangements. Had he realized, wrote Sankey on 7 June 1937, when he had just received a copy of the *Setting*, that 'there was such a mass of learning behind it and that there was a man who knew it all, I am afraid I should have feared to rush in'.[39] That is hardly a mere pleasantry or a patronizing remark in the circumstances, and it reflects what had been the truth at the time. Morgan, one of the greatest of many great lay people who have served the Church in Wales, was frequently frustrated beyond words by the obtuseness and indecision that he encountered in the Church in Wales – but he conceded that Green was 'one of the few who realised what yet had to be done' in the disestablished province – and Morgan lists as necessities the division of dioceses, amalgamation of benefices, a central examination for ordinands, a clergy superannuation scheme, tribunals and the problem of episcopal palaces.[40] Green shared this forward-looking policy and he had the capacity for creative administrative changes whilst, at the same time, preserving what was essential to catholic order in the new province.

Where Green was not forward-looking, but revealed a reactionary or at best static view of canon law and theology, was his attitude towards society – in particular the social changes that had taken place since the death of Queen Victoria. One of his little-known addresses was published in the Report of a special meeting of the Llandaff Diocesan Conference at Cardiff on Tuesday 18 June 1918. In a long speech Green delivered on the possible admission of women to Church institutions (particularly the Governing Body), he declared that '[w]oman is distinguished from man by her capacity for maternity. For that end her physical nature is constituted. The fact dominates her life. For about forty years Nature never ceases to remind her of it'.[41]

---

39 Edwards, *Archbishop Green*, 57.
40 Ibid.
41 *Report of a Special Meeting of the Llandaff Diocesan Conference* (Cardiff, 1918), 21.

Green considered that his strongest argument against the admission of women to the Governing Body was that such an idea was a new one. He was anxious whether 'the Church in Wales can safely lead the way to innovation'. He said: '[i]t has amazed me to find the suggestion that there is no positive bar'. His argument continued with the following exposition of some fundamentals of canon law: '[w]hatever reply might be made by Dogmatic Theology, no student of Canon Law nor even of Moral Theology would venture to minimize the force of the Common Law of the Church'. This, he said,

> . . .rests largely on custom, unbroken custom;. . .But custom, it may be replied, can be changed by legislative process. Certainly: and if the custom be a mere provincial custom, I suppose a Provincial Synod can alter or modify it. But when the custom is universal, it requires ecumenical action to alter it, before the alteration can assume an acceptable form.

He concluded: '[f]or four Welsh Dioceses to lead the way in an innovation of this kind is, to my mind, ridiculous. If there is any thing of permanent value in the Woman Movement, the question must claim the attention of the Church at large, and the final decision will rest with it'.[42] In other words, there was no precedent for the Welsh Church to act unilaterally and Wales was too small to create one. On this occasion Green's static view of the past did not prevail. The debate has an unmistakably contemporary ring to it.

Green and Clerical Discipline

Though he spends a great deal of time on the composition and powers of the Provincial Court, the only cases it had heard before 1937 were those brought by Green himself, concerning clerical indiscipline. The first was *Cook's Case* (1925).

The Provincial Court met at the Pump House, Llandrindod Wells, on 28 September 1925, to hear a petition from Green as Bishop of Monmouth under what was then chapter VII, section 46 of the Constitution: 'If any incumbent shall be absent from his benefice for. . .two consecutive months without the permission of the Bishop, it shall be competent for the Bishop to call upon him to return'; moreover, 'if at the expiration of one month he shall still be absent, it shall be competent for the Bishop to declare the benefice vacant'. Green

42 Ibid., 26–27.

alleged that Christopher Cook, the longest-serving incumbent in Wales (Vicar of Llanfihangel Pont-y-moel for seventy-four years and Rector of Mamheilad for seventy years), was 'childish and nearly deaf and blind and incapable of managing any affairs' and had 'not for many years past done any clerical duty'. Green proposed that adequate maintenance could be made for Cook by a pension under the provisions of the Welsh Church Act.

Presided over by Lord Justice Bankes, the other five judges of the Provincial Court were Mr Justice Sankey, the Dean of St Asaph, the Archdeacon of St David's, Mr D.F. Pennant and Canon Joyce. The court heard evidence from the Registrar of the Diocese of Monmouth and Cook's children (Revd W.G. Cook and Miss Cook), and decided that Cook should resign so that proper arrangements could be made for the pastoral care of the parishioners. Cook would be allowed to continue to live at Mamheilad Rectory, and to receive a pension of £118.10s. per annum. He was then declared to be incapacitated by permanent infirmity from the due performance of the duties of his office.[43]

The second was initiated by Green as Bishop of Bangor in 1933, concerning the misconduct of the Vicar of Dolwyddelan. By chapter VII,43(b), as it then was, '[t]he Bishop may remove an incumbent for any reason which, in the judgment of the Provincial Court, renders his continuance in office grievously prejudicial to the welfare of the Church'. This is 'provided that, failing other employment, he shall receive such maintenance, if any, as the Court shall recommend to the Representative Body'. Evidence was brought against the vicar in the form of petitions to Green from the parishioners and a presentment from the churchwardens to the Archdeacon of Bangor and to the Archdeacon's Court (held at Conwy on 19 April 1932). The vicar's disagreement with his parishioners had caused serious breakdown in pastoral relations within the parish. The vicar had committed assaults, used threatening behaviour and abusive language towards several parishioners, and had damaged property of one churchwarden (for which the vicar had been convicted in the Magistrate's Court at Betws-y-coed on 15 April 1933 – he had been bound over in the sum of £20 for twelve months). The Provincial Court, sitting at the Old Vicarage, Bangor, on 1 August 1933, held the vicar liable. Green delivered his sentence of deprivation on

---

43 *Register of the Provincial Court of the Church in Wales*; J.D. Evans, 'Parson Cook of Llanfihangel Pontymoel', *Gwent Local History, 59* (1985), 23–30.

8 August 1933. The vicar was a young incumbent whom Green had instituted three years before.[44]

Conclusion: Green in Perspective

Green's *Setting* was not written from a lawyer's point of view. Green's aim was to show how disestablishment left the Welsh Church very much in the same position as the early Church in Wales. A major theme for Green was historical continuity. He used the Stubbs argument to support the idea of an indigenous canon law – the local Church must be able to create its own independent law. The work is a commendable effort to show how the essential features of catholic order have been preserved in the Church in Wales in spite of disestablishment and have been enhanced by that process. Where it is enlightened by the pastoral insights that Green acquired as an incumbent, a rural dean, an archdeacon, a bishop and an archbishop, it is a rich quarry of information and guidance for his successors. The appendices provide models of ecclesiastical forms for all sorts of occasions arising from Green's own experience in ecclesiastical administration. There are even a couple of historical essays to justify his own interpretation of the catholicity of the Church in Wales.

Charles Green's interest in canon law may be said to have been a lifetime's fascination arising from his educational background and his political associations. This interest was intensified by the historical circumstances which had forced upon all Anglo-Catholics the need to be aware of the state of the ecclesiastical law. As a Welsh priest, Green's perceptions were sharpened by the political circumstances which led to the disestablishment and disendowment of the Church in Wales in 1920. However, Green made no reference in his own writings to the revision of the Roman Catholic *Codex Iuris Canonici* of 1917. (Though he began collecting, in 1917, cuttings from the Law Reports of *The Times* which he catalogued in his own library under 'Ecclesiastical Legal Points' – with reference to such cases as marriage discipline, the payment of tithes and clerical indiscipline.[45]

Green was present at the working parties in Sankey's home drafting the Constitution which was generally approved by him – though the precise extent to which his own ideas prevailed is

44 *Register of the Provincial Court and Official Handbook of the Church in Wales* (1933).
45 The book is to be found in the Library of St Michael's College, Llandaff.

not now clear. There was a need, at that time, for a commentary on the Welsh Constitution such as Green's. But, not surprisingly, it is in need of modernization. However, it is more surprising, in view of Green's claim in 1935 that disestablishment had not isolated the Church in Wales, that there was not more communication between the Church of England and the Welsh Church on the subject of canon law.[46] Again, Green makes no reference to the authorities on canon law then active in England – nor, indeed, was any reference made to Green's pioneering work in the Report of the Archbishops' Commission on the Canon Law of the Church of England in 1947. Furthermore, the Report itself had followed on much the same lines as Green's *Setting*.[47] Nor did Archbishop C.F. Garbett of York, the Chairman of the Commission of 1947, make mention of Green in his book *Church and State*.[48]

To conclude, some of the central elements of Green's conception of canon law discussed here might be summed up in this way. The canon law of the Church was a vehicle to provide for the episcopacy principle: canon law had to be based on a notion of the Church as episcopal. The canon law had also to be an indigenous law, fitting the nature of the Church. But his notion of canon law was of a system of rules essentially coercive in nature. He stressed too the positive aspects of the relationship between Church and State – the law of the State must not be ignored as a direct source of canon law.

In the library of Charles Green at Newport and in Bangor there was a series of handsomely bound green volumes containing the publications since 1904 of the Canterbury and York Society. These were the edited printed registers of the medieval bishops and arch-

46 C.A.H. Green, *Disestablishment and Disendowment* (reprinted from the *North Wales Chronicle*, 11 October 1935).
47 The Report has sections on the *ius antiquum* and the *ius novum* and, like the *Setting*, contains a lengthy historical survey. Indeed, Green had been awarded the degree of Doctor of Civil Law by the University of Oxford for the *Setting*: see Edwards, *Archbishop Green*, 91.
48 C.F. Garbett, *Church and State in England* (London, 1950): see 227–8 for Garbett's view that 'In addition to State Law the members of a Church are under another law, the law of the Church, which imposes upon them regulations from which other citizens are free ... Those who dislike them can resign or withdraw from their membership; for in our day there is no longer compulsion for anyone either to join a Church or to remain within it; of their own free will they can transfer their membership to some other religious society, or if they so wish they can remain outside all Churches. The canons of the Church affect only its members, and chiefly those who hold office within it; they have been made for its spiritual welfare and for the sake of its good order.'

bishops from the thirteenth to the sixteenth centuries.[49] They contain much information about the administration and style of a medieval bishop. The model of episcopacy and ecclesiastical government that Green transposed to the disestablished Church in Wales was fundamentally that of the medieval bishop. That model is as difficult to explain to posterity as the statue in the cathedral at St David's.

---

49 I.J. Churchill, *Canterbury Administration*, 2 vols (London, 1933); C.J. Offer, *The Bishop's Register* (London, 1929).

4

A Facilitative Canon Law: The Problem of Sanctions and Forgiveness

NORMAN DOE

A common perception of canon law is that of a set of rules, commanding and forbidding, whose object is coercive, to compel obedience to the Church's orders by means of threats of sanction. This concept of canon law has proved to be one of the many obstacles it faces to full acceptance as a legitimate function of the Church's right to manage itself.[1]

It is the purpose of this essay to examine two issues in the context of the law of the Church in Wales. First, it is proposed to emphasize that canon law is not simply a set of orders backed by threats – rather, fundamentally, it is facilitative, to enable the Church to do things. Secondly, accepting that sanctions are used in a limited area, the essay seeks to expose a problem intrinsic to those aspects of canon law which do involve the use of sanctions – the relationship between the employment of sanctions in canon law and the principle of forgiveness. The basic difficulty is this: does the imposition of a legal penalty for the violation of canon law conflict with the duty to

1 For the Church's right to create laws for itself, see *The Report of the Archbishops' Commission on Canon Law: The Canon Law of the Church of England* (London, 1947), 3. For the Roman Catholic view, stated by Pope John Paul II, at the promulgation of the new Code of Canon Law in 1983, see the Apostolic Constitution *Sacrae Disciplinae Leges*, in J.A. Coriden, T.J. Green and D.E. Heintschel (eds.), *The Code of Canon Law: A Text and Commentary* (London, 1985), xxiv–xxvi. See also the Code itself, Canons 129, 330, 331. The scriptural texts to which appeal is most commonly made, to authorize the use of canon law, are: Matt. 16:19; 18:18; 19:28; 28:18; Luke 10:16; 22:28–30; John 20:21. For Paul's acceptance of the use of judicial power in the Church, see 1 Cor. 6:1–6.

forgive? The question is whether the use of sanctions and the requirements of forgiveness are actually incompatible, whether forgiveness is an alternative to sanctions, or whether they might coexist.

The Characteristics of Canon Law

Common to definitions of canon law is the idea that the law of the Church is composed of three species of rule: rules created by the Church for itself, rules created by the State for the Church and those demands which God places upon the Church, demands which are commonly described in modern theology as comprising the divine law.[2] These rules, classically, have been expressed as either commands or prohibitions – rules which impose duties or obligations upon those to whom they are addressed. The idea of rules as precepts and prohibitions, binding on the members, clearly appears in the canon law of the Church in Wales. Some rules are in the form of commands – such as the duty of churchwardens to maintain order in the church or 'the duty of the incumbent and the [Parochial Church] Council to consult together and co-operate in all matters of concern and importance to the parish'. Other rules, though these are less numerous, are in the form of prohibitions – such as the rule that a Parochial Church Council is forbidden to make any 'formulation or declaration of doctrine', or the rule that an incumbent 'shall not make any structural alteration or addition to the parsonage or to the permanent fittings thereof without the consent of the [Diocesan Parsonage] Board'.[3] The distribution and sharing of responsibility, amongst lay and clerical members of the Church, is an important function of canon law – and the word 'responsible' appears time and time again in the law of the Church in Wales.[4]

As well as duty-imposing rules directed to individuals or bodies,

2   For the idea of a divine law in modern theology, see, for example, P.S. Minear, *Commands of Christ* (Edinburgh, 1972), 12–15; J.Knox, *The Ethic of Jesus in the Teaching of the Church* (London, 1961), 48–51,97–99. For definitions incorporating the three sources, see (for Anglican ideas) G.E. Moore and T. Briden (eds.), *Introduction to English Canon Law* (2nd. edn., Oxford, 1985), 9; for a Roman Catholic view, see G. May, 'Ecclesiastical law', in K. Rahner (ed.), *Encyclopedia of Theology* (London, 1981), 395, and P. Huizing, 'Church and state in public ecclesiastical law', *Concilium*, 8(6) (1970), 126 at 129.
3   Constitution, VI,17(2); VI,22(2); VI,22(3); X,17(f).
4   The concept of responsibility usually attaches to the performance of acts: ibid., IV,40(2)(a); X,17(c),(d),(e); X,39; for one body being responsible to another, see VI,29. The list is not exhaustive. For the development of responsibility in Roman Catholic canon law, see T.P. Doyle's remarks in *Commentary*, 795.

occasionally there is reference to what appears to be a fundamental principle of the law of the Church in Wales – decisions and acts must be carried out only in so far as they promote the good of the Church – for instance, the Diocesan Conference may repeal or alter any regulation made by a Parochial Church Council 'to provide against the admission of any principle inexpedient for the common interest of the Church in Wales in the diocese'.[5] Similarly, according to chapter VII, section 46, of the Constitution, a bishop may remove an incumbent for any reason which 'renders his continuance in office grievously prejudicial to the welfare of the Church'. Work is needed to identify and define precisely the nature and scope of this sort of principle.

However, it is misleading to conceive of the canon law of the Church in Wales, or canon law generally, as being composed entirely of commands and prohibitions. It is essential to discard this distorted view of canon law. In secular legal thought notions of law instead stress its facilitative nature – law exists to enable individuals to do things, 'to provide individuals with facilities for realising their wishes' – this is the starting point for the law relating to contracts, wills or marriage.[6] (Though it is not denied, of course, that within the general framework of the law relating to contracts, for example, many rules will be concerned with prohibiting parties from performing certain acts as well as commanding or enabling them to do things.)

The same is true in modern canonical thought. Canon law is not simply about commanding and forbidding. It exists to serve the purposes which are appropriate to the Church, its view of itself, its nature and mission (as we see in Antony Lewis's essay). In Anglican thought it has been suggested that the canon law aims to promote the Church's 'purpose as an institution for the help of [people] in their following of our Lord. . .to have such laws in force as to assist it in its work of training up the followers of our Lord'.[7] When Pope John Paul II promulgated the Code of Canon Law in 1983, he stressed that canon law 'facilitates. . .an orderly development in the life of both the ecclesial society and of the individual persons who belong to it'.[8] There is a rich literature in Roman Catholic canonical theory offering a diversity of views about the purposes of canon

5 Constitution, IV,43; see too II,33; II,57; VII,46(3); *Rules of the Courts*, I,27(c).
6 H.L.A. Hart, *The Concept of Law* (Oxford, 1961), 27.
7 *Report of the Archbishops' Commission on Canon Law* (1947), 5.
8 *Commentary*, xxiv-xxvi.

law: some writers (Georg May) suggest that law might be used by
the Holy Spirit as one of His ways in organizing Christian life; some
(Robert Ombres) suggest that canon law is a guide to the faithful to
salvation; others (like John Alesandro) offer a more aggressive
outlook and see canon law as determining and protecting the rights
and obligations of members of the Church; some (such as José Setien)
propose a pragmatic view of canon law based on the idea that it
exists to eliminate and control tensions in the Church; others emphasize the pastoral work of canon law (like Paul Winninger), claiming
that its main function is to effect the work of mission.[9]

Much of the law of the Church in Wales is intended to provide a
range of facilities for its members. Let us consider a collection of
single rules to illustrate each point. The Constitution is designed to
give the Church the power to regulate its life. It creates institutions
to help manage the Church – it creates the Governing Body, the
orders, the church electorate, the courts, for example. It confers
legislative, executive and judicial powers on these institutions –
chapter II, section 33 states that 'the Governing Body shall have the
power to make. . .constitutions and regulations for the general
management and good government of the Church'. But it also
imposes limits (substantive and procedural) on the exercise of these
powers – by section 36 of the same chapter, '[t]he Governing Body shall
have the power to make new articles, doctrinal statements. . .pro-
vided that no such action shall be taken except by a bill [proce-
dure]. . .backed and introduced in the Governing Body by a majority
of the Order of the Bishops'. The Constitution defines the relations
of one institution to another – 'no proceeding of the Governing Body
shall interfere with the exercise by the Archbishop of the powers and
functions inherent to the office of metropolitan, nor with the exercise
by the Diocesan Bishop of the powers and functions inherent in the
Episcopal Office' (II,32). The Constitution also attempts to facilitate
the operation of the elective principle and the majority principle in
the government of the Church in Wales.[10]

The law of worship (contained primarily in the *Book of Common*

9 See: G. May, 'Ecclesiastical law', 395; R. Ombres, 'Faith, doctrine and Roman
Catholic canon law', *Ecclesiastical Law Journal*, 1(4) (1989), 33 at 33,37; for
J. Alesandro, see *Commentary*, 6,20,21; J. Setien, 'Tensions in the Church',
Concilium, 8(5) (1969), 35–41; P. Winninger, 'A pastoral canon law', ibid., 28.
10 See, for the elective principle, for example: II,5,6,29; for the majority
principle, which appears in so many forms (as simple and special majorities): II,
34(1) and (2),38(5),41,50,52; III,26 – esp. (b); IV,32.

Prayer for Use in the Church in Wales 1984) provides a framework for corporate worship: it enables us to benefit from the use of forms of service; by the law of worship, providing for the 'regular and systematic reading of Holy Scripture and meditation upon it both the clergy and people are encouraged to grow in the knowledge and love of God'.[11] The canons of the Church in Wales provide for the possibility and development of ecumenical relations – such as the frequent establishment by canon of communion between the Church in Wales and other Churches, allowing communicants of other Churches to be 'admitted to the Holy Communion in the Church in Wales' and vice versa. Indeed, a study of the canons 'for covenanting between the Church in Wales and other churches for union in Wales' provides a useful general statement of the doctrinal stance of the Church in Wales.[12] As we saw in chapter 2, the disestablishment legislation itself can be conceived positively as a liberating law. The law exists to provide the people with access to the sacraments – such as the regulation by which a bishop 'may permit a lay person to assist the incumbent or other priest in the administration of the elements of the Holy Eucharist'. Again, regulations have been made 'to provide resources for training for the ordained ministry of the Church in Wales'. These are facilities, arranged by means of the canon law, crucial to the liturgical, pastoral, missionary and sacramental life of the Church.

Finally, canon law is about the conferring and protection of rights for all members of the Church – the ability or facility to do things (or not to suffer them). For example, the Parochial Church Council has the 'right to make representations to the Bishop concerning the affairs of the Church' (VI,22(5)) and qualified electors 'have the right

11 *The Book of Common Prayer for Use in the Church in Wales* (1984), v: 'The law of worship of the Church in Wales is contained in the Book of Common Prayer' (ibid).
12 These provisions were promulgated by canon in 1974. The Church in Wales covenants, for instance: to 'recognize in one another the same faith in the Gospel of Jesus Christ found in Holy Scriptures, which the creeds of the ancient Church and other historic confessions are intended to safeguard'; to 'recognize one another as within the one Church of Jesus Christ'; 'to seek a mode of Church government which will preserve the positive values for which each has stood, so that the common mind of the Church may be formed and carried into action through constitutional organs of corporate decision at every level of responsibility'. The canon states, however, 'that nothing herein contained shall affect or be deemed to affect the faith, discipline, articles, doctrinal statements, rites, ceremonies or formularies of the Church in Wales'.

to attend, speak and vote at Vestry Meetings' (VI,13). Indeed, the subject of rights has made an important mark (in recognizing, respecting and acting on the value of individuals in the Church) in recent years in Roman Catholic Church law.[13]

In short, much of the public aspect of the life of the Church in Wales is the product of Church law – and it is within this facilitating law, as a simple attempt to organize, that the public dimension of Christian life is provided with a form and structure and is enabled to develop. Canon law as duty-imposing is merely one aspect of a predominantly facilitative Church law. It is a distortion to think of canon law as having to do solely with orders backed by threats.

The Use of Sanctions in Canon Law

Whereas canon law is primarily facilitative, it is in the area of duties – commands and prohibitions – that the use of sanctions mainly operates. In this area canon law can be conceived in terms of orders backed by threats. This view of law, typified by the criminal law in the secular sphere, is one in which rules are treated as imposing duties on individuals (or bodies). In turn, a sanction is the consequence which is prescribed in the event of the non-observance of a substantive duty-imposing rule – and the duty may be imposed on an individual, an office-holder, or a body. A sanction is a response to some act or omission having the effect of disadvantaging its object. For merely organizational or facultative rules, of course, talk of sanctions will be inappropriate: there will be no sanction.

Sanctions might be imposed in a variety of settings – for the non-performance of duties, for acts which are prohibited, and for the violation of rights conferred by canon law. Moreover, the sanction itself, whether contained in the rule imposing the duty or elsewhere, might be in a variety of forms.

Sanctions may be applied to the clergy. According to chapter XI, section 18 of the Constitution the Provincial Court has the power to determine, amongst other things, a charge against any member of the Church in Wales for teaching or professing doctrine incompatible with that of the Church in Wales, 'neglect of duties, or conduct

13 F. Morrisey, 'Is the new code an improvement for the law of the Catholic Church?', *Concilium*, 185 (1986), 35, for a brief discussion of the 'charter of rights'; P. Lombardia, 'The fundamental rights of the faithful', *Concilium* 8 (5) (1969), 42. For individual rights see, for example: B. Primetshofer, 'The right of assembly in canon law', ibid., 47; P. Huizing and K. Walf, 'What does the "right to dissent" mean in the Church', *Concilium*, 158 (1982), 3.

giving just cause for scandal or offence', and 'wilful disobedience to or breach of any of the provisions of the Constitution'. Further, by section 25 of the same chapter, '[a] judgment, sentence or order of the Provincial Court may include deprivation or suspension from any preferment, office or any membership of a body and the right to vote in the Church in Wales'. However, the Court cannot deprive a cleric of office or suspend from performance of duties but may recommend one or both of these to the bishop who may make such an order on the recommendation as he thinks fit.

Sanctions might also be applied to lay members. By chapter XI, section 28 it is the duty of every member of the Church in Wales to attend and give evidence, when duly summoned to do so, at any trial or investigation held under the authority of the Constitution. However, '[i]f any member of the Church in Wales shall wilfully and without sufficient cause neglect or refuse to attend and give evidence', the Provincial Court may declare vacant any office in the Church in Wales (including membership of any body) to which that member has been elected or appointed. It might also 'declare that such member be deprived of or suspended from the right to vote in the Church in Wales'. It is, then, a constitutional offence for a lay person to fail to give evidence without sufficient cause, to which the sanction of deprivation or suspension applies. Arguably, as chapter XI, section 18 applies to any member, so too all lay persons holding office who are in neglect of duty, commit acts giving just cause for scandal or offence, or wilfully disobey or break any of the provisions of the Constitution, might be deprived of or suspended from office. It also seems that excommunication by a bishop is permissible – though not judicial excommunication.[14]

In relation to both clerics and the laity, chapter XI, sections 34 and 35 sum up the position: 'the power of the Archbishop, a Diocesan Bishop, the Provincial Court, the Special Provincial Court and the Supreme Court shall include that of passing sentence of monition, suspension or expulsion from office in the Church. . .in Wales'; '[t]he Bishop of the diocese shall have the power to suspend from office, until the hearing and determination of a case, any person holding office in his diocese against whom a charge is pending, and

14 C.A.H. Green, *The Setting of the Constitution of the Church in Wales* (London, 1937), 118, 165. For other examples of removal, see Constitution, III, 17 and III, 34. It seems that the possibility of extra–judicial excommunication in the canon law of the Church of England is not excluded: see Halsbury, *Laws of England*, vol. 14, *Ecclesiastical Law* (4th edn., London, 1975), para. 1384.

to make arrangements for carrying out the duties of that office during such suspension'.

Other forms of sanction may be applied in relation to ordinary members not necessarily holding office. For example, the name of a communicant member of the Church in Wales may be removed from the electoral roll of a parish for a variety of reasons: these include when that person 'becomes a member of any religious body which is not in communion with the Church in Wales'.[15] It is a matter of debate whether, having application to any member, the offences prescribed in chapter XI, section 18 are capable of being committed by lay members not holding office.

Sanctions might also be suffered by institutions. According to chapter IV, section 18 of the Constitution, '[t]he Diocesan Board of Finance with the approval of the Bishop shall have the power to place on a defaulters' list a parish which culpably neglects to meet its financial obligations': but in this event, if an incumbency is suspended (for instance), the bishop must make provision for the spiritual needs of the parish (VII,6(3)). Indeed, a body such as a Parochial Church Council might suffer sanctions: the Provincial Court may suspend any body of the Church in Wales (except the Governing Body or the Representative Body) 'for neglecting or refusing to obey any judgment, sentence or order. . .of the Arch-bishop, Diocesan Bishop or any Court of the Church in Wales' – to be valid the order of suspension must be made with the consent of the bishop (XI,27).

Sanctions might also be expressed in the form of invalidity, as when acts and decisions of committees must be approved by some body – if they are not then they are treated as invalid.[16]

Finally, sanctions may be pecuniary. For example, an incumbent is responsible for the results of any negligence by him (or his household) and for wilful damage done or allowed to be done by him to any part of the parsonage. When the incumbent is in violation of this rule forbidding negligent or wilfully damaging acts, he is responsible for carrying out to the satisfaction of the Parsonage Board necessary repairs, and if he fails so to do the Board can order

15 Constitution, VI, 2(6).
16 See ibid. III, 32: decisions of committees appointed by the Representative Body must be ratified by that body 'to become valid'; see also II,38(7) (a bill lapsing); IV,36 (Diocesan Decree invalid) and VII,28 (nominations of clergy) and VII,31 ('[n]o clergyman shall be instituted to a cure while a petition or suit respecting his nomination thereto is pending'). Sometimes rules specifically provide that procedural irregularity will not invalidate: II,81; III,31; V,8; VIII,27; IX,16.

the work to be done: 'and the cost thereof shall be a debt due by the incumbent to the Representative Body and may be set off against any sum due or become due by it to the incumbent' (X,17,20).

Justifications for Sanctions

Similar forms of sanction exist, of course, in other systems of canon law – rebuke, suspension, deprivation, excommunication – and these exist in the main in the area of discipline as well as for breaches of specific canonical rules. Indeed, for the English canonist Garth Moore the existence of sanctions is what converts canon law into genuine law: 'the lawyer must at least concede that, in the human field, canon law is real law inasmuch as it is enforced by sanctions'.[17]

It is rarely the case, however, in relation to Welsh canon law, that the law of the Church itself justifies the use of sanctions. Only occasionally are justifications incorporated into rules which impose duties or sanctions. For example, a bishop may remove an incumbent for any reason which, in the judgment of the Provincial Court, 'renders his continuance in office grievously prejudicial to the welfare of the Church' (VII, 46). The rule justifies the sanction of removal here as for the good of the Church: the Church functions better when its clergy are not neglectful. But this is unusual. Rather, it is to the theoretical works of canonists in other systems to which we must turn in order to seek justifications for the use of sanctions.

The Anglican canonist Herbert Box argues that '[t]he sanctions the Church possesses and the penalties it can inflict are purely spiritual'. He says that '[o]bedience is to be enforced, not positively by material means, but negatively by exclusion from spiritual privileges'.[18] Box relies on some scriptural texts to support the idea. First, the teaching of Jesus:

> If your brother commits a sin, go and take the matter up with him, strictly between yourselves, and if he listens, you have won your brother over. If he will not listen, take one or two others with you, so that all facts may be duly established on the evidence of two or three witnesses. If he refuses to listen to them, report the matter to the congregation; and if he will not listen even to the congregation, you must then treat him as you would a pagan or a tax gatherer. I tell you this: whatever you forbid on earth shall be

17 Moore and Briden, *Introduction*, 1.
18 H. Box, *The Principles of Canon Law* (Oxford, 1949), 25.

forbidden in heaven, and whatever you allow on earth shall be allowed in heaven.(Matthew, 18:15-17)

Box also uses Paul who instructed the Church at Corinth, concerning an individual who committed fornication and incest, that 'a man who has done such a deed should have been rooted out of your company. . .The old leaven of corruption is working among you. Purge it out. . .You are judges within the fellowship. Root out the evil-doer from your community' (I Cor. 5:1,2,7,13).

A more utilitarian approach was proposed in the Church of England's *Report of the Archbishops' Commission on Canon Law* in 1947. This suggests that:

[s]ince the Church is for the most part made up of ordinary frail human beings, the rules and regulations must be something more than exhortations, which anyone is at liberty to set aside when he thinks fit, or directions which can be disobeyed with impunity – otherwise members of the Church will only obey them when it is convenient.

Rather, 'they must be laws with penalties attached in case of their non-observance, where those who are accused of disobeying the laws of the Church can be tried'.[19]

Somewhat more varied and sophisticated justifications appear in Roman Catholic canonical thought. For the sake of convenience these might be summarized as follows. According to Canon 1312 of the 1983 Code of Canon Law the Church has its own inherent right to constrain with penal sanctions Christ's faithful who commit offences, and, by Canon 1317, '[p]enalties are to be established only in so far as they are really necessary for the better maintenance of ecclesiastical discipline'. The modern canonist Alesandro maintains that penalties are intended to help Christians to appreciate the disparity between their attitudes and actions and the values of the Gospel proclaimed by the Church: '[i]n this sense, penalties are meant to be tools of the external forum to bring about personal repentance and reconciliation with the community'.[20] Sanctions are also justified as deterrence: by Canon 1326 'a judge may inflict a more serious punishment than that prescribed in the law or precept when. . .a person, after being condemned. . .continues so to offend that obstinate ill-will may prudently be concluded from the circumstances'. Some Roman canonists suggest that penalties are

19 *Report*, 4.
20 *Commentary*, 19.

retributive and avenging, such as E. Taunton, who, writing at the beginning of this century, argued that '[p]unishment is the vengeance for evil doing, and it is devised for the amendment of man', and canonical 'censures are sometimes used as vindictive punishments'.[21]

Other canonists, like Thomas Green, suggest that sanctions exist 'to protect the integrity of the community's faith, communion and service'. It is 'imperative that there be some kind of framework to restore peace and order and to integrate the offending party within the life of the community'.[22] Otherwise, if the Church remained inactive to 'significant breaches of its faith or order. . .its identity as a sign of God's kingdom would be seriously jeopardized'. Condemning offences by means of sanctions allows the Church 'to be fair to its own members who joined a reasonably well-defined community and have definite expectations from it'. The use of sanctions is also important for ecumenical purposes: if left unenforced it is 'not fair to those outside the community who wish to understand its purposes and the means it uses to realize them'. Perhaps most importantly, Green suggests that 'if the Church's penal activity is to reflect its redeeming, healing character, its primary focus must be to affirm ecclesial unity through faith and charity'. Petrus Huizing agrees, adding that sanctions simply combat hypocrisy. How can the Church be taken seriously, be respected, and comment on secular ills, evils and indiscipline, if its own life is not characterized by discipline?[23]

In a nutshell, according to Thomas Green, sanctions seek to achieve two things: 'medicinal penalties' emphasize 'reconciliation of the offender with the community', and 'vindictive penalties' focus 'more on restoring community order, repairing scandal, and deterring would-be violators of ecclesiastical discipline'.[24]

---

21 E. Taunton, *The Law of the Church* (London, 1906), 539,540. The idea is also hinted at by L. Gerosa, 'Penal law and ecclesial reality: the applicability of the penal sanctions laid down in the new code', *Concilium*, 185 (1986), 60.
22 *Commentary*, 893f.
23 P. Huizing, 'Crime and punishment in the Church', *Concilium*, 8(3) (1967), 57.
24 In the Roman Catholic Code 'censures' are the 'medicinal' penalties (such as excommunication) and deprive the offender of ecclesiastical goods – like the sacraments – and they are operative until there is a change of heart on the part of the offender; with 'expiatory' penalties (replacing the 'vindictive' penalties under the 1917 Code), such as deprivation of office, the emphasis is on remedying damage done to social values in the Church and on deterrence: see *Commentary*, 906–9. The use of penalties in Roman canon law is treated very much as a last resort after pastoral measures have failed: Code, Canon 1341.

The Principle of Forgiveness

In 1988 the Bench of Bishops of the Church in Wales issued a statement on homosexuality. It explained that, basing its teaching on scripture, Christian tradition and the example of Jesus, the Church identifies as sinful promiscuity, fornication, adultery and homosexual acts: '[a]s with all sinful practices, such actions call for repentance – a turning away from such practices – with the assurance of forgiveness and healing for those who repent'. The bishops, distinguishing between homosexual orientation, which was not sinful, and homosexual practice, which was, stressed 'the responsibility of leaders in the Christian community to lead an exemplary lifestyle which will not give offence to the Gospel'. 'No Christian is exempt from this, but it is especially important that the ordained ministers of the Church should endeavour to embody those moral values which are central to Christianity'. Consequently, the bishops stated that '[i]f any serious moral or spiritual charge can be substantiated, an ordination candidate will not be accepted for ordination and a cleric will not be allowed to remain in office. Such moral failings would include unrepentant promiscuity, fornication, adultery and homosexual practice'. However, the bishops agreed that we all need to be reminded that 'the Gospel calls us all to repentance, to support and up-build one another within the body of Christ, and offers to each one of us forgiveness and healing according to our particular need'.[25]

This succinctly represents a fundamental problem for canon law. In the statement, the sanction to which the bishops refer, that of removal of a cleric against whom charges of moral misconduct are substantiated, and the demand upon us all to forgive, appear together. It is the purpose of the remainder of this essay to examine this basic problem for canon law. Can the Church impose sanctions at the same time as being obedient to the demand for forgiveness? First, we must analyse the elements of forgiveness.

Forgiveness occupies a central place in Christian theology. It is evident in the teaching of both Jesus and the Apostles.[26] Jesus uses forgiveness, broadly, in two contexts: in relations between humankind and God and in human relationships, summed up in the Lord's Prayer: 'And forgive us our sins; for we too forgive all who have done us wrong' (Luke. 11:4). Similarly: 'if your brother wrongs you, reprove him; and if he repents, forgive him. Even if he wrongs you

25 *Theologia Cambrensis*, 1 (Michaelmas, 1988), 16.
26 V. Taylor, *Forgiveness and Reconciliation* (London, 1948), 2.

seven times in a day and comes back to you seven times saying "I am sorry", you are to forgive him' (Luke, 17:3–4; Matt. 18:15, 21, 22). Jesus' teaching on forgiveness is also to be found in his parables (Matt.18:23–25; Luke, 15:11–32; 16:19–31; 18:10–14). In so far as the sayings of Jesus can be treated as part of the 'law of God', as 'what God requires of us', as laying demands upon us,[27] within the setting of human relations forgiveness is conceivable as a requirement, command or duty of divine law. The duty to forgive is also found in Paul's teaching: 'Let all bitterness, and wrath, and anger, and clamour, and evil speaking, be put away from you, with all malice. And be ye kind one to another, tender-hearted, forgiving one another, even as God for Christ's sake hath forgiven you' (Eph. 4:31–2); be 'long-suffering. . .forbearing one another, and forgiving one another' (Col. 3:12–13). We can begin to see the problem for canon law.

The object of forgiveness is when one person wrongs or injures another – as Studzinski says: '[f]orgiveness is a response to suffering which an individual has incurred at the hands of someone else'.[28] So, what must we do to forgive? Modern theologians offer a host of solutions. Some of the ideas most commonly used are these. First, forgiveness requires individuals to eradicate resentment felt against those who have injured us. Murphy says 'forgiveness is primarily a matter of changing how one feels with respect to a person who has done one an injury' – forgiveness is 'a matter of overcoming, on moral grounds, the resentment a self-respecting person quite properly feels when suffering an injury'.[29] Hampton, on the other hand, goes further. Overcoming resentment is only a prelude to forgiveness: the victim must overcome resentment and 'reapprove' of the wrongdoer and see the wrongdoer 'as still decent, not rotten as a person, and someone with whom he may be able to renew a relationship': 'forgiveness is precisely the decision that he [the wrongdoer] is not bad (even though his action [is])'.[30]

Secondly, some regard forgiveness as involving the relaxation of penalties or the cancelling of debts. For the Roman Catholic theologian Virgil Elizondo, for instance, forgiveness is 'an act of generosity which deliberately overlooks what has been done in order to remove

27 J. Knox, *The Ethic of Jesus*, 97, 98; P.S. Minear, *Commands of Christ*, 9.
28 R. Studzinski, 'Remember and forgive: psychological dimensions of forgiveness', *Concilium*, 184 (1986), 12 at 15, 16.
29 J.G. Murphy and J. Hampton, *Forgiveness and Mercy* (Cambridge, 1988), 167.
30 Ibid., 35–87.

the obstacle to our friendship and love. . .It is not for us to judge or punish. . .forgiveness is love surpassing righteousness and divine mercy transcending human justice'; Studzinski too argues that forgiveness is 'a process in which the forgiver chooses not to retaliate but rather respond in a loving way to the one who has caused some injury'.[31] This view accords with Paul's instruction that 'ye ought rather to forgive him, and comfort him. . .that ye would confirm your love toward him' (2 Cor. 2:7, 8).

However, modern theologians also consider that not only must forgiveness involve action on the part of the forgiver. The wrongdoer, too, must repent for the duty to forgive to be discharged. Repentance is often described as a precondition to forgiveness. Jesus himself, of course, refers to the two together – 'if thy brother sins, rebuke him; and if he repents, forgive him' (Luke, 17:3). The Protestant theologian H.R. MacIntosh saw repentance, 'the act of turning from sin', as a 'precondition to our being forgiven'.[32] Indeed, Murphy argues that 'repentance does not give one the right to be forgiven', but 'there is a sense in which it [repentance] may make resentment inappropriate', and, therefore, forgiveness appropriate.[33] By way of contrast, Hampton suggests that an individual's repentance may 'morally oblige you to reaccept him on the grounds that he has now become a person who has repudiated the action and who thus merits moral respect'.[34]

Two final points must be stressed. Our forgiving of another's injury against us is in itself a precondition to God forgiving us – the idea was expressed by Jesus (Mark, 11:25; Matt. 6:15) and appears in modern theology.[35] In short,(in the words of R.S. Franks) forgiveness effects 'a restoration of the sinner to communion with God; it is the breaking down of the barriers between them'.[36] In human relations, theologians identify a set of purposes: for some, like Virgil Elizondo and Paul Lehmann, forgiveness effects reconciliation and healing; Studzinski agrees, adding '[r]econciliation comes as the culmination of the forgiveness process. The forgiver is willing to start a new relationship with the injurer'; Studzinski also considers that

31 V. Elizondo, 'I forgive but I do not forget', *Concilium*, 184 (1986), 78; for Studzinski, ibid., 15.
32 H.R. MacIntosh, *The Christian Experience of Forgiveness* (London, 1927, Reprinted 1947), 236.
33 Murphy and Hampton, *Forgiveness and Mercy*, 24, 29.
34 Ibid., 41.
35 Taylor, *Forgiveness and Reconciliation*, 15.
36 R.S. Franks, *The Atonement* (1934), 156.

forgiveness frees us from the desire for retaliation and feelings of guilt in holding resentment towards the wrongdoer; Murphy suggests we forgive in order to reform the wrongdoer and bring him to repentance.[37] When viewed as healing and reconciling, the duty to forgive and actual forgiving are quite definitely functions of the pastoral life of the Church – forgiving is a pastoral activity of the Church.[38]

Sanctions and Forgiveness: A Dissonance?

It is a difficult question whether the use of sanctions in canon law offends the principle of forgiveness. From the materials examined here, two opposing sets of ideas emerge. On the one hand we have the idea that the duty to forgive forbids the use of penal sanctions. This is clearly the case when sanctions involve retaliation or resentment. This is because forgiveness requires the overcoming or eradication of resentment and the creation of new relationships. In secular legal thought, some retributivist theories of punishment do involve vengeance, retaliation and suffering. Those theories of sanction in canon law based on retaliatory or vindictive retribution would be in conflict with the divine-law principle of forgiveness, and, therefore, an invalid use of the Church's legislative and judicial power. The law of the Church is, after all, subordinate to the authority of divine law.[39] Thus, a concept of sanction (like that of Taunton) which sees canonical censures as 'vengeance' or 'vindictive punishments' is unacceptable. This type of outlook is in line with the notion in retributivist theory that punishment 'institutionalizes certain feelings of anger, resentment and even hatred that we typically direct toward wrongdoers' (Murphy), or that 'punishment is a conventional device for the expression of attitudes of resentment and indignation' (J. Feinburg).[40]

37 Elizondo, 'I forgive', 78; P. Lehmann, 'Forgiveness', in J. Macquarrie and J. Childress (eds.), *A New Dictionary of Christian Ethics* (London, 1986), 233; R. Studzinski, 'Remember and forgive', 13, 19; Murphy and Hampton, *Forgiveness and Mercy*, 30.
38 See generally, MacIntosh, *Christian Experience*, 276–8 and J.C. Hoffmann, *Ethical Confrontation in Counselling* (Chicago, 1979), 2.
39 See, for example, *Marriages between Anglicans and Roman Catholics: A Guide for Members of the Church in Wales from their Bishops* (Church in Wales Publications, Penarth, 1971), 7; the idea appears in Anglican and Roman thought: see R. Ombres, 'Faith, doctrine', 41 and Moore and Briden, *Introduction*, 2, 3. For the idea in the Roman Catholic Code, see, for example, Canon 24.
40 Murphy and Hampton, *Forgiveness and Mercy*, 8; J. Feinburg, 'The expressive function of punishment', *The Monist*, 49(3) (1965), 397–423

This view of sanctions opposes directly the idea of forgiveness as overcoming and excluding resentment – there can be no punishment in avengeful retribution and, at the same time, the overcoming of hatred and resentment. If the purpose of canonical penalties were retaliation and expressing hatred and resentment this would be wholly incompatible with the duty to forgive. As Studzinski says, '[t]o forgive is to move beyond the principle of retaliation'.[41] Indeed, Elizondo treats this form of penalizing as a participation in sin: in allowing vindictive punishments the law reproduces and propagates sin, vengeance and retaliation. Rather, the demand of forgiveness is that 'we make the radical and definitive break with the natural ways of justice and begin to enjoy the justice of God which in this life repays curse with blessing, injury with pardon, theft with gift, insult with praises and offence with forgiveness'.[42] This exclusion of the possibility of retaliatory penalty and forgiveness finds a parallel in the teaching of Paul (Rom. 12:17).

On the other hand, it is arguable that the use of sanctions does not offend the principle of forgiveness in certain circumstances. When the reason for punishing, when its objective or purpose, is something other that retaliatory or giving vent to resentment, then the imposition of penal sanctions is not incompatible with forgiving. When penalizing does not involve resentment, there is no clash with forgiveness which, after all, involves the overcoming of resentment. It must be remembered that, predominantly, modern theories of sanction in canon law (advanced by Roman Catholic canonists like Alesandro and Green) concentrate on motives other than resentment – that is, deterrence, symbolizing opposition to bad acts, and sanction as stimulus for repentance.

The root of this argument is, in effect, that sanctions and forgiving operate in two different spheres. Hampton maintains, for instance, that when we impose sanctions 'to reaffirm a victim's equal worth' or to deter the commission of prohibited acts, then the victim may make the demand for sanction and still forgive since 'forgiveness is a change of heart towards the wrongdoer in which one drops any emotions of hatred or resentment towards him and his deed'.[43] In short, 'one can want to vindicate the value of the victim and still decide to see the wrongdoer. . .as nonetheless decent, and so welcome him back. "I love you and forgive you, but you can't have the car

41 'Remember and forgive', at 13.
42 Ibid., 70–2, 77, 78.
43 Murphy and Hampton. *Forgiveness and Mercy*, 147–8.

for a week", a parent might say to a wayward teenager'. Again, forgiveness does not condone something bad (like neglect of duty), 'because forgiveness is precisely the decision that he [the wrongdoer] is not bad (even though his action [is])'. The forgiver never gives up opposition to the wrongdoer's action – imposing sanctions symbolizes this opposition. If penalizing concerns the disapproval of bad acts, and forgiveness the approval of persons, there is no dissonance.[44] Once more, the teaching of Paul seems to imply the possibility of penalizing and forgiving (2 Cor. 2:5–10).

First and foremost, canonical theories of sanction involve the objective and operation of healing and reconciliation. As such, the use of sanctions and the principle of forgiveness actually meet in terms of their objective – reconciliation. Canonical sanctions, along with forgiveness (and repentance), are merely contributions towards the healing of wounds inflicted on the Church and its members by wrongdoing and injury. Together, sanctions and forgiveness are attempts to contribute to the healing of wounds: when sanctions are not seen as retaliatory and based on resentment, but as deterrent, symbolic opposition to acts, stimulus for repentance, and healing, there is no incompatibility with forgiveness. Whereas retributivist penalties perpetuate resentment (the opposite of forgiveness), and cannot coexist with forgiveness (the eradication of resentment), sanctions directed towards reconciliation (by reaffirming the value of the victim, by deterring, by being seen as part of the working out of repentance) strengthen the work done by the victim in trying to undo and heal by forgiving.

Forgiveness in Canon Law

In order to render more practical our discussion as to whether there is room for sanctions and forgiveness in the canon law of the Church in Wales, let us examine some actual rules and their sanctions. This will help to identify what would be required by each set of opposing ideas about the possible dissonance between sanctions and forgiveness. It will also help to clarify that there are some fundamental difficulties in discussing forgiveness and the application of sanctions.

First, let us take for example the hypothetical case of an office-holder in the Church in Wales who persistently neglects to perform the duties attached to that office. The Church has created the rule

44 The idea of punishing and forgiving is certainly a hallmark of some atonement theories: see, for example, J. Stott, *The Cross of Christ* (Leicester, 1986), 131.

forbidding neglect of duties as part of its choice to distribute responsibilities. For a violation of this rule under chapter XI, section 18 of
the Constitution, as we have seen, sanctions might include (subject
to the provisions of the Constitution) monition, suspension or even
expulsion from office. Now, if a sanction is imposed to express
resentment or anger against the individual for neglecting his duties
the imposition of the sanction is not legitimate as it offends the
principle of forgiveness. However, according to some canonical
theories, the sanction may exist to deter others from doing the same,
to symbolize opposition to the act, or to stimulate the offender to
recognize the injury to the Church and be sorry for it – these need
not involve resentment. This is not at odds with the duty to forgive
– resentment can be eradicated (forgiveness) and the sanction can be
carried out. The object of each is to heal and produce reconciliation.
But the process is dependent on the motive of the participants.

Secondly, take, for example, a hypothetical case contemplated in
the Bishops' *Statement on Homosexuality* (1988). A cleric commits
adultery: according to the bishops this may provide grounds for
removal from office (again, it is an act which arguably falls under
'conduct giving just cause for scandal or offence' within chapter XI,
section 18). In this case there is a problem about the elements of
forgiveness. Let us assume that the cleric is removed for motives other
than resentment or anger – (according to one account) there is no
offence to the principle of forgiveness. However, in order for the duty
to forgive to be discharged, several things must be clarified. We are
clear that there has been an offence. But who is injured by that
offence? Who has the duty to forgive? Where is the evidence of
resentment that must be overcome in forgiving? Arguably partners
to those involved in the adultery are victims – and presumably they
are under a duty to forgive. But it is not they who impose the sanction
– the Church imposes the sanction. Now, let us apply the theory that
says sanctions offend the principle of forgiveness – the argument is:
we must not penalize we must forgive. For the Church to be able to
forgive it must have the right to forgive *as victim*. For this theory to
work it must be clearly established that the Church is victim – it
seems possible that the Church is wounded by a cleric committing
adultery, not least in the diminution of respect it might suffer in the
eyes of those outside the Church. The opposite account says, of
course: as the Church imposes the sanction without anger or resentment, so too it can forgive in the event that resentment exists. But
how do we identify corporate resentment?

These sorts of difficulties clearly raise the question whether for-giveness is in issue at all or is an appropriate issue for some violations of rules and for some uses of sanction. This is certainly the case with many rules to which sanctions are attached. When a parish culpably neglects its finances, and an incumbency is suspended, when the 'sanction' of invalidity is imposed on a body for failing to follow the legal procedure in making a decision – where is the injury, where is the resentment, where is the victim? These must clearly be identified before the duty to forgive can be discharged.

In point of fact, there is a host of other questions upon which we must be clear: can evidence of repentance function to relax the imposition of a sanction, as operates in some areas of Roman Catholic canon law?[45] After all, the bishops in their statement implied that only a cleric who had committed unrepentant promis-cuity might be removed. What is the role of absolution? Again, in the Roman Catholic Church it is arguable that the Church is under a duty to forgive imposed by canon law (when it is conceived as victim), provided that conditions including the repentance of the wrongdoer are met; indeed, it may be in Roman Catholic canon law, that the repentant injurer has a right to absolution, based on the general right of the faithful to the sacraments (here, the sacrament of penance).[46]

Conclusion

The view of canon law in general, and the law of the Church in Wales in particular, as *fundamentally* coercive and duty-imposing, a collec-tion of rules whose effect is to limit the freedom of Christ's Church, is misleading. It is important to recognize that canon law is in the main facilitative – it is an attempt by the Church to help organize the life of the Church by providing all types of facilities – liturgical, pastoral, ecumenical. And in so doing it provides, by supplying

45 See, for release from censures (like excommunication), Code, Canon 1347(2): 'The guilty party is to be said to have withdrawn from contumacy when he or she has truly repented the offence and furthermore has made suitable reparation for damages and scandal or at least has seriously promised to do so.' No equivalent principle is stated in Welsh canon law. See also Canon 1152: in relation to adultery, '[i]t is earnestly recommended that a spouse, motivated by Christian charity and solicitous for the good of the family, should not refuse to pardon an adulterous partner and should not sunder the conjugal life'.
46 Canon 843(1): 'Sacred ministers may not deny the sacraments to those who opportunely ask for them, are properly disposed and are not prohibited by law from receiving them.'

frameworks, the opportunity for the growth of its members. Moreover, it is important for the Church in Wales, in order to convey the idea of the legitimacy of its own law, to expose this quality of canon law. However, it is equally important for the Church to recognize that it has chosen to employ sanctions as part of its canon law. Here, it is more difficult to accept a view of law as duty-imposing backed by sanctions. One of the difficulties this poses is the apparent contradiction with the duty to forgive.[47] It is to be emphasized that an acceptance of the use of sanctions together with the working out of forgiveness is possible only if we view the objectives of sanctions and forgiveness as meeting – in the eradication of resentment and in the effecting of reconciliation. Both sanctions and forgiveness, along with repentance, are merely contributions to the healing of wounds suffered by the Church.[48]

[47] It is to be noted that the problem of (a) forgiving and penalizing; or (b) forgiving or penalizing, is ultimately one of conscience. Welsh canon law must recognize this. Since the problem of sanction is treated at present as one for the Church, it must also be recognized as a problem for the conscience of those in authority, whose function it is to impose sanctions. After all, in the context of our discussion, the choice between forgiving *or* penalizing and that of forgiving *and* penalizing depends upon motive. If in penalizing there is no resentment, there can be forgiveness and there is no offence to conscience. If this is not possible, the law must create a discretion to be exercised in conscience by Church authorities. In the event that the authority considers in conscience that there is a conflict between applying sanctions and forgiving, then the law ought to allow the relaxation of sanction, *for that reason.* If there is no conflict, in the conscience of the authority, by genuine acceptance of the idea that they are compatible, then sanction and forgiveness are possible.

[48] This notion of healing might be accommodated neatly within the general idea of the Church's pastoral role as having to do with (in part) healing wounds between its members: see generally, S. Pattison, *A Critique of Pastoral Care* (London, 1988). In the Church of England there has been, in recent years, a steady output of legislation dealing with pastoral matters: see for example the Pastoral Measure (No.1) 1968; the Sharing of Church Buildings Measure (No.2) 1970; and the Pastoral Measure (No.1) 1983: for discussion of elements of these see Moore and Briden, *Introduction*, 45, 47, 103, 110, 168.

5

Cognitive Faith and the Problem of Mental Handicap in Canon Law

REVEREND JOHN A. GRIFFITHS

In recent years, several eminent theologians and writers have begun to examine the Christian Gospel and the theological issues regarding persons with mental handicap.[1] By its very nature, mental handicap forces the theologian to examine the meaning of concepts such as *faith* and *understanding* in the Christian context.[2] Similarly, from the viewpoint of the principle of love, the individual Christian is required to establish the extent to which the Church – as much as society – protects or disadvantages persons with mental handicap in its working out, with God's grace, of the Gospel in the world. Law is one of the most tangible materials by which is made visible both the protection and the disadvantaging of groups in the ecclesiastical and the secular spheres alike. This essay is an examination of canon law in the light of a developing awareness of the role of cognition in faith and of Christian and secular attitudes towards persons with mental handicap. An analysis of canon law helps to identify how the mind of the Church is formally expressed in relation to these issues, and to indicate the degree to which the Church, by its law, actually protects the interests of those with mental handicap. By looking at

---

1 F.M. Young, *Face to Face* (London, 1985); F.M. Young, *The Crooked Timber of Humanity: The Challenge of the Handicapped* (Norwich, 1987); S. Hauerwas, *Suffering Presence* (Notre Dame, Illinois, 1986); F. Bowers (ed.), *Let Love be Genuine: Mental Handicap and the Church* (London, 1985); J. Vanier (ed.), *The Challenge of L'Arche* (London, 1982); B. Easter, 'Communication and Community' (Unpublished Ph.D. Thesis, University of Birmingham, 1983).
2 R. Bultmann, *Faith and Understanding* (London, 1969).

canon law, we see more clearly how the Church treats, in a practical way, the issue of mental handicap.

Cognitive Faith

In this section we shall examine some of the difficulties that exist in defining cognitive faith and explore some key areas where the issue of cognitive faith is of particular relevance.

Faith and belief

There are two distinct uses of the term *faith* in the Christian setting. The 'faith which is believed' *(fides quae creditur)* is the *objective* application of the term to describe the body of truth and complex of doctrine found in the Creeds, the accredited Councils' definitions, the teachings of the Church Fathers, the formularies and, primarily, the Bible. It represents the material of belief – this is *expressed* faith. On the other hand, the 'faith by which one believes' *(fides qua creditur)* is more of a *subjective* application of the term to the process of the human response to God's *divine truth*, and the activity which leads to belief. It involves the medium of belief – this is *experienced* faith. The relationship between these two uses of the term has been the subject of extensive discussion, in terms of their interdependence, their relative antecedence, and their revelatory significance.[3]

Faith and reason

The development and fullness of *experienced* faith is said to require an act of the will and, variously, the use of intellect and reason. The activity which leads to belief is regarded by orthodox theologians as a supernatural (rather than a natural) action on the part of God in the human soul, made effective by the immediate operation of His grace in the context of Christian revelation. The role of intellect and reason in faith became a preoccupation in the Middle Ages, and the voluntary element in faith was emphasized by Reformation writers in terms of personal trust (or *fiducia*). The Anglican Thirty-nine Articles refer favourably to the teaching of justification by faith alone, while holding faith to be a supernatural act.

3   Ibid.; E. Schillebeeckx, *Revelation and Theology*, vol. II, *The Concept of Truth and Theological Renewal* (London, 1968); A.T. Hanson and R.P.C. Hanson, *Reasonable Belief* (Oxford, 1980); J.H. Newman, *An Essay in Aid of a Grammar of Assent*, edited by I.T. Ker (Oxford, 1985), 70.

The dignity of human reason, particularly in terms of its capability to know the existence of God and to ascertain the historical credentials of Christian revelation, has been firmly asserted. At the same time, the strictly supernatural character of revelation and the nature of faith-commitment as essentially different from an intellectual assent (based on rational evidence) have been emphasized.

Roman Catholic theology since the Second Vatican General Council in the 1960s has moved towards a somewhat reduced reliance on propositional and epistemological aspects of faith, and has reopened the possibility of showing the concrete significance of revelation and faith for humankind and society. Aquinas maintained that '[r]eason need not be the origin of faith. . .though it does test and verify it'.[4] Newman stated that '[f]aith is an intellectual consent under the impulse of the human will which is moved to this [consent] by God's grace'.[5] Statements such as these have retained their significance and relevance in pointing to the underlying concept of the supernatural character of faith as a human response to divine revelation. In this humans are bound to yield '[t]he full homage of intellect and will to God who reveals Himself'.[6] And through His own self-communicating God gives 'to all joy in assenting to the truth and in believing it'.[7] God's universal salvific will results in the offer of grace as gratuitous and supernatural. Everyone receives the grace necessary to keep the commandments,[8] the first impulse coming from grace,[9] and leading to faith which is necessary for justification.[10] Humankind must respond to grace actively, freely and co-operatively.[11] Aided by grace, humans must prepare for justification;[12] faith alone without *conversion* is not sufficient.[13]

4 Aquinas, *Summa Theologiae*, 2a, 2ae, 2, 9.
5 J.H. Newman, *Fifteen Sermons Preached Before the University of Oxford* (London, 1868), 183.
6 First Vatican General Council: Third Session, *Dogmatic Constitution Dei Filius on the Catholic Faith* (1870), Ch. 3.
7 Second Council of Orange (529), *Canons on Grace*, 7; see also Second Vatican General Council, *Dogmatic Constitution: Dei Verbum* (1965), Ch.1 p. 5.
8 Second Council of Orange (529), *Conclusion Redacted by Caesarius of Arles* (The teaching of tradition on predestination).
9 The Sixteenth Council of Carthage (418), 4, 5.
10 The General Council of Trent: Sixth Session, *Decree on Justification* (1547), Ch. 6, 'The manner of preparation'.
11 The *Indiculus* (? 435–42), 9.
12 The General Council of Trent, ibid., Ch. 5, the necessity for adults to prepare themselves for justification and the origin of this justification.
13 Ibid., Ch. 11, the observance of the commandments, its necessity and possibility; ibid., *Canons on Justification*, 9, 12–14, 19–21.

Faith and understanding

The process of justification and conversion therefore implies an active response by individuals. This in turn implies a degree of conceptual understanding – an act of cognition – which is to be used for the activation of this response. Thus, faith – in the same way that sensation through a mediating response becomes perception – moves from experience to understanding. The understanding or cognitive aspect of faith is clearly a developmental feature [14] which suggests disposition, intention [15] or interior participation.[16] This has particular significance in relation to the sacraments.[17]

Cognitive faith and the sacraments

According to Roman Catholic theology, '[i]t is necessary that the faithful come (to the sacrament) with proper dispositions, that their minds should be attuned to their voices, and that they should cooperate with divine grace lest they receive it in vain'.[18] The sacraments not only presuppose faith, but also nourish, strengthen and express it.[19] Correlative to the emphasis on Christ's presence and action in the sacraments, the Second Vatican Council stressed the personal encounter of Christ with individuals in the signs of the Church, and the role of faith in the so-called *sacraments of faith (sacramenta fidei)*: '[T]hey do indeed impart grace, but, in addition, the very act of celebrating them most effectively disposes the faithful to receive this grace in a fruitful manner, to worship God duly, and to practise charity'.[20] The Council maintained that it was 'of the highest importance that the faithful should easily understand the sacramental signs, and should frequent with great eagerness those sacraments which were instituted to nourish the Christian life'.[21]

14 J.W. Fowler, *Stages of Faith: The Psychology of Human Development and the Quest for Meaning* (San Francisco, 1981).
15 Pius X, *Decree Sacra Tridentina* (1905), decree on daily communion.
16 *Instruction of the Sacred Congregation of Rites on Sacred Music and the Sacred Liturgy* (1958).
17 Pius XII, *Encyclical Letter: Mediator Dei* (1947).
18 The Second Vatican General Council, *Constitution: Sacrosanctum Concilium* (1963), Constitution on the Sacred Liturgy, 11.
19 Ibid., 59.
20 John Paul II, *Letter to the Bishops of the Church Dominicae Cenae* (24 February, 1980), 6; John Paul II, Homily at the Inaugural Mass of the National Eucharistic Congress, Fortaleza (8 July, 1980) (English text: *L'Osservatore Romano* (English edn.), 11 August 1980, 7).
21 The Second General Council, 59.

Cognitive faith – in terms of a degree of understanding of the significance of experience and the cooperative initiation of a personal response to grace – is implicated as a precondition to receiving the sacraments.[22] The principal exception is infant baptism.[23] The fact that infants cannot yet profess personal faith does not prevent the Church from conferring baptism upon them since in reality it is in the Church's own faith that they are baptized.[24] As St Augustine put it: 'When children are presented to be given spiritual grace. . .it is not so much those holding them in their arms that present them. . .as the whole company of saints and faithful Christians'.[25] In other words, presentation is done 'by the whole of Mother Church'.[26] Nevertheless, while aware of the efficacy of the faith operating in the baptism of infants, and of the validity of the sacrament, the Church also recognizes the limits to this practice and requires not only parental consent to the baptism but also serious assurance that appropriate opportunity for the development of faith will be available to the child.[27]

The discernment of cognitive faith

The relationship between the 'faith by which one believes' and the 'faith which is believed' becomes particularly significant when cognitive faith – achieved through maturational development and catechetical formation, and facilitated by grace – comes to be examined with a view to determining the disposition, intention or interior participation of the recipient of the sacraments. Almost invariably, this has been achieved by means of the examination of learned expressions of the 'faith which is believed'. Consequently, for example, in English canon law, confirmation candidates must be 'ready and desirous to be confirmed. . .of sound discretion' and

22 The General Council of Trent: Thirteenth Session, *Decree on the Most Holy Eucharist* (1551), *Canons on the Most Holy Sacrament of the Eucharist*, 11.
23 John Paul II, *Instruction on Infant Baptism (Pastoralis Actio) of the Sacred Congregation for the Doctrine of the Faith* (20 October 1980), 14.
24 *Summa Theologiae*, 3, 69, 3.
25 Augustine, *Epistles*, 98, 5, J.P. Migne (ed.) *Patrologia Latina* (1844–55), 33, 362.
26 Ibid.
27 John Paul II, *Instruction*, 15; J.L. Segundo, *A Theology for a New Humanity*, vol. IV, *The Sacraments Today* (Dublin, 1980), 76–81. For a discussion of the role of the Church in baptism in relation to the Church in Wales, see R.L. Brown, 'Baptismal concern: a call for baptismal discipline within the Church in Wales', *Theologia Cambrensis*, 2 (2) (1990), 3: the article contains an interesting proposal for the amendment of Welsh canon law.

have 'come to years of discretion'.[28] Moreover, 'a minister having a
cure of souls must diligently seek out children and others whom he
thinks meet to be confirmed, and instruct them in the Christian faith
and life as set forth in the Bible, the Book of Common Prayer and
the Catechism'. In addition, 'the godparents of baptised infants are
to take care that they are brought to the Bishop to be confirmed as
soon as they can say the Apostles' Creed, the Lord's Prayer and the
Ten Commandments, and are further instructed in the Church
Catechism'.[29]

Mental Handicap

The Mental Health Act 1983 classes as 'mentally handicapped' those
with an IQ of seventy or below, and the most generally accepted
definition of mental handicap is that of the American Association on
Mental Deficiency: 'significantly sub-average general intellectual
functioning existing concurrently with deficits in adaptive behaviour
and manifested during the developmental period'.[30] The expression
'significantly sub-average' is defined here as approximately IQ seventy or below. 'Adaptive behaviour' relates to 'the effectiveness or
degree with which individuals meet the standards of personal and
social responsibility expected for their age and cultural group', and
'developmental period' relates to ages between birth and eighteen
years. Mental handicap, therefore, is an impairment of intellectual
function – of cognitive development – with concurrent secondary
difficulties in the areas of personal and social adaptation.

The typical scenario begins with a child born as a slow learner,
possibly with accompanying physical impairment (such as deafness
or blindness). Following a childhood without the aid of adequate
special intervention, the child emerges as a youth who has developed
problems related to incompetence, frustration, inexperience and
over-dependence. Intervention in the form of varieties of institu-

28 Halsbury, *Laws of England,* vol 14, *Ecclesiastical Law* (4th edn., London,
1975), para.999.
29 The similarities with Church in Wales practice may be noted in the Orders
of Service and associated rubrics relating to the administration and celebration
of the sacraments published in *The Book of Common Prayer for Use in the
Church in Wales* (Penarth, 1984), vols I and II. See also the Roman Catholic
Code of Canon Law (1983), Cans.752-4; E. Schillebeeckx, *Christ the Sacrament
of the Encounter with God* (London, 1963), 108–9.
30 A.M. Clarke, A.D.B. Clarke and J.M. Berg (eds.), *Mental Deficiency: The
Changing Outlook* (4th edn., London, 1985); H.J. Grossman (ed.), *Classification
in Mental Retardation* (Washington, 1983).

tional care is then likely because of difficulties of handling at home and the possibility of remedial training being more accessible. This move in itself, however, can create an additional layer of problems for the adult whose existence becomes characterized by a lack of decision-making, little contact with 'ordinary' behaviour, reduced privacy and possessions, and communal living arrangements.[31]

This layering of problems has become more widely appreciated, together with the recognition that the abilities of mentally handicapped people have been significantly underestimated by professionals and parents alike. People with mental handicap are essentially persons with learning difficulties arising out of specific or general intellectual impairment. Their learning takes longer because it often requires more extensive repetition of much simpler elements of learning through the medium of several sensory inputs and expressed in terms of concrete (rather than abstract) operations – or even intuitively. It may indeed have lower ceilings of ultimate attainment than the learning of those without handicap, but there is increasing awareness of its overall potency, subject to the limits of opportunities afforded to its growth. Broad guidelines, based on Piaget's model of intellectual development,[32] would suggest that the person with mental handicap, while in more profound cases operating at a sensorimotor level (normally equivalent, chronologically, to ages from birth to eighteen months), will generally operate at least at the pre-operational level (eighteen months to four years) with development towards intuitive reasoning (four years to seven years), and in milder cases will advance into formal operations of concrete (seven to eleven years) and even simple abstract (eleven years onwards) thinking.[33]

Status in secular law

In many areas of law, factors which interfere with either the freedom of the will or the clarity of understanding will have distinct legal consequences, such as the capacity to make contracts or liability for criminal acts. For example, the celebrated (but much criticized) case of *M'Naghten* (1843) resulted in the evolution of rules governing the role of insanity in criminal law. These include the idea that, if a

---

31 A. Heron and M. Myers, *Intellectual Impairment: The Battle Against Handicap* (London, 1983).

32 J. Piaget, *The Origins of Intelligence in the Child* (London, 1953).

33 Clarke, Clarke and Berg, *Mental Deficiency*, 751; Heron and Myers, *Intellectual Impairment*.

defendant in a criminal case was 'labouring under such defect of reason from disease of the mind, as not to know the nature and quality of the act he was doing', by which the defendant did not 'know the difference between right and wrong', he will be able to avail himself of the so-called defence of insanity.[34] In the criminal law a defect of reason may be a factor determining mental handicap. In practice, moreover, in this context, the use of expert evidence – usually in the form of intellectual assessment employing the M'Naghten approach – will be used to determine the individual's status. In the criminal law, too, a mentally handicapped person might be able to plead diminished responsibility as a defence – in relation to homicide the Homicide Act 1957 prescribes that a person shall not be guilty of murder 'if he was suffering from such abnormality of mind (whether arising from a condition of arrested or retarded development of mind or any inherent causes or induced by disease or injury) as substantially impaired his mental responsibility for his acts and omissions' (section 2(1) of the statute).

Generally, secular law has moved with medico-psychological knowledge and has responded to sociological pressures. Recently these have involved many developments in parliamentary legislation relating to the mentally handicapped, in all manner of areas: community care arrangements, particularly in terms of residence and educational or training opportunities, employment, guardianship, hospital care and treatment – today the law recognizes in and confers upon the mentally handicapped a very wide range of rights.[35] This legal framework is in general agreement with the United Nations Declaration on the Rights of Mentally Retarded Persons (1971): a mentally handicapped person 'has a right to proper medical care and physical therapy and to such education, training, rehabilitation and guidance as will enable him to develop his ability and maximum potential' (Art. 2). There has also been increasing recognition of the parallel between the movement for civil rights of persons with mental

---

34 (1843) 10 Clark and Finnelly 200; see also W.S. Holdsworth, *A History of English Law*, 16 vols (London, 1922–66), VIII, 433.
35 B.M. Hoggett, *Mental Health Law* (2nd edn., London, 1984): for community care see 25, 284; for the role of the Development Team for the Mentally Handicapped (1976), 214; for education, 294–7; employment, 298; guardianship, 53, 182, 203, 278, 300, 302; for hospital care, 7, 8, 24–25; treatment, 201–3; and rights generally, 284–86. For the purposes of modern health legislation, see C. Unsworth, *The Politics of Mental Health Legislation* (Oxford, 1987), 6f. See also generally, M. Roth and R. Blugrass (eds.), *Psychiatry, Human Rights and the Law* (Cambridge, 1985), and T. Whitehead, *Mental Illness and the Law* (Oxford, 1983).

handicap, and those of other groups who have campaigned with some success against discrimination and disadvantage – in particular women, ethnic and religious minorities. Although 'participation and equality' was the slogan of the International Year of Disabled Persons (1981), very few governments have passed legislation against discrimination of people with mental handicap.[36]

Christian approaches to mental handicap

The gradual advance of medico-psychological knowledge and language has led to the differentiation of mental handicap and mental illness. This in turn has permitted a Christian account of mental handicap which does not imply moral defect. For centuries the historical type for both mental illness and mental handicap had been that of the *sinner* and the *possessed.*[37] In the case of mental handicap, this was eventually replaced by that of the *infant* or the *child.* This emphasized the prevalence of the concept of developmental arrest in the person with mental handicap. It promoted a paternalism toward such persons, and an implicitly custodial and compensatory approach toward their integration or care. In line with the socio-political enlightenment already outlined, this concept and its accompanying attitudes have largely changed during the present century through the acknowledgement that differences between individuals do not mean inequality in the eyes of God. As Pope Paul VI puts it: '[t]he credibility of the Church is at stake. How can she contribute to the integration of the handicapped in modern society if she does not work within her own ranks to recognise them as full members?'[38] The Church became more clearly regarded not, in the first place, as 'a highly organised, articulate and mature group of people seeking to help others', but rather as 'a community which seeks to integrate within itself the weak and the powerless and the inadequate as well as the strong and active'.[39]

In order to comprehend what humankind united in one family

---

36 W. Wolfensburger, 'Social role valorisation: a proposed new term for the principles of normalisation', *Mental Retardation*, 21 (1983), 234–9; Clarke, Clarke and Berg, *Mental Deficiency*, 751–2.

37 Matt. 19:22.

38 Paul VI, *Address to the Conference of the International Catholic Child Bureau, Rome* (October, 1973) (English text: *L'Osservatore Romano* (English edn.), 18 October 1973, 12).

39 G.F. Moede (ed.), *The Unity of the Church and the Handicapped in Society,* World Council of Churches Study Encounter, No.17, No.7, 4 (Geneva, 1971), 5.

means, it should be possible to look at the Church to see in her, as in a model, the beginnings of such a unity. Again, according to Moede, '[t]he Churches should examine their practices to ensure that their treatment of the handicapped is indeed such as to manifest the nature of the Kingdom to men in the world'. Moreover, churches should make sure that 'it is not only doctrinally but also practically possible for the handicapped to participate as fully as they are able in the life of our congregations. They should allow the handicapped and their needs to share in setting the tone of Church life, as they certainly did of Jesus's ministry'.[40]

In this way, the type for the mentally (and physically) handicapped has become 'the poor, the maimed, the lame and the blind'.[41] There is little or no emphasis on the causative factors of mental handicap here, but considerable stress on their poverty of competence, of ability and of development. More importantly, there is an explicit call for the acceptance of their differences, for their integration into the community, for their being embraced first as brothers and sisters. Wilson captures well the fundamental problem: '[t]he Church is not the gathering together of the competent who are going to do things for the incompetent'. Rather, 'she is the gathering together of the competent and incompetent (and who is to say which is which?) in such a way as to be the sign of unity for mankind as a whole'.[42]

With this embrace, and as a necessary corollary, the relief of need becomes an essential activity, and the Church will necessarily undertake to care for the mentally handicapped as she would for all the *poor*. There is also a new dynamic implied here: the mentally handicapped are no longer 'permanent infants' with arrested development, but have (in common with the materially, physically and spiritually *poor*) an array of needs upon which their continuing development depends. For them, the intellectually or cognitively *poor*, these needs have their focus in the communicative, educative and catechetical processes. The nature of cognitive faith represents the field of opportunity and challenge for the Church in its care for her mentally handicapped members.[43]

In most recent years, it may be suggested that the type for the

---

40   Ibid., 4.
41   Luke 14:13–14.
42   D. Wilson, 'The church, the eucharist and the mentally handicapped', *Clergy Review* (February, 1975), 73.
43   Schillebeeckx, *Christ the Sacrament of the Encounter with God*, 109–12.

mentally handicapped has rather become that of the *oppressed* or the *downtrodden*.[44] In line with secular developments in the area of human rights, particularly of minority groups, and also in parallel with adjustments in approaches to poverty and injustice, the focus of a number of authors and theologians has shifted from the acknowledged needs of the individual to the processes (or systems) by which they have been (and continue to be) progressively deprived of the opportunities and resources necessary for the realization of their individual potential and role.[45] Thus, the Church's ministry is interpreted as involving the liberation of the oppressed. Indeed, the challenge to theology 'does not come primarily from the man who does not believe, but from the man who is not a man, who is not recognised as such by the existing social order' – in short, it may be that '[t]he question is not how to speak of God in an adult world, but how to proclaim Him as Father in a world that is not human'.[46] Practically speaking, this sort of liberation theology is biased in terms of its support for the revolutionary struggle of the oppressed and sees exclusively in the poor and oppressed the *locus theologicus* – the place where God is working and truth is revealed.[47] Nevertheless, in extending the type for the mentally handicapped so as to include that of the oppressed, it ensures that the Church and theology give due cognizance to the dangers of oppressive systems and their inadvertent perpetuation.

Canon Law and Mental Handicap

The teaching of the Church may be said to be distilled in its canon law,[48] and the traditional teaching of the Church in relation to its approach to persons with mental handicap lies within canon law – and in the doctrinal documents which form the basis for instruction and the interpretation of canon law. The law and constitution of the Church in Wales do not treat of such persons to any greater extent

44 Ps. 9:9; Luke 4:18; Jas. 2:6.
45 G. Gutierrez, *A Theology of Liberation* (London, 1974); A. Fierro, *The Militant Gospel* (London, 1977); J.L. Segundo, *The Liberation of Theology* (Dublin, 1977).
46 G. Gutierrez, 'Liberation, theology and proclamation', *Concilium*, 6 (1974), 68–9.
47 A. Cussianovich, *Religious Life and the Poor* (Dublin, 1979).
48 See, for example, chapter 2 above for the view of theology *in* canon law in the work of the Roman Catholic canonist R. Ombres: *supra*, p.46.

than does English canon law,[49] and this, in turn, together with the Thirty-nine Articles of the Church of England, and its formularies as its principal doctrinal summary, fails to specify any developed or systematic approach to their status and condition beyond that which has been referred to already. This is in some contrast, however, to the canon law of the Roman Catholic Church which, certainly from a practical viewpoint, commends itself to jurist and student alike. The review and reform of the Code of Canon Law of the Roman Catholic Church, completed in 1983, provides as contemporary and comprehensive an instrument as one might hope to find.[50]

With regard to questions relating to cognitive faith and problems associated with the approach of the Church to persons with mental handicap, the Code of Canon Law cannot be said to provide a systematic treatment, but, as the following summary review is intended to demonstrate, contains extensive (if not always explicit) reference to some central issues.

Roman Catholic canon law and mental handicap

The Code of Canon Law employs a set of key expressions which are relevant here: 'those who are of feeble mind' (Can. 1550), 'those who lack the use of reason',[51] those with 'only an imperfect use of reason' (Cans. 1324(1), 1345), 'those who lack sufficient use of reason' (Can. 1095), those who 'suffer from. . .psychological infirmity',[52] those 'who have not reached the use of reason' (Can. 914), those who are 'incapable of personal responsibility' (Cans. 852(2), 99), 'the mentally. . .handicapped' (Can. 777(4)), 'those burdened with special difficulties' (Can. 529(1)), those 'incapable of a human act' (Can.

49 Halsbury, *Laws of England*; G.E. Moore and T. Briden, *Introduction to English Canon Law* (2nd edn., London, 1985); E.J. Bicknell, *A Theological Introduction to the Thirty–Nine Articles of the Church of England* (2nd edn., London, 1939).
50 See generally, J.A. Coriden, T.J. Green, and D.E. Heintschel, *The Code of Canon Law: A Text and Commentary* (London, 1985). For guidance on the place of the mentally handicapped generally in the Church of England, see M. Bayley, *The Local Church and Mentally Handicapped People* (London, 1984), a report published for the General Synod Board for Social Responsibility. This report was debated by the General Synod of the Church of England in July 1984. The following motions were passed: 'That this Synod: (a) welcomes the development of policies aimed at enabling a greater number of mentally handicapped people to live in the community; (b) notes that fresh resources need to be made available if these aims are to be realised; (c) commends the Report to the dioceses for their study and action'.
51 Code, Canons 99, 1322, 1323, 1478.
52 Ibid., Canons 1041(1), 1044(2).

171(1)), and those 'lacking active voice' (Can. 171(1)). All of these may be interpreted as referring to persons with mental handicap.

The personal and legal status of these categories of person is presented in Canon 44, according to which '[w]hoever habitually lacks the use of reason is considered as incapable of personal responsibility and is regarded as an infant'. Moreover, by Canon 97(2), 'a minor who has not completed the seventh year of age is called an infant and is considered incapable of personal responsibility' – 'on completion of the seventh year, however, the minor is presumed to have the use of reason'. In contrast, 'a person who has completed the eighteenth year of age has attained majority' (Can. 97(1)). There is only an implied suggestion that persons with mental ages equivalent to the specified chronological ages would be treated comparably.[53]

By way of contrast, the canon law also explains the Christian status of these people. Under Canon 204(1) 'Christ's faithful. . .since they are incorporated with Christ through baptism' are called 'each according to his or her particular condition, to exercise the mission of God entrusted to the Church to fulfil in the world.' The baptized have 'equality of dignity and action', whereby they 'contribute, each according to his or her own condition and office, to the building up of the Body of Christ' (Can. 208), as well as obligations, responsibilites and rights.[54] Every member of the Church has the right to be 'assisted by their pastors from the spiritual riches of the Church, especially by the Word of God and the Sacraments' (Can. 213). Again, each person has the right and duty 'to acquire the *knowledge* of Christian teaching which is appropriate to each one's capacity and conditions' (Can. 229). The pastor is to be 'especially diligent in seeking out. . .those burdened with special difficulties' (Can. 529(1)) – those, that is, 'who cannot sufficiently avail themselves of the ordinary pastoral care' (Can. 771(1)).

It is in this context that the facilitative function of canon law (described in chapter 4 above) comes to the fore – in the context of catechetical formation and education. In the terms of Canon 777(4), the parish priest is under a canonical duty to ensure that 'as far as their condition allows, catechetical formation is given to the men-

53 As a general guideline, an individual with mental age (MA) 18 would be labelled mentally handicapped if he/she was of chronological age (CA) at least 25. An individual of CA 18 would be so labelled if assessed as MA 13 or below. The mentally handicapped person of MA 7 is likely to be at least CA 10.
54 Code, Book II, Part I.

tally. . .handicapped'. Local ordinaries, therefore, must ensure that 'catechists are duly trained. . .have an appropriate knowledge of the teaching of the Church. . .and both the theory and practice of the principles of pedagogy' (Can. 780). Thus, 'where it is suitable, the diocesan bishop is to provide for the establishment of schools catering for special needs' (Can. 802(1)).

The handicapped and the sacraments in Roman canon law

The sacraments, in Roman Catholic canon law (treated as 'actions of Christ and of the Church'), are 'signs and means by which faith is expressed and strengthened, worship offered to God and. . .sanctification is brought about' (Can. 840). Baptism validates admission to the other sacraments and, together, baptism, confirmation and the Holy Eucharist are required for full Christian initiation (Can. 842). The sacraments may not be denied to those who 'opportunely ask for them, are properly disposed and are not prohibited by law from receiving them' (Can. 843(1)). All members of Christ's faithful have a duty 'to ensure that those who ask for the sacraments are prepared for their reception. . .through proper evangelisation and catechetical instruction' (Can. 843(2)). In order to examine the role of handicap more closely, in relation to the sacraments, it is necessary to set out some of the central rules about their administration.

In Roman canon law, baptism 'is necessary for salvation, either by actual reception or at least by desire' (Can. 849). The canonical provisions on adult baptism apply to 'all those who, being no longer infants, have reached the use of reason'; and 'one who is incapable of personal responsibility is regarded as an infant even in regard to baptism' (Can. 852). An adult intending to receive baptism is admitted to the catechumenate (Can. 206) and 'brought through the various stages of sacramental initiation' (Can. 851(1)). The parents and sponsors of a child who is to be baptized 'are to be suitably instructed on the meaning of this sacrament and the obligations attaching to it' (Can. 851(2)). An adult must have 'manifested the intention to receive baptism, be adequately instructed in the truths of the faith and in the duties of a Christian, and tested in the Christian life over the course of the catechumenate. The person must moreover be urged to have sorrow for personal sins' (Can. 865(1)). In danger of death, an adult may be baptized if, 'with some knowledge of the principal truths of the faith, he or she has in some manner manifested the intention to receive baptism and promises to observe the requirements of the Christian religion' (Can. 865(2)) in the event of recovery. Generally, an adult 'immediately after receiving baptism, is to be confirmed, to participate in the celebration of the Holy Eucharist and to receive Holy Communion' (Can. 866). For an infant to be baptized, parents must give their consent and there must 'be a well-founded hope that the child will be brought up in the catholic religion' (Can. 868). If the infant is in danger of death, 'it is to be baptized without delay' and 'aborted foetuses, if they are alive, are to be baptized, as far as this is possible' (Cans. 867, 871).

The diocesan bishop is under a canonical duty to ensure that the sacrament of confirmation 'is conferred upon his subjects who duly and reasonably request it' (Can. 885(1)). Again, in order to receive confirmation 'a person who has the use of reason must be suitably instructed, properly disposed and able to renew the baptismal promises' (Can. 889(2)), and the sacrament is to be conferred on the faithful 'at about the age of discretion' (Can. 891).

The most venerable sacrament is the Holy Eucharist and the other sacraments are directed to it (Can. 897). Christ's faithful are to hold it in the highest honour, to take an active part in its celebration, to receive the sacrament with great devotion and frequently, and to reverence it with the greatest adoration (Can. 898). In 'the eucharistic assembly the people of God' all unite in its celebration, to participate in their own way according to their orders and liturgical roles (Can. 899(2)). Indeed, as we have seen, 'any baptized person who is not forbidden by law may and must be admitted to Holy Communion' (Can. 912). For Holy Communion to be administered to children, it is required that they have sufficient knowledge and be adequately prepared, 'so that according to their capacity they understand what the mystery of Christ means and are able to receive the Body of the Lord with faith and devotion' (Can. 913(1)). Moreover, it is the duty of parents and the parish priest to ensure that 'children who have reached the use of reason are properly prepared and, having made their sacramental confession, are nourished by the divine food as soon as possible'. It is also the duty of the parish priest 'to see that children who have not reached the use of reason, or whom he has judged to be insufficiently disposed, do not come to holy communion' (Can. 914).

The sacrament of penance requires that the faithful be 'so disposed that, repudiating the sins they have committed and having the purpose of amending their lives, they turn back to God' (Can. 987). These are 'bound to confess, in kind and in number, all grave sins committed after baptism,. . . of which after careful examination of conscience they are aware' (Can. 988). All the faithful 'who have reached the age of discretion are bound faithfully to confess their grave sins at least once a year' (Can. 989). For the reception of the sacrament of order, one who suffers from 'psychological infirmity, because of which he is. . .judged incapable of being able to fulfil the ministry' is regarded as irregular, and is further impeded from the exercise of orders – dispensation from all irregularity is reserved to the Apostolic See alone (Cans. 1041, 1044, 1047).

Marriage between the baptized 'has been raised to the dignity of a sacrament and is brought into being by the lawfully manifested consent of persons who are legally capable' (Cans. 1055, 1057). A man must be at least sixteen years of age and a woman fourteen in order to enter marriage validly (Can. 1083). In terms of matrimonial consent, 'those who lack sufficient use of reason, those who suffer from a grave lack of discretionary judgment' concerning the essential matrimonial rights and obligations to be mutually given and ac-cepted, and those who 'because of causes of a psychological nature are unable to assume the essential obligations of marriage' are incapable of contracting marriage (Can. 1095). The contracting parties must be 'at least not ignorant of the fact that marriage is a permanent partnership between a man and a woman, ordered to the procreation of children through some form of sexual co-operation' and this ignorance is not presumed after puberty (Can. 1096). However, provided it does not determine the will, error concerning the sacramental dignity of marriage does not vitiate matrimonial consent (Can. 1099). Indeed, 'the internal consent of the mind is presumed to conform to the words or the signs used in the celebration of a marriage', given that the spouses express their matrimonial consent in words or, if they cannot speak, by equivalent signs (Cans. 1101(1), 1104(2)).

The role of cognition is also crucial in relation to offences and punishment in Roman Catholic canon law. According to Canon 1322 of the Code, 'those who habitually lack the use of reason, even though they appeared sane when they violated a law or precept, are deemed incapable of committing an offence'. Equally, a person is not liable to a penalty who, when violating a law, has not completed the sixteenth year of age, or was 'without fault, ignorant of violating the law or precept', or 'lacked the use of reason' (Can. 1323). Similarly, penalties prescribed in canon law must be diminished or substituted by a penance if the offence was committed by one who had 'only an imperfect use of reason, or was a minor' (Can. 1324). Indeed, whenever the offender had only an imperfect use of reason, the judge can refrain from inflicting any punishment if he considers that the person's reform may be better accomplished in some other way (Can. 1345). Minors and those who lack the use of reason are able to appear before a tribunal only through their parents, guardians or curators. But, interestingly, in cases where spiritual (and related) matters are involved, if the minors have the use of reason, they can plead and respond without the consent of parents or guardians – if they have completed their fourteenth year, they can appear on their own behalf (Can. 1478). Moreover, minors under fourteen, and those of feeble mind, are not admitted to give evidence – they can be heard, however, if in the view of the judge it is appropriate for them to be heard (Can. 1550).

Conclusion

From this summary of Roman Catholic canon law it is evident that, even as regards terminology, there is no systematic treatment of persons with mental handicap – there is no separate section on the place and rights of such people in Roman canon law. Several general comments may, however, be made. First, the chronological age of seven, or its mental equivalent, would be regarded as the watershed for the attainment of the use of reason and discretion, as well as the capacity for personal responsibility. Expressions of intention, disposition, knowledge, understanding, judgment and consent (except where otherwise stated) are presumably treated as valid from this age onwards, consonant with accepted psychological models. The implication for the concept of cognitive faith would be that expressions of belief on the part of the person with mental age seven are admissible – although they must conform with Christian teaching and truths of the faith, and be reflected in due reverence, devotion and adoration, imparted by catechetical formation. This cognitive faith would appear to be a necessary precondition to the reception of the sacraments, with the exception of infant baptism.

Secondly, however, the phrase 'according to each one's capacity and condition', and its equivalents, would seem to furnish the canon law with flexibility and discretionary breadth to ensure that the concept of cognitive faith is not employed to the disadvantage of any group or individual, particularly those with mental handicap. It embodies a markedly protective ethic for the potentially disadvantaged. Thirdly, the explicit reference to the obligatory provision of catechetical formation for the mentally handicapped – again, as far as their condition allows – to the appropriate training of catechists, and even to the provision of educational resources for those with special needs, represents the ultimate level of protection for such persons. It is the closest Roman canon law comes not only to a systematic treatment of their needs and status but also to the anti-discriminatory measures advocated by socio-political reforms.

Fourthly, marriage has been made conditional upon specific chronological age and the Code's provisions with regard to matrimonial consent contain several other remarkable features: (1) the correlation between ignorance and puberty must be regarded as an aberrant anomaly; (2) the relationships between error – particularly in terms of the 'sacramental dignity of marriage' – the determination of the will, and consent might, when applied to the other sacraments, prove illuminatory in considerations of the requirement of cognitive faith and its discernment; and (3) the presumed conformity of internal consent to the words or signs used in the celebration of the sacrament has similar potential application to issues of cognitive faith and the sacraments.

Fifthly, the discretionary powers of the judiciary in terms of the reform of offenders and the admissibility of evidence in cases concerning spiritual matters indicate further protective enlightenment in the Code as it might be applied to persons with mental handicap.

At first reading, the Code of Canon Law appears to treat persons with mental handicap as infants, and the provisions on personal status, the apparent requirements of cognitive faith and the several references to chronological age, contribute to this impression. Nevertheless, the static arrest in development which the employment of the infant as the type for the mentally handicapped generally suggests, is absent from the tenor of the law. The explicit provisions for the mentally handicapped, in particular, signify a dynamic of potential growth, development and nurture, more in accord with the type of the poor. Those rules using phrases such as 'according to his or her capacity and condition' contribute to a more conspicuous recognition of the individual, his or her personal encounter with God, and his or her needs. And they run counter to the custodial or paternalistic generalizations which tend to result from the use of the type of the infant.

There are clear indications, furthermore, that all baptized persons are Christ's faithful with 'equality of dignity and action' and rights as well as duties. This conforms with the notion of the Church as the 'competent and incompetent acting together in the building up of the Body of Christ'. The Code elucidates the requirement to embrace the intellectually *poor* and to provide for their needs.

Wilson lays great emphasis upon these and similar features of the canon law and of associated doctrinal documentation when advocating a less restrictive approach to the reception of Holy Communion by persons with mental handicap.[55] He argues that the use of the term 'devotion', as a primary condition for reception, overrides the argument relating to the use of reason in that devotion is primarily an act of affection or will and does not necessarily involve the discursive faculty of the mind. Wilson insists that the criterion of devotion appropriate to the individual's age, capacity, condition or development permits reception for all but the most profoundly handicapped. For him, the Holy Eucharist is the fullest expression of the unity of the Church as the Body of Christ and, as such, membership of the Body demands reception of the sacraments. Similarly, the union with Christ and with each other in the Holy Eucharist is a union of love from which inevitably flows the attitude of service and care for the mentally handicapped members: 'the God–man's expression of love with all its consequences',[56] and the sacramental relationship is entered into by means of the physical, the concrete, the intuitive and the emotional – all of which are accessible to the mentally handicapped.

Wilson reminds the reader that: '[t]he essential in the celebration of the sacrament is not what man does: it is enough if he is welcoming according to the limits of his possibilities. It is Christ who sanctifies him to whom the sacrament is administered'.[57] Wilson maintains that not only do all baptized persons have the right to receive the Holy Eucharist as God's gift, but that it is the ancient tradition of the Church to share the Holy Eucharist with those who have no 'intelligent' awareness, and that, in effect, as with infant baptism, the faith and intention of the community can count for that of the mentally handicapped person. While he would thereby criticize the current reformed Roman Catholic Code for its failure to remove all apparent restrictions on the reception of the sacraments, Wilson is nevertheless likely to congratulate the reformers for their emphasis upon individual encounter with God, individual circumstances, ca-

---

55 Wilson, 'The church, the eucharist'.
56 Schillebeeckx, *Christ the Sacrament of the Encounter with God*, 84.
57 Mgr. Boillon, cited in D. Wilson, 'The church, the eucharist', 76.

pacities and conditions, including the requirements relating to catechetical provision.

Macquarrie is more likely to regard the continuing requirement
of cognitive faith as the significant feature of the reform. His
anxieties relate to 'indiscriminate communions' and the 'serious
decline in the spirit of reverence in recent years'.[58] Macquarrie
emphasizes the role of preparation, both in terms of appropriate
catechesis and of individual disciplines of contrition, penance and
fasting, in the development of the attitude of reverence. In this way
he might be regarded as extending the notions of poverty and
incompetence to the majority of worshippers, and as bringing to the
need for nurture a renewed universal perspective which he shares
both with Wilson and the Roman Catholic Code itself.

The theology of liberation and the type of the oppressed, as the
root notion for the handicapped person – inasmuch as they extend
beyond the option for the poor – do not find extensive articulation
in the Code, and no attempt is made to shift selectively the *locus
theologicus*. However, if the provisions of canon law are read
positively and not from a perspective of disadvantage, the principle
of liberation (or freedom) for the individual emerges. This is when
requirements and necessary conditions are perceived as promoting
protection and opportunities for nurture and development appropriate to the needs of the individual. The freedoms to 'exercise the
mission of God entrusted to the Church to fulfil in the world', to
'equality of dignity and action', to 'contribute. . .to the building up
of the Body of Christ', to be 'assisted. . .from the spiritual riches of
the Church', and 'to acquire the knowledge of Christian teaching'
are all ensured. Ultimately, the requirement of cognitive faith also
respects the liberty of the individual – and allows the freedom of
individual response. The person with mental handicap is not richly
endowed with the personal freedoms which others take for granted
– such as those of abstract thought, fluency and articulation – but
Roman Catholic canon law goes some way towards protecting what
freedom he or she has as a person and as a child of God. This
protection ensures his or her participation as a right, and this
participation reveals to all the universality of the Church, the unity
of humankind and the love of God for every person. This is one of
the values to which all systems of canon law ought to aspire.

One of the tragedies, in Roman Catholic canon law, of the rule

58 J. Macquarrie, 'Baptism, confirmation, eucharist', in J. Greenhalgh and E.
Russell (eds.), *Signs of Faith, Hope and Love* (London, 1987), 57.

that it is 'the duty of the parish priest to see that children who have not reached the use of reason, or whom he has judged to be insufficiently disposed, do not come to Holy Communion' (Can. 914), is that it discredits canon law. It militates against the positive interpretation and appreciation of the protective function of canon law for the individual – and, arguably, offends the Gospel.[59] It highlights, further, the problems involved in the discernment of faith on the part of priests, teachers, catechists and parents, and the implication that the onus of responsibility for the enforcement of the law in this regard lies with the priest. It is to be hoped that such discernment of faith and understanding of the law will be aided by appropriate guidelines and exercised with due sensitivity to the capacities and conditions of the persons concerned. The operation of grace has no less relevance for these processes than for the sacraments themselves and for the sometimes unusual signs and sounds with which persons with mental handicap express their appreciation, devotion and reverence for the mystery of the sacraments and the desire to share in them.

Breadth of approach in discernment and interpretation need not imply vagueness or imprecision, and the intuitive processes or concrete operations of the mentally handicapped generally ensure that this is not a danger. This same phenomenon applies to the adaptations of catechetical processes and the liturgy made with full participation of the mentally handicapped in mind.[60] The needs of the mentally handicapped call for immediacy, vividness and essential purity of meaning in Word and Sacrament through a process of rediscovery of basic principles and truths of the Christian faith which can be helpful to all.

59 Matthew 19:13–15.
60 B.J. Easter, 'Sacraments and mentally handicapped people', *Liturgy*, 9, No.5 (1985), 190–9; B.J. Easter, 'The bottom of the barrel or essential humanity?' *Crucible* (July/September, 1986), 122–30; D. Wilson, 'Symbols and readings – reflections from celebrating mass with mentally handicapped people', *Liturgy*, 9, No.5 (1985), 181–9; S. Clifford, *Invitation to Communion* (Leigh-on-Sea, 1980); S. Clifford, *Called to Belong* (Leigh-on-Sea, 1984); S. Clifford, *St. Joseph's Mass Book* (London, 1985).

6

The Jus Liturgicum *of the Bishop and the Church in Wales*

REVEREND JEFFREY GAINER

Central to the life of the Christian Church is the worship of the people of God and central to that worship is the ordinance variously described as the Lord's Supper, the Eucharist, the Mass or the Divine Liturgy. Worship plays a crucial role in forming Christians and the old Latin tag *lex orandi, lex credendi* fitly indicates that between prayer and belief there is an intimate connection and that Christian authority is exercised above all in a liturgical context.[1] The influence of the liturgical movement in this century, the shift from a static conception of Christian worship with a consequent spate of new liturgical forms and the emphasis on the corporate nature of worship have all underlined the importance of the eucharistic community. At the same time various churches have felt the need to regulate change so that development does not cause division and clearly in an episcopal Church, bishops have a key role in maintaining the 'unity of the Spirit in the bond of peace'.[2]

Just as the forms of worship are important, because they serve to mould people at a deeper level than the purely conscious, so the role

1 G. Wainwright, *Doxology* (London, 1980), 218–83. See also the important declaration made in 1948 by the Anglican bishops: 'This essentially Anglican authority is reflected in our adherence to episcopacy as the source and centre of our order, and the Book of Common Prayer as the standard of our worship. Liturgy, in the sense of the offering and ordering of the public worship of God, is the crucible in which these elements of authority are fused and unified in the fellowship and power of the Holy Spirit': *The Lambeth Conference 1948* (London, 1948), 84–5. See also P. Moore (ed.), *The Synod of Westminster* (London, 1986), esp. 73f.

2 Eph. 4:3.

of the leadership of worship is important because it shapes the way in which worship is presented. In this context the bishop has a vital part to play. His ministry is essentially liturgical. He is 'the chief minister of the sacraments of the New Covenant' and when he is ordained the Holy Spirit is invoked upon him in order that he may glorify God in the midst of His people and offer spiritual sacrifices acceptable unto the Lord.[3] Thus, the bishop has the right to be the celebrant of the Eucharist and to preach; he is the minister upon whom falls the responsibility for so ordering liturgical worship that the communion of the faithful is deepened and divisions avoided. He admits the baptized to eucharistic communion by the laying-on-of-hands in Confirmation and where, sadly, need arises he excludes the impenitent from such communion.[4] As a Bishop of Oxford put it on the occasion of the consecration of a former Warden of St Michael's College, Llandaff: 'as the leader of worship in his diocese, the bishop is charged with the duty of ensuring that the clergy who, under his guidance, call the faithful to serve, love and worship the Lord, are in things material as in things spiritual duly equipped for that task'.[5]

The emphasis on the bishop's liturgical presidency has deep Christian roots and whilst it has been obscured over the centuries there are indications of a welcome revival of interest in the subject. It is in this context, and that of the law of the Church in Wales, that we discuss: (1) the key issue of what exactly is the bishop's *jus liturgicum* - his rights in liturgical worship; (2) the *jus liturgicum* at the time of the Reformation; (3) its position at the time of disestablishment; (4) the exercise of the *jus liturgicum* since 1920; (5) the principles underlying its use; and (6) two controversial matters settled.

The Jus Liturgicum

To answer the question 'What is the *jus liturgicum*?' we have to be truly radical. From earliest days, the bishop has been the focus of unity, as the celebrated letters of Ignatius show: 'If the prayer of one

3 *The Book of Common Prayer for Use in the Church in Wales* (1984), 'The Ordination of Bishops', II, 716.
4 *Book of Common Prayer* (for the Celebration of the Holy Eucharist), General Rubrics (3). Compare the 1662 Book of Common Prayer, Rubrics at the beginning and end of the Order of the Administration of the Lord's Supper.
5 A Sermon entitled 'Beauty and Bands', preached on 6 January 1954 at the Consecration of the Very Reverend William Glyn Hughes Simon as Bishop of Swansea and Brecon, in K.E. Kirk, *Beauty and Bands* (London, 1955), 13f.

or two individuals has such efficacy, how much more is that of the bishop together with his whole Church?' He continues: 'Abjure all factions, for they are the beginning of evils. Follow your bishop, every one of you, as obediently as Jesus Christ followed the Father'. Moreover, 'make sure that no step affecting the Church is ever taken by anyone without the bishop's sanction. The sole eucharist you should consider valid is one that is celebrated by the bishop, or by some person authorised by him'. Nor is it permissible, says Ignatius, 'to conduct baptisms or love feasts without the bishop'.[6] Again, the earliest order for ordination, that of Hyppolytus' *Apostolic Tradition*, states: 'Let him be ordained bishop who has been chosen by all the people; and when he has been named and accepted by all, let the people assemble, together with the presbytery and those bishops who are present, on the Lord's Day'.[7]

The bishop is not an isolated agent. If he is the natural liturgical president, nonetheless he exercises his ministry *within* the Body of Christ, not above or apart from it, and his decisions about the ordering of worship are to be such as promote the unity of the same Body. Much is often made of the monarchical episcopate found in the pages of Ignatius, but it is a constitutional monarch that Ignatius portrays. Note how often obedience to the bishop *and* presbyters is desiderated.[8] And as the *Apostolic Tradition* reminds us, the *original* duty of a presbyter (or priest) was to assist the bishop in governing the Church. The ordination prayer for a priest has as its central petition: 'Look upon your servant, and impart the Spirit of grace and counsel of the presbyterate, that he may help and govern your people with a pure heart'.[9]

Though it may surprise some, it was only in the later, medieval

6 Ignatius, *Epistle to the Ephesians*, 5; *Epistle to the Smyrnaeans*, 8 (conveniently translated in Maxwell Staniforth, *Early Christian Writings* (Harmondsworth, 1968), 77, 121). See also F.R. McManus, 'The juridical power of the bishop in the constitution on the sacred liturgy', *Concilium* 2 (1) (1965), 18.

7 G.J. Cuming, *Hippolytus: A Text for Students*, Grove Liturgical Study, 8 (Bramcote, Nottingham, 1976), 8. Paul Bradshaw sees the composition of the *Apostolic Tradition* as a 'clear sign' of an attitude which was concerned to conserve and regulate in matters of worship: see his essay 'Authority and freedom in the early liturgy', in K. Stevenson (ed.), *Authority and Freedom in Liturgy*, Grove Liturgical Study, 17 (Bramcote, Nottingham, 1979). See also the essay by R. Williams, 'Authority and the bishop in the Church', in M. Santer (ed.), *Their Lord and Ours: Approaches to Authority, Community and the Unity of the Church* (London, 1982).

8 *Epistle to the Ephesians*, 20; *Epistle to the Magnesians*, 6, 7; *Epistle to the Philadelphians*, 8.

9 Cuming, *Hippolytus*, 12.

Roman ordination services that authority was given to the presbyter to offer the eucharistic sacrifice, and this because in essence it is the bishop who is the natural head of the eucharistic assembly. In his absence presbyters are authorized to act as his representatives. But the original ministry of a presbyter was to assist the bishop in the governing of his diocese.[10] As Dom Gregory Dix put it: 'The presbyter only acquires liturgical functions by degrees, and then rather as the bishop's representative than as his assistant.'[11]

All this has an important bearing on the *jus liturgicum*. If the bishop has an inherent capacity to order divine worship to the edification of the Lord's people, nonetheless he is to be aware that for due exercise of this authority within the worshipping community, there needs to be a recognition of the legitimate place of custom and a sense of the need to regularize custom by obtaining the assent, or at least acquiescence, of the wider Christian community, and especially of the presbyterate. Likewise, the presbyterate cannot act as if the bishop did not exist.

Jus liturgicum is indeed part of the larger *jus* which allows or forbids custom *(consuetudo)*. It is abundantly clear that in the medieval Western Church there was great diversity of liturgical custom, and as the great Roman liturgical scholar J.A. Jungmann says: 'Over and over during medieval times the phrase of St. Gregory is reiterated: *in una fide nil officit ecclesiae consuetudo diversa.*'[12]

Now, a custom operates within a community of faith. The idea that all Christian communities have ever worshipped in exactly the same way, or that this is a laudable aim which can be procured by legislation, is vain indeed. As Jungmann shows, customs varied considerably. Prayers varied and this is not surprising since they were handed down not in writing but by word of mouth. Indeed, even

10 For a further discussion of this point, see H.J.M. Turner, *Ordination and Vocation* (Worthing, 1990), 63. The point was used in 1897 by the Archbishops of Canterbury and York in replying to the papal condemnation of Anglican orders (see *Saepius Officio*, XII, Church Literature Association, London, 1977). In reply to Leo XIII's observation that the English ordination service omits the conferring of the specific power of 'consecrating and offering the true Body and Blood of the Lord in that sacrifice which is no nude commemoration of the sacrifice offered on the cross', Their Graces noted that the earlier Roman ordination services (Hippolytus; the old Roman Sacramentary) likewise omit this specific donation.
11 G. Dix, *The Shape of the Liturgy* (London, 1945), 33–4.
12 J.A. Jungmann, *Mass of the Roman Rite* (New York, 1951), I, 98; see St Gregory the Great's *Epistle*, 1.43 (Migne, *Patrilogia Latina*, LXXVII, 497). The phrase may be translated as: 'As long as the Church preserves one faith, there is nothing inconsistent about a divergence of customs.'

bishops did not hesitate to insert absolutely private prayers in the course of the mass. Such a one was Bishop Gandulph of Rochester who daily said a second mass in the presence of his monks and after the Gospel sat down and gave himself over entirely to his devotions and sighed and wept – whilst the choristers sang the offertory.[13]

However, despite the diversity of usages and customs, medieval canon law did not recognize an individualistic approach to worship. True, a practice might be introduced by an individual or group, but it did not become a legally established custom, customary law, until it was rooted in the community. A period of time was necessary before it acquired the status of lawful custom – there was often considerable debate amongst canonists about the period which conferred validity on usage as customary law – and forty years was a common opinion. Moreover, before the custom could become valid (and this was also the position with temporal customs in medieval law) it had to be reasonable. In addition it had to be approved by the legislator.[14] Indeed, in modern Roman Catholic canon law these populist and validity notions can be found: '[a] custom introduced by a community of the faithful has the force of law only if it has been approved by the legislator'; '[n]o custom which is contrary to divine law can acquire the force of law'; and '[a] custom which is contrary to or apart from canon law, cannot acquire the force of law unless it is reasonable; a custom which is expressly reprobated in the law is not reasonable' (Cans. 23, 24, 25). As we shall see, these ideas become of critical importance for the operation of the *jus liturgicum* in the Church in Wales.

In the course of time certain centres standardized their liturgical books and these became popular elsewhere. It became possible for bishops to authorize particular liturgies for their own dioceses. This is what happened in Wales. So, in 1233 Bishop Iorwerth (Gervase) adopted the *Use of Sarum* for the diocese of St David's.[15] This power,

---

13 J.A. Jungmann, *Mass of the Roman Rite*, 98. However, bishops' idiosyncrasies in this regard were often condemned. So, for example, Origen urged bishops to refrain from introducing their own peculiar ideas into their eucharistic prayers and pleaded that they should 'remain in the conventions': Origen, *Conversation with Heracleides*, cited by R.P.C. Hanson, 'The liberty of the bishop to improvise prayer in the eucharist', *Vigiliae Christianae*, 15 (1961), 173–6.

14 For a fuller discussion of this point, see R.C. Mortimer, *Western Canon Law* (London, 1953) – generally, Ch. 5, 'The characteristics of canon law'. For the same problem in medieval secular law, see N. Doe, *Fundamental Authority in Late Medieval English Law* (Cambridge, 1990), 78–83.

15 J. Fisher, 'The pre-Reformation services of the Church in Wales', *The Directory and Year Book of the Church in Wales* (Cardiff, 1925), 33.

that is the right to determine the form and manner of public worship, is clearly an expression of the *jus liturgicum*. The diversity of uses and their express sanction in a diocese by the bishop led to a situation which is reflected in the preamble to the 1662 Prayer Book headed 'Concerning the Service of the Church': 'And whereas heretofore there hath been great diversity in saying and singing in Churches within this Realm; some following Salisbury use, some Hereford use, and some the use of Bangor, some of York, some of Lincoln; now from henceforth all the whole Realm shall have but one use'.[16]

The Reformation Settlement

The settlement of worship was not finally made until the Act of Uniformity 1662, which provided that a new Book of Common Prayer be made obligatory from St. Bartholomew's Day 1662 in 'this Realm of England, Dominion of Wales, and Town of Berwick of Tweed'.[17] It ordered that a Welsh version of the Book be ready for use in the 'Dioceses and Places in Wales, where the Welsh is commonly spoken or used' by 1 May 1664. Amongst all the upheavals three things stand out. First, the Reformation was an act of State - the monarch was determined to be master in his own house.[18] By sweeping away papal jurisdiction, Henry VIII was resolved to exercise an equivalent control over State and Church. This is evident in the preamble to the Act in Restraint of Appeals 1533: 'Where by divers sundry old authentic histories and chronicles, it is manifestly declared and expressed, that this Realm of England is an Empire'. In consequence, it continued:

> [it] hath been accepted in the world governed by one supreme head and king, having the dignity and royal estate of the imperial crown of the same, unto whom a body politic, compact of all sorts and degrees of people divided in terms and by names of spirituality and temporality, be bounden and ought to bear, next to God a natural and humble obedience .[19]

16 Mentioned first in the Preface to the Book of Common Prayer (1549).
17 13 and 14 Car II, c.4. See also above, ch. 1, n.6.
18 See, for example, Article 37 of the Thirty-nine Articles, which declares that 'the Queen's Majesty hath the chief power in this Realm of England, and other her Dominions, unto whom the chief Government of all Estates of this Realm, whether they be Ecclesiastical or Civil in all causes doth appertain, and is not, nor ought to be, subject to any foreign Jurisdiction'.
19 24 Henry VIII, c.12. See G.R. Elton, *The Tudor Constitution* (2nd edn., Cambridge, 1982), 353.

Secondly, the Reformation settlement of worship was part of an attempt to exercise social control through the Church. In all the doctrinal variations unleashed by the Reformation, the English monarchs saw the danger of instability. As with the common law in the early medieval period, they sought one use – for the Provinces of Canterbury and York - which would encompass all their subjects in the one Church. Control of church worship was an integral part of the monarch's strategy to be master in his own house.

Thirdly, by inclination Henry VIII and, later, Elizabeth I were conservative in matters of religion and they sought to emphasize the continuity of the Church. By so doing they also hoped to counteract the arguments of the Roman polemicists. The Submission of the Clergy Act 1533 provided that such canons, constitutions and ordinances synodal or provincial being already made, which were not 'contrariant or repugnant' to the laws, statutes and customs of this realm, nor to the damage of the king's prerogative, were still to be used and executed as they were before the making of the Act. This is crucial. In all the Reformation changes, much of the canon law of medieval England and Wales remained – including the *jus liturgicum* of the bishop. True, it was much circumscribed by the emphasis upon the royal supremacy, but certainly did not become extinct. It is essential that this point be underlined. As appears in Halsbury: 'The constitutions contained in Lyndwood, the general usages of the Church and certain portions of the canon law admitted by those usages are still part of the law of the Church of England.'[20] And, we may add, by virtue of s.3(2) of the Welsh Church Act 1914 and the continuing applicability of pre-1920 English ecclesiastical rules (see chapter 7 below), so too for the Church in Wales – unless, that is, altered by the canon law of the Church in Wales since 1920.[21]

It must not be supposed that custom became of no effect in the four ancient dioceses of Wales in the period between the Reformation and disestablishment. The bishop's *jus liturgicum* still applied.

20 Halsbury, *Laws of England*, vol. 14, *Ecclesiastical Law* (4th edn., London, 1975), para. 304. See also the statement in *Martin* v. *Mackonochie* (1868) LR 2 A&E 116 at 153 *per* Sir Robert Phillimore. See generally, R.H. Helmholz, *Roman Canon Law in Reformation England* (Cambridge, 1990).

21 An interesting example of this is the canon to amend the canon law relating to the solemnization of Holy Matrimony (promulgated on 22 April 1987). By virtue of the authority expressed in s.3(2) of the Welsh Church Act 1914, the Governing Body repealed the canon *ut nullus filiam suam* of the Council of Winchester 1076 to allow deacons to officiate at the service of Holy Matrimony. Clearly there would be no need to repeal a pre-Reformation canon unless this was deemed to be still valid and in force.

It was exercised in various ways. For example, to determine the true manner in which the Prayer Book services should be carried out. The preamble headed 'Concerning the Service of the Church' (already referred to) has these words: 'And forasmuch as nothing can be so plainly set forth, but doubts may arise in the use and practice of the same; to appease all such diversity (if any arise) and for the resolution of all doubts, concerning the manner, how to understand, do and execute, the things contained in this Book', the parties that doubt 'shall alway resort to the Bishop of the Diocese, who by his discretion shall take order for quieting and appeasing of the same; so that the same order be not contrary to anything contained in this Book. And if the Bishop of the Diocese be in doubt, the he may send for the resolution thereof to the Archbishop.'

The *jus liturgicum* could also be used to authorize services not provided for in the Prayer Book. These services are additional to those in the Prayer Book and are doctrinally at harmony with them. What happened at the Reformation was that the *jus liturgicum* of the Anglican bishops was confined by the royal supremacy – just as in the Roman communion at the same time (and by a parallel process) the Roman Catholic bishop found his authority limited by the superior legislative authority of the pope.[22] However, the *jus liturgicum* still covered such matters as authorizing forms of service for consecration of churches and other services which in pre-Reformation days would have been included in the pontifical – the book containing the services that the bishop alone needed. However, such services authorized by the bishop were in addition to the Prayer Book and were not services as substitutes for the Prayer Book provisions. The bishop's *jus* does *not* include an absolute freedom to ordain *any* service he may choose *instead* of the synodically agreed forms – to do so would undercut the principle in church life that a decision affecting the whole body of the faithful should be ratified by its consent.

The last principle was accepted by the great seventeenth-century liturgists. After the Reformation, many liturgical scholars welcomed the fact that parliamentary authority had been given to the Church's Prayer Book. In part this was done to emphasize the authority of the

22 *Codex Juris Canonici*, Canons 1257–61 (1917 Code). The bishop at this time was limited to authorizing extra-liturgical prayers, the watching over observance of the laws and the prevention of superstition and abuse. The principle was clear: 'It belongs to the Apostolic See alone both to compile and to approve liturgical books.' See further A.G. Martimort, *The Church at Prayer* (New York, 1968) esp. Ch.4 on liturgical law, 58ff.

common liturgy after the upheavals of the Commonwealth. But, it must be noted, the Anglican divines concerned stressed that the authority on which the Prayer Book rests is not statute law but that of the bishops and clergy in provincial synods: 'the king and parliament only establishing by the civil sanction what was there done by ecclesiastical authority'.[23] The authority of the Prayer Book comes from the Convocations and is binding in *foro conscientiae*. Parliament had no hand in drawing it up – the bishops principally were responsible for that – and so Parliament gave it confirmation of temporal law.[24] It is fair to say, therefore, that the bishops assembled at Lambeth in 1920 failed to appreciate that their liturgical authority is not arbitrary when their *Fourth Report* recommended that 'it should be recognised that full liberty belongs to Diocesan bishops not only for the adaptations and additions alluded to above [that is, by previous Lambeth Conferences] but also for the adoption of other uses'. They were, however, on much safer ground when they went on to declare:

> . . .in the exercise of this liberty care should always be taken: (a) to maintain a scriptural and catholic balance of Truth; (b) to give due consideration to the precedents of the early Church; (c) to observe such limitations as may be imposed by higher synodical authority; and (d) to remember with brotherly consideration the possible effect their actions may have on other Provinces and Branches of the Anglican Communion .[25]

23 C. Wheatly, *A Rational Illustration of the Book of Common Prayer of the Church of England* (Oxford, 1839), 31. Interestingly enough, the Welsh version of the Book of Common Prayer (1664) produced in accordance with the Act of Uniformity 1662 was not presented to Parliament nor was it annexed to the Act like the English version. Its use rests upon the action of the Bishops of Wales and the Bishop of Hereford in translating the English book and subsequently permitting its use. See A.O. Evans, *A Memorandum on the Legality of the Welsh Bible and the Welsh Version of the Book of Common Prayer* (Cardiff, 1925), and especially the Introduction to the Welsh Prayer Book of 1841, 41–48, 158–9.
24 For a valuable discussion of the seventeenth-century High Church divines' attitude to the liturgy, see G.W.O. Addleshaw, *The High Church Tradition: A Study in the Liturgical Thought of the Seventeenth Century* (London, 1941), esp. Ch. 5.
25 Lord Davidson of Lambeth, *The Six Lambeth Conferences 1867–1920* (London, 1929), 88. The Fourth Report deals with 'Missionary problems', and its third section deals specifically with liturgical variations. Interestingly, a few years after this conference a colonial bishop, Dr Westcott of Calcutta, showed a keen awareness of the limitations upon his *jus liturgicum* when he sought advice from the English liturgical expert, Walter Frere: see R.C.D. Jasper (ed.), *Walter Frere: His Correspondence on Liturgical Revision and Construction* (London, 1954), 259f.

There can be no doubt that a bishop's liturgical authority includes the right to authorize services additional to those in the Prayer Book. But the *jus liturgicum* does not extend to authorizing unilaterally services contrary to the Prayer Book or services which are already covered by the Prayer Book.

The Church is a living body, an organization, and her liturgical life cannot be entrapped in statute law. Instead the Church has the means of avoiding anarchy and regulating innovation by due synodical procedure in which the bishops take the initiative in preparing changes. Thus, the changes effected at the Restoration were endorsed by the Convocations on 20 December 1661. The bishops acting in synod obviously carry more weight than an individual bishop acting in a possibly eccentric or injurious manner. So at this period it was customary for bishops to put out services needful in the Church's life – such as consecration of churchyards – but it is no accident either that the practice of each bishop drawing up consecration orders stopped when the Convocations issued one in 1712.

Moreover, there is evidence, at this time, that individual bishops were prone to consult traditional practices when in doubt as to how to interpret the Prayer Book rubrics. Thus, Cosin, Bishop of Durham (1660–72), said: 'Let ancient custom prevail, the thing which our Church chiefly intended in the review of this service'.[26] In testy mood, he explained:

And it is to be noted, that the book [that is, the Prayer Book] does not everywhere enjoin and prescribe every little order, what should be said or done, but take it for granted that people are acquainted with such common, and things always used already. Let the Puritans then here [that is, in the matter of how to recite and respond to the liturgy] give over their endless cavils.

A little later he mentions the 'laudable custom' of the people repeating the third collect for grace. In this regard, Cosin was true to the spirit of Canon 30 of the Constitutions and Canons Ecclesiastical 1603, which explains the lawful use of the sign of the cross in baptism:

Nay, so far was it from the purpose of the Church of England to forsake and reject the Churches of Italy, France, Spain, Germany or any such like Churches, in all things which they held and practised, that, as the Apology of the Church of England confesseth, it doth with reverence retain those ceremonies, which doth neither endamage the Church of God, nor offend the minds of sober men.

26 Cosin, *Works*, V, 65, Library of Anglo-Catholic Theology (Oxford, 1855).

The Church departed from them only 'in those particular points, wherein they were fallen both from themselves in their ancient integrity, and from the Apostolic Churches, which were their first founders'.

It is, therefore, no accident that in the period when the Convocations failed to meet (and for some time after their revival), Erastianism rather than a sound grasp of liturgical principle took hold of those responsible for interpreting ecclesiastical law. The sad result of this was a foolish and ill-fated attempt to restrict the Church's worship to the Prayer Book so interpreted as if it were a statute – rather than as a manual of worship for use in the worshipping community.[27] The result of such a misguided approach can be seen, for example, in the decision of the Judicial Committee of the Privy Council which overturned the judgment of Phillimore in *Martin* v. *Mackonochie* (1868). The Privy Council cited *Westerton* v. *Liddell* (1855): 'In the performance of all services, rites and ceremonies ordered by the Prayer Book, the directions contained in it must be strictly observed; no omission and no addition can be permitted', since the object of the Act of Uniformity was to produce 'an universal agreement in the public worship of Almighty God'.[28]

It is ironic that, at about the same time the Anglican Churches overseas were making tentative efforts to provide for synodical government which would ensure the Church's control over its worship, there was a mistaken attempt to restrict artificially the Church's worship at home. It is also pertinent to observe at this juncture that whilst the Church in Wales at disestablishment took over English ecclesiastical rules as obtaining in 1920 (with certain specified exceptions), its Constitution expressly declared that 'the courts of the Church in Wales shall not be bound by any decision of the English courts in relation to matters of faith, discipline or ceremonial'.[29]

27   Compare the warning of the late Chancellor E.G. Moore in Moore and Briden *Introduction,* 59, 60: 'When dealing with the Book of Common Prayer it must be remembered that, although it has statutory authority, it is not itself an Act of Parliament and should not be construed as such. Its rubrics ... must be interpreted with the elasticity which directives usually require.'
28   For the protracted litigation, see (1868) LR 2 PC 365; (1869) LR 3 PC 52; (1870) LR 3 PC 409. For *Westerton* v. *Liddell et al* (1855) 1 Jur NS 1178.
29   Constitution, XI,36. This proviso presumably accounts for the canon promulgated on 22 April 1987 to allow deacons to officiate at weddings, since, in *R* v. *Mills* (1844) 10 Cl & Fin 534, the court ruled to the same effect on the grounds that the pre-Reformation canon law had fallen into desuetude. The Church in Wales – not being bound by this decision – has therefore resolved the matter by canonical enactment rather than by a decision of the English court. In the same

In sum, the period leading up to disestablishment led to a narrowing of the exercise of the bishop's *jus liturgicum* not least because a nervous reaction to ritualism moved some to conclude that the bishops could not be trusted to curb liturgical deviations.[30]

The Jus Liturgicum *and Disestablishment*

What happened to the *jus liturgicum* (defined by C.A.H. Green as 'the right to determine the form and manner of public worship') at the time of the disestablishment of the Church in Wales?[31] At the time of disestablishment many were fearful about the future. However, thanks to the wisdom, hard work and learning of those who contributed to its making, a constitution was devised which has lasted (in its main features) to the present day. Yet, it is important to realize the motives and aims of the drafters of the Constitution. These were expressed, in a homely way, by Sankey in a speech on 9 January 1918:

> In the building of a house you are necessarily circumscribed, because you have to comply with various natural laws and bye-laws. Our house we have already built. Our house is the scheme for the Governing Body, and you were naturally restricted when you came to consider and pass this scheme. . ... The reasons you were restricted were two-fold: (1) it was quite impossible for you to do as you liked, because you could not do anything to imperil your communion with other branches of the Catholic Church; (2) you had to take care that the scheme you made for the Governing Body was one which harmonised with the rules and principles of other branches of the Catholic and Apostolic Church.[32]

(29 contd.) spirit, it may be noted that whilst the Welsh Church Act 1914, s.3(2), allowed the Church in Wales to set up its own courts and, with the consent of the Archbishop of Canterbury, to allow appeals from its Provincial Court to the Court of the Arches, no provision for this is made in the Constitution.

30 Compare, for example, the attitude of Sir William Harcourt, a noted anti-ritualist, who repeatedly criticized the bishops for their failure to control clergy who introduced liturgical customs he deemed more characteristic of Rome than of Canterbury: G.K.A. Bell, *Randall Davidson* (Oxford, 1938), 327f. Harcourt wrote to the Bishop of Winchester (23 September 1898), 'For myself I would willingly trust the present Bishop of Winchester, but I should certainly not have the same confidence in the contiguous Sarum. You would have a special service approved on one side of the road and disapproved on the other side.'

31 C.A.H. Green, *The Setting of the Constitution of the Church in Wales* (London, 1937), 14.

32 Speech of Mr Justice Sankey to the Governing Body of the Church in Wales, *Western Mail* (Cardiff, 9 January 1918), 7.

Here, Sankey expressed the conviction that the Church in Wales was a sound part of Catholic and Apostolic Christendom – and by virtue of this fact had definite limitations placed upon its freedom of action.[33]

Charles Green, reflecting on the situation in his *Setting of the Constitution of the Church in Wales* (1937), underlined the role of the bishops. Constitutionally, the Welsh bishops were 'without a Province and without a Metropolitan'. In this situation 'the bishops alone had the authority and the power requisite for the crisis'. As we saw in chapters 2 and 3, Green argued: 'Interpreted in the light of past history, the Constitution of the Church in Wales neither confers, nor is meant to confer, any authority or power upon the Bishops which did not already belong to them, by Divine Commission.' As such, 'all ministrations, clerical or lay, in the Church, derive their validity from the Bishop, in whom is vested the plenitude of Apostolic authority and power'.[34] This emphasis on the episcopal authority is expressed in the Constitution: 'Subject to the Constitution no proceeding of the Governing Body shall interfere with the exercise by the Archbishop of the powers and functions inherent in the Office of Metropolitan, nor with the exercise by the Diocesan Bishop of the powers and functions inherent in the Episcopal Office.'[35] Here, the Constitution does not *confer* authority upon the bishop (how could it?), but simply *acknowledges* his authority and what has been true in the Church since early days.

As we have seen, as far as the control of worship is concerned, the bishop does not have *carte blanche*: he has to govern his diocese in accordance with canon law.[36] He can give authoritative interpretation of rubrics. The bishop may authorize services *praeter legem* but not services *contra legem*. Moreover, he is to be guided in the exercise of the *jus liturgicum* by custom – custom which is communally

33 Compare Sankey's words spoken after the acceptance of the Constitution in April 1922: 'The Church in Wales is a Catholic and National Church. As a Catholic Church you are not at liberty to consult your own desires or do as you like. You are a branch of the great Catholic and Apostolic Church, with explicit creeds and determined traditions. See to it, then, that you discount innovations which may impair your own communion with others': cited by D.T.W. Price, *A History of the Church in Wales in the Twentieth Century* (Penarth, 1990), 22.
34 *Setting*, 13, 15.
35 Constitution, II,32; see also II, 2, 3.
36 See the statement of Martin I (649–55) which expressed a typical sentiment among early popes: 'We cannot transgress the ecclesiastical canons; on the contrary, we are their defender and protector, not their violator', *Epistle 9*, Mansi 10:823, cited in P. Granfield, *The Limits of the Papacy* (London, 1987), 70.

acceptable, profitable in itself and of long standing. Furthermore, since (as Green says) 'the Province of Wales is only one Province in the Catholic Church', the bishop will (like all members of the Governing Body), in all his doings, feel himself 'under a mental inhibition to refrain from acting contrary to Catholic Tradition'.[37]

Another restriction upon the bishop results from 'the vestiges of establishment'.[38] Whilst it is clear that the intention behind the 1914 Act was to make a clean break between Church and State in Wales, some qualifications were made and these exist in the areas of marriage and burial. Section 23 of the 1914 statute provided that, from disestablishment, 'the law relating to marriages in churches of the Church of England (including any law conferring any right to be married in such a church) shall cease to be in force in Wales and Monmouthshire, and the provisions of the Marriage Acts 1811 to 1898...shall apply to marriages in churches of the Church in Wales'. However, s.6 of the Welsh Church (Temporalities) Act 1919 repealed this so that the Church in Wales clergy still hold a privileged position with regard to the solemnization of Holy Matrimony. Yet, one consequence of this is that 'in exceptional circumstances, the Archbishop of Canterbury can grant a special licence which permits the solemnization without Banns, at any convenient time or place, of a marriage according to the rites of the Church in Wales'. Once more, neither the bishops nor the Church in Wales could change the doctrine of matrimony from the contractual one expressed in the Prayer Book service. This understanding of matrimony (deriving ultimately from the Roman law of contract) is a characteristically Western feature, and underlines the parliamentary legislation which controls the Church in Wales in this regard. The Church in Wales and its bishops are not free to change this Western tradition.[39]

The Jus Liturgicum *After Disestablishment*

For the first thirty years or so after disestablishment, the Welsh bishops were content to adopt a cautious policy. Indeed, at the time of the controversies over the Prayer Book revision, they felt it expedient to remind members of the Governing Body that:

37 *Setting*, 203.
38 This is an expression used by T.G. Watkin, 'Vestiges of establishment: the ecclesiastical and canon law of the Church in Wales', *Ecclesiastical Law Journal*, 2 (1990), 110. See also *supra*, chapter 2, pp. 33–38.
39 See generally T.A. Lacey, *Marriage in Church and State* (London, 1947), 23.

We [the diocesan bishops] are of the opinion that, as the decisions of the Convocation of Canterbury, made since Disestablishment, and the measures of the National Assembly of the Church of England, have no authority nor force in the Province of Wales, it is now and will always be illegal to use any Book of Common Prayer other than that accepted by the Governing Body of the Church in Wales at its creation.

This was so, in the Province of Wales, 'until and except such Book of Common Prayer be revised or altered by the Governing Body under the Bill procedures as prescribed' in the Constitution.[40]

This statement is of more than antiquarian interest. From time to time, for example, it is suggested that a Welsh bishop can legally authorize a collection of services for use in his diocese which could be used instead of the Prayer Book. This is incorrect. The *jus liturgicum* emphatically does not extend to authorizing services – such as the eucharistic rites of other provinces – which are already provided for in the Prayer Book unless there is a canon duly promulgated to that effect by the Governing Body. The statement is also of importance as indicating the ancient principle that canon law applies to territory (the Province of Wales) as well as to persons. It cannot be argued, for instance, that a Welsh cleric, including a bishop, is free to do certain things in a non-Anglican place of worship which would, if carried out in a church of the Church in Wales, constitute a breach of canon law. The canon law binds every member of the Church in Wales – including bishops – wherever they may be if they are within the Province of Wales.[41]

Indeed, the territorial principle is grounded in ancient tradition. The Apostle Paul greeted his fellow Christians in a particular locality, in Rome, Corinth or Philippi, for example. Likewise, Holy Scripture describes the Christians as being gathered *epi to auto* (Acts 1:15; 2:1; I Cor. 11:18, 20; 14:23; Luke 17:35) which denotes 'altogether' and 'in one place'.[42] This accounts too for the ancient rule that there be but one bishop *in one place* and one celebration of the Eucharist

40 Minutes of a meeting of the Governing Body held on 19 April 1927, p. 2. The bishops alluded to the Constitution of the Church in Wales, II,30. See also E. Lewis, *Prayer Book Revision in the Church in Wales* (Penarth, 1958), 22f.
41 Compare the Roman Catholic Code of Canon Law (1983), Canons 12 and 13, esp. 12(3): 'Without prejudice to the provisions of can. 13, laws enacted for a particular territory bind those for whom they were enacted and who have a domicile or quasi-domicile in that territory and are actually residing in it.'
42 See W. Bauer, *Greek–English Lexicon of the New Testament* (Chicago, 1979), 288.

on the Sunday. All this was intended to emphasize and uphold the unity of the faithful.[43]

The Jus Liturgicum *in Recent Years*

Whilst caution prevailed in the years immediately following disestablishment, the last thirty years have seen major liturgical changes in all the Western Churches. The Roman Catholic Church has produced a mass in the vernacular; there has been a keen interest in the forms of worship common in the patristic era and an attempt to get behind Reformation controversies by drawing upon primitive liturgy. Clearly the danger in all this would be fracture as uncontrolled experiment led to excesses. In Wales the bishops took action early on to avoid such a situation and have consistently obtained the consent of the legislature, the Governing Body, for liturgical changes and developments. This wise policy, which is based upon the ancient principle that worship – which affects all – should be approved by all, resulted in a new Welsh Prayer Book (1984), superseding the old (1662) Book of Common Prayer. The situation in Wales is therefore different from that obtaining in England, where the Book of Common Prayer (1662) remains the legal norm,[44] although other services may be authorized, under English canon law, as *alternatives* to the Prayer Book – provided that they do not indicate any departure from the doctrine of the Church of England in any matter.[45]

However, at times the bishop's *jus liturgicum* has come into prominence. One particular matter that recurred from the 1960s was that of the admission of non-Anglican Christians to Holy Communion. On 27 September 1962 and 24 September 1969, statements of the Bench of Bishops of the Church in Wales were brought before the Governing Body. These statements made provision *inter alia* for a baptized communicant member of a Trinitarian Church not in communion with the Church in Wales, in certain circumstances, to receive Holy Communion in the Church in Wales, subject to the oversight of the diocesan bishop. In the 1962 debate Archbishop Morris said: 'We hold that the power of dispensation, the exercise of economy in particular circumstances not envisaged by those who

43 See J. Zizioulas, *Being as Communion* (St Vladimir's Seminary Press, Crestwood, New York, 1985), esp. 145f. and 247f. See also J. Meyendorff, *Catholicity and the Church* (New York, 1983), ch.7.
44 Canons Ecclesiastical of the Church of England (1964–70), Canons A3, A4 and A5.
45 Ibid., Canons B1(d), B2 and B3

made a particular rule or rubric, is a power inherent in the office of a bishop'. Moreover, said Morris 'we think that we could have done this without coming to the Governing Body at all, but out of respect for the Governing Body and our desire to know whether we are expressing the general mind of the Church in Wales as represented here or not . . . '.[46]

Objections were made at the time that the permission so granted should be effected by bill procedure. The ground for this was the rubric in the 1662 Prayer Book after the order of confirmation which reads: 'And there shall none be admitted to the Holy Communion until such time as he be confirmed, or be ready and desirous to be confirmed'.

There has been dispute over the years whether this rubric states a rule applicable only to those baptized in the Church of England – or whether it includes those Christians commonly designated Nonconformists. Much, of course, has depended on the importance assigned to confirmation.[47] And with the influence of the Tractarian movement (with its concern for a strict application of the Prayer Book rubrics) a distinct reluctance to use this rubric to grant permission to offer Holy Communion to non-Anglicans became evident.[48] It is doubtful whether the Prayer Book rubric does grant permission to Nonconformists to receive Holy Communion although this did become a practice of certain clergy in the Church of England. Indeed, Archbishop Tait's ruling of 1870 to the effect that the rubric applies 'solely to our own people, and not to those members of foreign or dissenting bodies who occasionally conform', was unconditionally rejected by the Legal Board of the Church Assembly in the 1960s.[49]

46 See T.C. Bryant, *Lawful Authority in the Church in Wales* (March 1978), a paper issued by the then Legal Assistant to the Governing Body; this should be consulted along with the *Further Report of the Working Group on Bill Procedure*, entitled 'The status of the *jus liturgicum* of the bishops in relation to the constitution' (issued to the Governing Body and dated November 1979). See also for Green, *Setting*, 113–4, for the idea of lawful authority equated with the *jus liturgicum*.

47 For a summary of the arguments, see the *Report of the Archbishops' Commission on Intercommunion*, 'Intercommunion today' (Church Information Office, London, 1968), esp. 29–45.

48 D. Stone summarizes the arguments in favour of the line of reasoning in the minority report of the committee and the Lower House of the Canterbury Convocation, Convocation Report No.591. This is reported in F.L. Cross, *Darwell Stone: Churchman and Counsellor* (Westminster, 1943), 419–32; see also, ibid., 209–10.

49 See Appendix IV of 'Intercommunion today', 157.

The statement by Archbishop Morris is, likewise, questionable.
The 'dispensing power' of the bishop cannot run counter to a specific
provision in the Prayer Book, especially when the bishop's discretionary powers allowed in 'Concerning the Service of the Church'
are limited by the proviso that 'his ordering shall not be contrary to
anything contained in this Book'.[50] But, as always, canon law, far
from being the desiccated study of legal niceties that it is alleged to
be, points to basic matters of corporate belief.[51] The intention of the
bishops responsible for the rubric was to answer the Puritan divines
who at the Savoy conference of 1661 had stated that 'confirmation
may not be made so necessary to the Holy Communion, as that none
should be admitted to it unless they be confirmed'. The bishops' only
concession to this was to include the words 'be ready and desirous
to be confirmed'.[52]

The consequence of all this is that the various statements by the
Bench of Bishops on intercommunion, made in the 1960s and 1970s,
whilst they may well have been acceptable to the majority of the
Governing Body, were nonetheless grounded in an apprehension of
the *jus liturgicum* that was (and is) not universally accepted. They
raised fundamental issues of faith and order - and as present-day
controversies show, it is (*pace* Hooker) impossible to draw a clear
dividing line between the two - since the manner in which a Church
orders its life expresses its apprehension of Christian truth.[53] Confirmation is not an optional extra – and every time an Anglican

50 See also Canons 9, 10, 11 and 27 of the Canons Ecclesiastical 1603. These
have not been repealed wholesale in the Church in Wales. See chapter 7 for the
Welsh Church Act 1914 and the problem of the applicability of pre–1920 rules
of English ecclesiastical law.
51 This was perceived by the Convocations in the discussions concerning
Resolution 42 of the 1930 Lambeth Conference. The Lower Houses did not
support the bishops' resolutions and no *synodical* decision was reached. The
bishops assumed that the admission of Nonconformists to Communion in
temporary circumstances 'should be left to the discretion of the Diocesan Bishop',
but, as Dr Sparrow Simpson has commented, 'the assumption is not easily
justified on constitutional principles' since the legislator in England is not the
bishops individually or collectively, but Convocation, which includes the Lower
House: Sparrow Simpson, *Dispensations* (London, 1935), 170–5. The matter has
since been resolved – but by proper synodical action: see Canon B15 of the
Canons Ecclesiastical (1964–70).
52 G.J. Cuming, *The Durham Book* (London, 1975), 229.
53 R. Hooker, *Of the Laws of Ecclesiastical Polity* (1594), edited by R. Bayne
(New York, 1907), III, x.10. It is mistaken to call the distinction between faith
and order the classical teaching of the Church of England. Such teaching is found
in her formularies which include, for example, statements as to the necessity to
maintain the threefold order of the Church. See Kirk, *Beauty and Bands*, 238–49.

congregation declares its belief at the Eucharist in the words of the Nicene Creed it is important to realize that what was denoted by the framers of the phrase 'one Baptism for the remission of sins' included not only the washing with water in the name of the Trinity but also the 'sealing' of this by the bishop in confirmation. The Welsh for 'confirmation' – Bedydd Esgob (bishop's baptism) – only reaffirms the point.[54]

Accordingly, a policy of extending Communion to non-Anglicans should have been implemented by bill procedure and not by a questionable use of episcopal discretion. This discretion, whilst applicable in the case of particular individuals in particular circumstances, cannot reasonably be held to cover whole groups of people, for such action would in effect constitute a general permission. It is clearly wrong for dispensation to be used either by a bishop individually or even the bishops collectively in a way that in effect makes a general change in the law. Such changes have to be made according to the Constitution of the Church and must be effected by promulgation of a canon. This point has now been taken both in England (Canon B15A) and Wales where synodical action in approving the new Prayer Book includes the express proviso that '[e]xcept with the permission of the bishop, no one shall receive Communion until he is confirmed, or is ready and desirous to be confirmed'.[55]

---

54 There is, however, a confusion in the Welsh Prayer Book (1984). The Catechism (Question 57) (vol. II, 698) declares confirmation to be 'the rite by which we make a mature expression of the commitment to Christ made at Baptism and receive the strength of the Holy Spirit through prayer and the laying on of hands by a bishop'. However, the actual order of confirmation clearly distinguishes the two parts: the former called 'The Renewal of the Baptismal Vows' and the latter only is called 'The Confirmation'. The order expresses the truth rather than the catechism. The post-Reformation practice of preceding confirmation with catechetical instruction and the renewal of baptismal vows may have much to commend it on pastoral grounds, but such a practice cannot be called the confirmation proper, since this consists in the 'sealing' of baptism by the bishop. This only is the ancient and primitive use. Thus Canon 60 of 1603 defines confirmation without one word about ratification of vows. See further, B.J. Kidd (ed.), *Selected Letters of William Bright* (London, 1903), 188–92. For a discussion of the various views of baptism, and its meaning in the early Church, see L.L. Mitchell, *Baptismal Anointing* (London, 1966). Mitchell's conclusion was: 'Baptism was a single rite. It consisted of several liturgical actions, of which the most prominent were the washing, the anointing, and the laying on of hands.'

55 The weakness in the argument of the Working Party on Bill Procedure is seen at Section 15 of the *Further Report* (November 1979), where it is declared that the bishops 'were making provision for persons who cannot be said to be bound by any rule or rubric of the Church in Wales'. But a bishop cannot dispense anyone who does not come within his jurisdiction.

Conclusion: Basic Principles and Problems

It is, then, evident that much confusion obtains as to the extent of the *jus liturgicum*. This discussion of the *jus liturgicum*, principally from a historical perspective, might be summarized in this way.

First, the bishop's *jus liturgicum* is inherent in his office – but is exercised constitutionally in association with his presbyters. There is a great need for a revival of the synod of the bishop and his presbyters to discuss matters liturgical (and otherwise). As the Convocation of York put it (in 1922): 'The bishop and his presbyters assembled for consultation constitute the diocesan synod proper' and 'the name should be reserved for that gathering'.[56]

Secondly, the bishop's *jus liturgicum*, (as Green says) 'the Apostolic Right and Power to determine the Form of the Rites, and the Ceremonies, to be used throughout his Diocese in Public Worship',[57] since it affects all in worship, being a common activity, should be so exercised as to be acceptable to the overwhelming majority of his diocese. It should not be used to favour incipient or developed congregationalism since this would damage the unity of the diocese. Moreover, the *jus liturgicum* is not a recipe for arbitrariness, and, hence, synodical approval of basic (and especially contentious) changes is required.

Thirdly, much confusion is caused by the failure of the Church in Wales to revise its canons and clarify the precise nature and scope of the bishop's *jus liturgicum*. This is further compounded by the rule in the Constitution that the Church in Wales is not bound by the old decisions of the English courts in matters of faith, discipline and ceremony.[58] Obviously, many of the 1603 Canons are obsolete and whilst partial changes can be made to meet new circumstances, the Welsh diocesan bishop still has no clear modern collection of canons to guide him in the exercise of his authority in liturgical matters. In this regard, the Church in Wales is far behind other disestablished Churches in the British Isles.[59] Moreover, the bishops would then be

---

56 H. Riley and H.R. Wilson (eds.), *Acts of the Convocations of Canterbury and York* (London, 1961), 9. The limits of the individual's initiative in liturgical matters are stressed by W.H. Frere. See J.H. Arnold and E.G.P. Wyatt (eds.), *Walter Frere: A Collection of His Papers on Liturgical and Historical Subjects* (Oxford, 1940), 179–81.

57 Green, *Setting*, 113.

58 Constitution, XI,36. See also A.J. Edwards, *Archbishop Green: His Life and Opinions* (Llandysul, 1986), 65–6.

59 The Church of Ireland revised its canons in 1870. The Scottish Episcopal Church issued a code of canons in 1925, 1928, 1929 and 1973.

able to determine with greater clarity what provisions of pre-Reformation canon law still apply.

Fourthly, there is a need for a much clearer expression of the binding force and effect and authority of custom, particularly in liturgical affairs. Whilst it is clear that the English courts in the nineteenth century moved away from the (Roman) canon law understanding of custom,[60] nonetheless the Welsh Church still acknowledges it.[61] So, for example, a canon promulgated on 17 September 1981 provided that 'it shall not be unlawful to continue the use of the form of the 1662 Order for Holy Communion, with such variations permitted by the ordinary as have been customary in the Church in Wales'. This, however, does not face up to the issue. Exactly what variations have in fact been customary? To what degree might local custom, apart from (as opposed to alongside) an exercise of the *jus liturgicum* by the bishop, authorize forms of liturgy? Can the bishop tacitly approve the use of a local liturgical custom by his inaction, or must approval be express? Again, how does the canon law safeguard against arbitrariness if one bishop permits one custom which conflicts with episcopal permissions and customs elsewhere in the province?

In fact, there is a great need to define what is meant by custom. The seventeenth-century liturgists were quite certain that custom did not mean allowing individual clergy (or bishops) to follow their own fancies. What they had in mind was not an individual minister's peculiar innovations (akin to the idea of personal prescription in secular law) which would imperil the principle of common worship, but rather such custom as was widespread in the Church, uniform in its features, and which issued genuinely from the community of the faithful.[62] In this regard, the Church of Rome has a much clearer expression (as we saw at the outset of this essay) of what is meant by custom in its new Code. It allows the principle *consuetudo est*

60   R. Bursell, 'What is the place of custom in English canon law?', *Ecclesiastical Law Journal*, 1(4) (1989), 12–26.
61   For example, the ratification of long-standing custom in the case of harvest festivals; the wearing of veils by female candidates at confirmation; the blessing of oils on Maundy Thursday. Custom is also recognized in relation to the numbers of churchwardens in the Constitution, VI,17. This has always been true in church life. So, whilst the 1549 Prayer Book included the use of the sign of the cross by the bishop at confirmation and the 1552 Prayer Book omitted it, nonetheless crossing was retained in practice and was considered to be at the bishop's discretion to use. See F. Proctor and W.H. Frere, *A New History of the Book of Common Prayer* (London, 1961), 605,n. 2.
62   See Addleshaw, *High Church Tradition*, 147, 148.

optima legum interpres (custom is the best interpreter of laws) but
goes on to specify what constitutes custom (Canons 23–8). Again,
in Roman Catholic canon law custom must be 'approved by the
legislator' (this could include tacit acceptance of a custom); it must
not be against the divine law; there must be at least thirty years'
observance of a custom that is apart from canon law *(praeter ius)*.
Not all customs in the Church in Wales are salutary, and some
awareness of the principles that underlie acceptance or rejection of
custom is needful in order to facilitate the judicious exercise of the
bishop's *jus liturgicum*.[63]

Always in discussing this issue, it is vital to bear in mind that canon
law, like liturgical forms, expresses the root beliefs of a Christian
community. Accordingly, a clear canon law will be a means to
facilitate the Church in Wales in determining, and presenting, what
it actually believes. A new code will not be all-sufficient and it will
still be that bishops have inherent powers to teach, preside and
sanctify the faithful, which will enable the Church to respond to new
circumstances and problems – providing always that the bishops
exercise such authority mindful of the benefit that a common,
ordered liturgy confers upon the People of God. Above all, all
Christians – bishops, priests, deacons and lay people – are called to
read the canons in the light of a true understanding of canon – that
is, discerning what is normative for the structure and the life of the
Church as the Spirit-filled Body of Christ.[64] That society, the Church,
exists to offer the sacrifice of praise and thanksgiving to the Blessed
Trinity. The true test of the fruitful use of the *jus liturgicum* is
whether it enables Christians to offer that sacrifice so that they are
drawn ever further to the life of loving personal communion which
exists within God Himself.

63 A provision such as that of approval by the legislator in Roman canon law
by implication affects the issue of whether the use of eucharistic rites (Roman or
the English Alternative Service Book) other than the Prayer Book is unlawful
since such use has not been authorized by the legislature of the Church in Wales,
the Governing Body.
64 See J.H. Erickson, 'The orthodox canonical tradition', *St Vladimir's Theological Quarterly*, 27 (3) (1983), 167.

7

The Status and Enforceability of the Rules of the Church in Wales

DAVID LAMBERT AND NORMAN DOE

In the field of constitutional and administrative law a central problem facing theorists and practitioners alike is that relating to the status and validity of rules. What sort of rule is that which permits Parliament the power to create any law it pleases? What sort of rule forbids the monarch to refuse assent to a bill passed by both Houses of Parliament? What is the relationship between domestic law, created by Parliament or the judges, and that created by European institutions? To what extent does European law prevail over United Kingdom law? To what degree are rules made by local authorities inferior to those made by central government? Equally, it seems that there are large areas of the canon law about which it is crucial to determine what sorts of rules comprise the *law* of the Church in Wales – principally, to identify the extent to which they can actually be enforced. In this essay, it is proposed to examine the nature of the rules of the Welsh Church: are its rules able to be treated appropriately as *laws*; or, rather, in virtue of actual difficulties surrounding their enforcement, are the rules of the Welsh Church more properly classified as non-legal rules or conventions? To this end, three basic accounts of the status of Welsh Church rules will be examined: the convention theory, the contract theory and the subordinate legislation theory.

The Convention Theory

Before work on the fabric of a church building can be carried out, permission must be obtained. This is a requirement of the canon law in both the Church in Wales and the Church of England. Permission is granted either by the use of an episcopal faculty or by means of an archdeacon's certificate – these allow acts to be performed which otherwise, if carried out without permission, would be a breach of canon law.[1] In England, the reports of cases involving faculties, which have been considered by the Consistory Courts, are peppered with decisions which include the use not only of aesthetic and sometimes doctrinal values and judgments, in determining the permissibility of work done on church buildings, but also of legal argument.[2]

In a recent case from the Chichester Consistory Court, in 1987, the Chancellor explained that:

> ...the Reverend Mr. Cross, with the churchwardens, directed the execution of major works to the ancient and fine church in his care without due authority. . .In my judgment this was a serious breach of his obligation of canonical obedience. He should appreciate that if he should ever again execute works to the Church of St. Thomas which require the authority of an archdeacon's certificate or a faculty, but without having that authority, he may. . . have to face proceedings.[3]

In relation to the churchwardens, the Chancellor said: 'The churchwardens. . .are not as lay men and women liable to such proceedings. They, however, should appreciate the pecuniary risks which they will run should they ever again execute such works without authority.' He added: 'If, therefore, the churchwarden, acting alone or with others, directs works to a church without the authority of an archdeacon's certificate or faculty, he may expose himself to grave financial liability and loss.' Thus, if 'damage were to result from alterations done to the fabric without a faculty, the churchwarden would be personally liable'.

In the Church in Wales, the question 'Do you clearly understand that no repair. . .to the fabric of the Church can be undertaken without first obtaining a faculty or archdeacon's certificate?' has very

1   For an excellent account of the Faculty Jurisdiction (Amendment) Rules 1987 and related law in the Church of England see G.H. Newsom, *Faculty Jurisdiction of the Church of England* (London, 1988), 180; 'the task of the ecclesiastical courts. . .is to ensure that the sacred uses are protected, that the parishioners are duly consulted, that the wider aesthetic interests of the public are considered, but remembering always that a church is a place of worship and not a museum', ibid., 5–6.
2   See J.D.C. Harte, 'Doctrine, conservation and aesthetic judgments in the Court of Ecclesiastical Causes Reserved', *Ecclesiastical Law Journal*, 1 (2) (1988), 22.
3   *Re St. Thomas à Becket, Framfield* [1989] 1 All ER 170 at 173.

often been answered with 'No'.[4] In point of fact, there are many examples of works being executed without following the Faculty Rules. Archdeacons and even bishops over the years seem to have given their blessing (without a formal faculty or certificate) to quite major work being undertaken in churches under their jurisdiction. It is sometimes recited how in the past an archdeacon, after attending evensong, would tour the church apparently agreeing to some remarkable proposals being executed purely as a result of informal conversations. The absence of any indication in the current Diocesan Index for Llandaff of a faculty or certificate is often explained because an elderly member of the congregation is able to recall the kindly archdeacon or bishop agreeing to the walls of the church being painted in colours which are not really suitable from an aesthetic point of view and which cause the walls to start crumbling after a little while because the paint is quite unsuitable. The financial cost to the Church, of unsuitable work being carried out without proper approval or consideration, is often substantial.[5]

A problem such as this, about the actual enforcement of rules relating to faculties and certificates, affords an interesting test to determine whether rules of the Church in Wales are actually laws. It is instructive to turn to the secular sphere of constitutional law to provide a context within which to discuss this problem.

According to classical constitutional theory, the constitution of the United Kingdom is composed of two types of rule – legal rules and non-legal rules or constitutional conventions. A rule can be identified as a legal rule, to use the ideas of H.L.A. Hart, because it belongs to the family of rules which compose the legal system.[6] It is recognized as a legal rule by incorporation in a parliamentary statute, or in a judicial decision, or in a piece of subordinate legislation (created by the executive under a power given in a statute by Parliament). These are formal signs by which we can ascertain that a rule is a valid legal rule. Now conventions are similar to legal rules in several respects. Conventions are treated as rules prescribing particular forms of conduct in those to whom they are addressed, and both conventions and laws may be rooted in acquiescence.[7] As Marshall argues, conventional rules may either impose duties – such

---

4 Articles of Inquiry of an Archdeacon's Visitation.
5 See Newsom,*Faculty Jurisdiction,* 180–187.
6 H.L.A. Hart, *The Concept of Law* (Oxford, 1961), 97—107.
7 G. Marshall, *Constitutional Conventions* (Oxford, 1984), 7; S.A. de Smith, *Constitutional and Administrative Law* (4th edn., Harmondsworth, 1981), 53; I. Jennings, *The Law of the Constitution* (5th edn., London, 1959), 74.

as the convention forbidding the monarch to refuse assent to bills or, to express it in the form of a precept, commanding the monarch to follow the advice of her ministers – or they may confer rights – such as the prime minister's right to cabinet secrecy.[8] In the words of Hood Phillips, conventions are 'rules of political practice which are regarded as binding by those to whom they apply'.[9]

However, legal and conventional rules have one fundamental difference. According to classical constitutional theory, legal rules are enforceable by the courts whereas conventional rules are not. Dicey, writing at the end of last century, maintained that laws 'are rules which (whether written or unwritten, whether enacted by statute or derived from the mass of custom, tradition, or judge-made maxims known as the common law) are enforced by the courts'.[10] Munro has recently refined this by his use of the more accurate notion that laws are *enforceable* by the courts – as some laws may not actually be *enforced*.[11] For Dicey, though, in the constitution, another 'set of rules consist of conventions, understandings, habits or practices which. . .are not in reality laws at all since they are not *enforced* by the courts'.[12] Hood Phillips agrees: conventions 'are not laws at all as they are not enforced by the courts'.[13]

Indeed, this Diceyan view that conventions are rules but ones which the courts do not enforce has been absorbed into judicial practice. For example, in *Madzimbamuto* v. *Lardner–Burke* (1969), the Judicial Committee of the Privy Council concluded that it was not entitled to take into account the convention requiring the United Kingdom Parliament to legislate for Southern Rhodesia only with the consent of that country.[14] Similarly, in the earlier case of *Adegbenro* v. *Akintola* (1963), Viscount Radcliffe explained that conventional rules did not impose restrictions on the Governor General of West Nigeria which the court would 'make it his legal duty to observe'.[15]

8 Marshall, *Constitutional Conventions*, 210.
9 O. Hood Phillips, *Constitutional and Administrative Law* (6th edn., London, 1978), 104–5.
10 A.V. Dicey, *Law of the Constitution* (1885) (10th edn., London, 1971), 23.
11 C. Munro, 'Laws and conventions distinguished', *Law Quarterly Review*, 91 (1975), 218.
12 Dicey, *Law of the Constitution*, 24.
13 O. Hood Phillips,*Constitutional and Administrative Law*,104.
14 [1969] 1 AC 645.
15 [1963] AC 614,630; for a possible reorientation of the classical view about the non–enforceability of conventions, see N. Doe, 'Non-legal rules and the courts: enforceability', *Liverpool Law Review*, 9 (1987), 173–88.

The example of the failure to obtain formal faculties or archdeacons' certificates, as prescribed by Welsh canon law, is simply one of many provisions of the rules of the Church in Wales which are not actually enforced. Though, happily, of course, the vast majority of the Church's rules are complied with, we shall see elsewhere in this volume references to the non-enforcement of Church rules.[16] This fact of life in the Church in Wales brings into question whether we should rather describe the rules of the Church, in Dicey's words, as conventions and 'not really laws at all since they are not enforced by the courts' or by anyone else.

Certainly the rules of the Church in Wales are commonly described as law, canon law. Indeed, the rules express the normal structure of laws and they might be recognized as valid rules of canon law by virtue of their incorporation in the Constitution, canons and regulations of the Church in Wales. This applies also to pre-1920 rules. These too might be found in statutes and the decisions of judges, for example. But, strictly, in relation to the pre-1920 sources, the Welsh Church Act 1914, of course, declared that 'the ecclesiastical law of the Church in Wales shall cease to exist *as law*' for the Welsh province.[17] They might form part of the *canon law* of the Church in Wales, unless and until they are altered by the Church in Wales – but they are not part of the *law of the land*, as are the rules of the established Church of England's ecclesiastical law. For the Welsh Church, pre-1920 rules, terminologically, are hybrids – though incorporated or located in statutes and cases they are merely, it might be argued, in the *form* of laws. Yet much of the pre-1920 Church law still constitutes the law of the land in England – but, for Wales, it has ceased to exist *as law*. For England it is still *ecclesiastical law*, but for Wales it is *quasi-law*, canon law but not the law of the land.[18]

If the test to determine whether a rule is a convention rather than a law is one of enforcement, actual enforcement, then, of course, many of the rules of Welsh canon law might fail that test. An argument may run along the lines that we cannot treat those rules of

16 Below, p. 183, n.36.
17 See Halsbury, *Laws of England*, vol. 14, *Ecclesiastical Law* (4th edn., London, 1975), para. 322. See also above chapters, 2 and 3, pp.31–2, 57–8.
18 This is analogous to the position in British colonies where 'a colonial legislature could depart from the rules of the common law without fear of challenge in the courts, and was not required to observe Acts passed at Westminster unless expressly or by necessary implication they applied to the colony': see E.C.S. Wade and A.W. Bradley, *Constitutional and Administrative Law* (10th edn., London, 1985), 420–1.

the Welsh Church as laws because of the actual non-enforcement of many of them. This would seem to be the obvious conclusion if we apply the test of enforcement. In other words, in so far as they are not actually enforced, the rules of the Welsh Church may indeed be merely conventions – this is so, it is stressed, only if we accept that the test to determine whether something is convention or law is on the basis of actual enforcement. However, it is submitted that such a test is not appropriate.

Many laws, in the secular field, are not actually enforced. Yet this does not mean that they are not laws. As Munro observed, rather, the test is one of enforceability – are these rules capable of being enforced by the courts? Are the rules of the Welsh Church, if violated, capable of being followed by proceedings. If a rule is capable of being enforced, even if it is not actually enforced, it is still law – this is simply because of its formal incorporation in the legal system, in statutes and judicial decisions. This is the position with the rules of the Welsh Church. The Church in Wales has the constitutional right to make canon law for itself and those rules, even if they are not actually enforced, are nevertheless capable of being enforced – most immediately by the courts of the Church in Wales. As the rules of the Welsh Church are enforceable, so they must be treated as closer in type to laws rather than to conventions. Rather, the problem of the non-application of the rules of the Welsh Church is really one of obedience and not one relating to their validity as laws.

The Contract Theory

The account, then, of Welsh Church rules as conventions, not enforceable by Church authorities, is an inadequate account of the status of those rules. It can be dismissed on grounds of their actual enforceability and on grounds of their incorporation into the Welsh canonical system. Another explanation of the status of these rules is to regard them as the terms of a contract, binding upon the members of the Church in Wales. This has profound implications for their enforceability outside the institutions of the Church in Wales, by the ordinary courts of the land.

In his *Setting of the Constitution of the Church in Wales* Charles Green employed what might be termed the 'contract theory' of Welsh canonical rules. Green based this idea on s.3(2) of the Welsh Church Act 1914. For Green, the 'ecclesiastical law of the Church in Wales "is binding on the members for the time being of the Church in

Wales in the same manner as if they had mutually agreed to be so bound, and shall be capable of being enforced in the temporal courts", in the same manner as any other Civil or Commercial Contract'.[19] As such, explained Green,

> [e]very person who uses the property of the Church in Wales, such as 'places of worship', or who claims the right to any service or privilege or blessing enjoyable by members of the Church in Wales, does, by making such use or by asserting such claim, tacitly and implicitly enter into the Contract set forth in the Ecclesiastical Law of the Church in Wales, and can be called to account for the Breach thereof.[20]

Indeed, as Green also explained, '[a]ll persons admitted to Holy Orders, and to ecclesiastical Cures or Offices, bind themselves explicitly to the Declarations required of them'.[21] Moreover, those who wish to be entered on the electoral roll of a parish are required to 'agree to accept and be bound by the Constitution of the Church in Wales'.[22] The Constitution itself states that all office-holders in the Church, clerics, deaconesses (in receipt of a pension from the Representative Body) and those on the electoral roll are bound by its provisions.[23] For Green, the contract is fictitious for pre-1920 rules, and implicit and explicit for post-disestablishment rules.

Elsewhere, in his book, Green refers to 'the Concordat or Contract implicit in the Ecclesiastical Law'.[24] Green clearly sees the fundamental basis of the Constitution, and this is a contribution to its authority, as consent. According to Green, under the Welsh Church Act 1914, in relation to pre-1920 rules, '[t]he Legal Contract, in all its terms and contents, is declared to be "subject to such modification

19 C.A.H. Green, *The Setting of the Constitution of the Church in Wales* (London, 1937), 98. The part of s. 3(2) of the Act which Green quoted actually referred only to enforcement in civil courts of rules 'in relation to any property' held by the Church.
20 Ibid., 98–9.
21 Ibid., 99.
22 Constitution, VI,3
23 Ibid.,I,2. As s.3(2) of the Welsh Church Act 1914 states that the then existing ecclesiastical law of the Church of England, as modified by the Constitution of the Church in Wales, shall be binding on 'the members for the time being of the Church in Wales', a more comprehensive expression, there seems to be a disparity between this provision and Chapter I, Section 2 of the present Constitution, which, arguably, addresses a more specific and perhaps limited class of member. This raises the difficult question of the legal meaning of membership of the Church.
24 Green, *Setting*, 117.

or alteration, if any, as after the passing of this Act may be duly made therein, according to the constitution and regulations for the time being of the Church in Wales"'.[25] 'The Constitution of the Church in Wales', he says, 'is the result of consultation and co-operation between the Welsh Bishops and their Clergy and Laity.' As such, it is 'a Solemn Covenant or Concordat between the Bishops of the one part, and the Clergy of the second part, and the Laity of the third part, that the Plenitude of Apostolic authority and power will be exercised in Wales in the manner set out in the Constitution'.[26] Again, he explains, 'by the Agreement or Concordat, set forth in the Constitution, the Bishops have contracted with the Clergy and the Laity that they will exercise their judicial powers only through the Courts as defined therein' – and they will not alter existing law except with the 'consent, co-operation and concurrence of the Clergy and Laity in the Provincial Assembly' (the Governing Body).[27]

A modern explanation of the rules of the Church in this form has also been offered by Thomas Watkin (in chapter 2 of this volume and elsewhere). Conceding that the pre-1920 rules, by initial agreement on disestablishment, 'may arguably have been fictitious', he states that 'the consent of the current membership to the Constitution is not'. As members entered on the electoral roll of a parish and all clerics 'have expressly consented to be so bound', for Thomas Watkin '[a]ny fiction. . .has long since been purged, and replaced by clear, express consent'.[28] He too suggests that 'the ecclesiastical law of the Church of England at the moment of disestablishment became binding upon the members of the Church in Wales in the form of a contract which the statute imposed upon them. This contract was to be binding upon them "in the same manner as if they had mutually agreed to be so bound"'. And, subsequently, 'the Church in Wales was to have full powers to alter and modify the terms of this contract, even when the terms were contained in an Act of Parliament'. That is, 'while the Church in Wales ceased to have an ecclesiastical law at disestablishment, that is a law made for it by the State, it had acquired a canon law' – this canon law, from disestablishment onwards, 'has been valid within the Church in Wales either because the church has

25 Ibid., 299–300.
26 Ibid., 14.
27 Ibid., 190.
28 T.G. Watkin, *Theologia Cambrensis*, 3 (1) (1990), 18–19. The observations were made in response to an article by N. Doe, 'Theology and the study of canon law: some fundamental problems', *Theologia Cambrensis*, 2 (2) (1990), 21 at 25, n. 15.

continued to accept its validity or because it has itself enacted it'.[29] The pre-1920 body of rules, therefore, argues Thomas Watkin, 'has ceased to exist as law and has become merely the terms of the contract which binds members of the church together as members of an unincorporated association'. Thus, he says (for example), 'any offence is committed against the terms of that contract not against the law of the land, and the only persons who can complain of that contract being broken are parties to it, that is members of the church'.[30] In short, Welsh canon law is 'in the eyes of the civil authorities no more than rules agreed upon by members of an unincorporated association for its internal government'.[31]

Implications of the Contract Theory

At this point it is necessary to examine the canon law, as the terms of a contract, within the context of the ordinary civil law. The normal kind of contract is a set of obligations constituted by agreement between two legal persons and giving rise to rights and duties imposed and conferred upon each as against the other party to the contract. However, it is possible to make a contract with a number of persons under which each party has rights and duties against each of the other parties to that contract. In a multipartite contract it is not essential that all parties should owe the same rights and duties to each other.[32] This is clearly the case with the canonical contract of the Church in Wales. Here each party has rights and duties to more than one other party and the performance of the contract is conditional upon each of the parties honouring his obligations. For example, as with the Church in Wales, when a person joins a members' club or some other unincorporated association (a body without a single legal personality), though he may have dealings only with officials (and may be unaware of the identity of other members), he actually contracts with them all – this has been clearly established by case-law.[33]

29 T.G. Watkin, 'Vestiges of establishment: the ecclesiastical and canon law of the Church in Wales', *Ecclesiastical Law Journal*, 2 (1990), 110 at 111 (the vestiges relate to the law of marriage and burial).
30 Ibid., 113.
31 Watkin, *Theologia Cambrensis*.
32 D.M. Walker, *The Law of Contracts and Obligations in Scotland* (London, 1979), 417 – the discussion is based upon English authorities.
33 See, for example, *Evans* v. *Hooper* [1875] 1 QBD 45; for unincorporated associations see, for instance, P.S. Atiyah, *An Introduction to the Law of Contract* (2nd edn., Oxford, 1971), 109.

Now, in civil law, '[t]he terms of the contract are laid down by the constitution and rules of the club or association, and admission and expulsion must be done in accordance with the rules'.[34] In other words, the parties are bound in a multipartite contractual relationship with all the other members on the terms of the constitution and rules of the association. What is important, however, is that these rules are enforceable, not only by the tribunals of the association itself, but by the ordinary courts. In this respect, as the rules of an association are enforceable in the civil courts, and that is the test to determine whether something is a law or not, those rules might legitimately be treated as *laws*. Thus, for the Church in Wales, though its rules can be enforced by the courts of the Church in Wales, if they are conceived as terms of a contract they are also effectively enforceable by the ordinary courts – they are enforceable against each member by each member. The rules of the Church in Wales, equally, might be treated as *legal rules* in the fullest sense – rules enforceable by the ordinary courts. Those rules may not come from the same source as normal legal rules, that is, statutes and judicial decisions, but, *as enforceable terms of the Church's contract,* they are of equal status to legal rules.

The implications for the Church seem to be that, as an alternative (or in addition) to enforcement or interpretation by the internal courts of the Church in Wales, the civil courts may be competent to enforce or interpret Welsh Church law as a matter of contract. Green himself had argued along these lines: 'although the ecclesiastical law is no longer recognized by the State to be part of the law of the Realm (as it was before Disestablishment), a legal remedy is provided for breaches of the said Legal Contract, wherever the arbitrament of the Church Courts is rejected.' Thus, he said, '[i]f a case of ecclesiastical discipline is carried into the Courts of the Realm, those Courts would say to the parties: "We have here to decide not whether the defendant has broken any Law, but whether he has broken his Contract"'.[35]

The civil courts' possible attitude to the enforceability of rules of the Church in Wales, as an unincorporated association, is indicated in the case of *Baker* v. *Jones and Others* (1954), which concerned the constitution and rules of the British Amateur Weightlifters'

34 J.F. Josling and L. Alexander, *Law of Clubs* (5th edn., London, 1984), 28f; Walker, *Law of Contracts*, 417. See also, S.M. Waddams, *The Law of Contracts* (Toronto, 1984), 47
35 Green, *Setting*, 300.

Association.[36] In this case Lynskey J said this: 'B.A.W.L.A. is an unincorporated association. It has no legal entity. The relationship between its members is contractual. That contract is contained in or to be implied from, the rules. The courts must consider such a contract as they would consider any other contract.' Now, explained Lynskey, '[a]lthough parties to a contract may, in general, make any contract they like, there are certain limitations imposed by public policy, and one of those limitations may be that parties cannot, by contract, oust the ordinary courts from their jurisdiction'.[37] He continued: 'The parties can, of course, make a tribunal or council the final arbiter on questions of fact. They can leave questions of law to the decision of the tribunal, but they cannot make it the final arbiter on questions of law. They cannot prevent its decisions being examined by the courts.' Lynskey cited a dictum of Denning LJ in *Lee* v. *Showmen's Guild of Great Britain* (1952): 'If parties should seek, by agreement, to take the law out of the hands of the courts and into the hands of a private tribunal, without any recourse at all to the courts in case of error of law, then the agreement is to that extent contrary to public policy and void.'[38]

The implications for the Church in Wales seem to be clear. Its rules might be treated as the terms of a contract between the members of the Church in Wales – or, the Welsh Church's contract is (to use Lynskey's expression) contained in, or to be implied from, the rules of the Church in Wales. As the terms of the contract are expressed as and in the rules of Welsh canon law, and as terms of such a multipartite contract are enforceable by the civil courts (as well as by the Church courts), so those rules might be treated as *legal rules* in the full sense – though, again, they do not derive from the same source as orthodox legal rules, such as statutes or common law – they begin life, so to speak, as the Welsh Church's private or internal canon law, made for the Church by itself, and they become or acquire the nature, as *terms of a contract*, of legal rules proper.

Indeed, there is perhaps a more refined analogy by which we might perceive Welsh canonical rules as legal rules proper. The 'articles of association' of a company (which, unlike an unincorporated association, has a legal personality) are, in civil company law, 'the domestic regulations of the company and govern its internal administration' – just like the canon law or constitution of any Church. Now,

36 [1954] 2 All ER 553.
37 Ibid., 558.
38 [1952] 1 All ER 1181.

according to s.14(1) of the Companies Act 1985, the articles, when
registered, bind the company and its members to the same extent 'as
if they respectively had been signed and sealed by each member, and
contained covenants on the part of each member to observe all the
provisions. . .of the articles'.[39] It has been held by the courts that
'[t]he nature of the statutory contract created by s.14(1) constitutes
a "social contract"' (for which injunctions and declarations may be
granted), and it has been held that 'the articles create a contract
binding each member of the company but that each member is only
bound *qua* member'.[40] Furthermore, '[t]he articles constitute a contract between individual members. . .enforceable through the
company'.[41] In s.14 of the Companies Act 1985 there is a clear
parallel with the express wording of 3(2) of the Welsh Church Act
1914. Again, as the rules contained in the articles of a company (an
incorporated association) might be treated as a species of legal rule,
in so far as they are enforceable in the ordinary courts by virtue of
a contract, so too might the rules of the Welsh Church (an unincorporated association), the rules of its canon law, in so far as they may
be enforceable by the ordinary courts as the terms of a contract, be
treated as a species of legal rule. Welsh Church canonical rules are
not legal rules by way of derivation (as they are not, at least as regards
post-disestablishment rules, contained in statutes or case-law), but
by way of recognition and enforceability by the civil courts.

Difficulties with the Contract Theory

The contract theory of the rules of Welsh canon law, however, is not
without its difficulties. Three are prominent. First, the so-called
contract which exists in relation to pre-1920 canon law, was *imposed*
by the Welsh Church Act – whereas contracts, of course, issue from
actual consent. Secondly, in order for parties to be able to agree to
the terms of a contract, those terms must be certain. Since the rules
set out in the Constitution, and the post-disestablishment canons and
regulations of the Church in Wales are easily identifiable, they are,
clearly, capable of being the subject-matter of an agreement – to
which, as Thomas Watkin says, the members of the Church in Wales

39 J.H. Farrar, *Company Law* (London, 1985), 99.
40 See the Australian cases of *Dutton* v. *Gorton* (1917) 23 CLR 362 at 395, and
Wood v. *W. and G. Dean Pty Ltd* (1929) 43 CLR 77, and the English case of
Hickman v. *Kent or Romney Marsh Sheep-Breeders' Association* [1915] 1 Ch 881.
41 J.H. Farrar, *Company Law*, 100; *Welton* v. *Saffery* [1897] AC 299.

can readily give assent. However, the Constitution of the Church in Wales, the Church's canon law, is not simply contained in these documents. The practical difficulties of ascertaining the rules of pre-1920 English ecclesiastical law (which by the disestablishment legislation ceased as law for Wales but still functions – unless and until altered – as a source of valid canonical rules) render the contract theory suspect. Moreover, if we accept, as we must, that the divine law is part of the canon law of any Church, then, because of the difficulties of ascertaining this (and who ascertains it) the contract theory again becomes questionable because of the uncertain subject-matter.[42] How can the members of the Church in Wales *actually* consent, or, indeed, be deemed to consent *tacitly*, to be bound by something that has not (yet) been comprehensively presented or expressed in a single, coherent form? If the contract theory is to make sense, then surely it is necessary for the Church to be provided with a formal and comprehensive publication of its pre-disestablishment canon law.

The third problem is this: would the ordinary courts decline the invitation to accept jurisdiction if actually called upon by members of the Church in Wales to enforce the terms of its contract, the rules of its canon law, if (for instance) the Church authorities themselves failed or refused to do so? There have been recent judicial dicta which suggest that the courts may decline to accept jurisdiction.[43]

The Subordinate Legislation Theory

The rules of secular law exist in a hierarchy. The provisions of a parliamentary statute are inferior to those of European law,[44] rules

---

42 For contracts created by oppression and the requirement of certainty, in civil law, see G.H. Treitel, *The Law of Contract* (6th edn., London, 1983), 40, 310f. Legally speaking, the allegation of imposition, however, cannot be sustained by virtue of the principle of sovereignty – Parliament can do (almost, see n.44 below) as it pleases.

43 See, for example, *R* v. *Football Association Ltd, ex parte Football League Ltd, The Times*, 22 August 1991. In this case Rose J said that the Football Association was a domestic body whose powers arose from, and existed only in, private law. He declined the invitation to accept jurisdiction to review the use of the Football Association's powers. However, this case may be distinguished in so far as the Church in Wales was created by means of parliamentary statute, the public law of the State. For a similar idea, see also *R* v. *Chief Rabbi, ex parte Wachmann* (1991) COD 309

44 For a discussion see, Wade and Bradley, *Constitutional and Administrative Law*, 136-8. See for domestic and European law, *R* v. *Secretary of State for Transport, ex parte Factortame Ltd* [1990] 2 WLR 818. See also N. Doe, 'The problem of abhorrent law and the judicial idea of legislative supremacy', *Liverpool Law Review*, 10 (1988), 113 at 116-8.

of judge-made law are inferior to statutes, and other laws (such as local by-laws) are inferior to the common law and statute. Now subordinate legislation is variously known as secondary or delegated or executive legislation. Parliament creates a statute and in the statute it may confer powers upon a person, body or institution which consequently, in turn, creates law – this law is subordinate legislation – such as rules and regulations made by ministers, statutory bodies and local authorities. In other words, by means of the statute (primary legislation) forms of subordinate or secondary law are created by executive or administrative bodies wielding legislative power which they have obtained from the parent statute.[45] Indeed, measured by volume, far more legislation is produced by the executive government than by the legislature.[46]

Within the constitutional framework of the separation of powers (of which there are several models), it might be said that the use of legislative power, derived from statutes, which is enjoyed by these executive bodies under the authority of statutes, is subject not only to the control of the originator of those powers, Parliament, but also it is subject to the control of the ordinary courts.[47] The courts have developed a series of principles by which they are able to control the use of executive power. Chief amongst these is the principle of *ultra vires* – rules and regulations not made within the enabling powers of the parent Act of Parliament are legally ineffective. The courts frequently have to determine the validity of delegated legislation by applying the test of *ultra vires*:

> Delegated legislation in no way partakes of the immunity which Acts of Parliament enjoy from challenge in the courts, for there is a fundamental difference between a sovereign and a subordinate law-making power. Acts of Parliament have sovereign force [subject to European law], but legislation made under delegated power can be valid only if it conforms exactly to the power granted.[48]

Thus, if an executive body makes a subordinate law which it is not permitted to make under the parent statute, this will render the rule substantively *ultra vires*, and if the body fails to follow the procedures for the creation of subordinate legislation this will be

45 J.A.G. Griffith and M. Ryle, *Parliament: Functions, Practice and Procedures* (London, 1989), 244.
46 H.W.R. Wade, *Administrative Law* (5th edn., Oxford, 1982), 733.
47 For the models of separation of powers, see, for example, G. Marshall, *Constitutional Theory* (Oxford, 1971), 100-3.
48 Wade, *Administrative Law*, 748.

procedural *ultra vires*.[49]

Moreover, just as with other kinds of administrative action, which the courts can treat as unlawful if it is considered to represent an unreasonable use of statutory powers (broadly, a use which Parliament did not intend),[50] so too can the courts condemn rules of subordinate legislation for unreasonableness. The courts naturally employ the assumption that Parliament could not have intended powers of delegated legislation to be exercised unreasonably, and if they are treated by the courts as unreasonable they might be considered as *ultra vires* and therefore void.[51] This practice has been used particularly in relation to local authority by-laws. For example, local authorities are empowered by statute to make by-laws for the good rule and government of their area and for the suppression of nuisances.[52] In the leading case of *Kruse* v. *Johnson* (1898), the court upheld the validity of a by-law against singing within fifty yards of a dwelling house (in this case the complaint was of an open-air religious service). Lord Russell explained:

> If. . .[by laws] were found to be partial and unequal in their operation as between different classes; if they were manifestly unjust; if they disclosed bad faith; if they involved such oppressive or gratuitous interference with the rights of those subject to them as could find no justification in the minds of reasonable men, the Court might well say, 'Parliament never intended to give authority to make such rules; they are unreasonable and *ultra vires*'.[53]

Such by-laws would be void.

Subordinate legislation, then, is that set of rules created by a body upon which power has been conferred, usually by Parliament under a statute, to make those rules – these rules are themselves subject to control by the ordinary courts. Can this be said of the rules of the Church in Wales? It is often said that the Church of England is 'by law established'.[54] In some fundamental respects this is also the case with the Church in Wales, for it too, in a constitutional sense, owes its legal origin to an Act of Parliament. Admittedly, the canon law

---

49 See D. Foulkes, *Administrative Law* (5th edn., London, 1982), 169.
50 See Wade, *Administrative Law*, 572.
51 Ibid.
52 Local Government Act 1972, s.235.
53 [1898] 2 QB 91.
54 G.E. Moore and T. Briden, *Introduction to English Canon Law* (2nd edn., Oxford, 1985), 11-17.

which the Church in Wales has created since 1920 has acquired its own validity because it has been created under powers recognized by the Constitution of the Church in Wales. This is the immediate authority, so to speak, of the rules of Welsh canon law. But the original authority of the rules of Welsh canon law is derived from the Welsh Church Act 1914.

According to the terms of the Welsh Church Act 1914, not only do the legislative and administrative organs of the Church in Wales derive their legal authority from the statute itself, but also it could be said that the rules which the Church in Wales creates for itself, its canon law, are in the nature of pieces of subordinate legislation. The Welsh Church Act s.13(1) states that:

> Nothing in any Act, or custom shall prevent the bishops, clergy and laity of the Church in Wales from holding synods or electing representatives thereto, or from framing, either by themselves or by their representatives elected in such manner as they think fit, constitutions and regulations for the general management and good government of the Church in Wales.

In other words, despite the negative framing of the provision – 'nothing. . . shall prevent' – rather than the more usual positive conferring of powers, the bodies of the Church in Wales themselves could perhaps be said in some sense to be analogous to statutory bodies exercising power under a parent statute – and the rules they make are made from a power given by statute. If this is so, these rules, the rules of Welsh canon law, appear to have the same status, and source, as rules of delegated legislation.

The consequences of this view are far-reaching. Internally, of course, if canonical rules or amendments of the Constitution are not effected according to the terms of (for example) the bill procedures prescribed by the Constitution of the Church in Wales, then they are *ultra vires*, and consequently the courts of the Church in Wales would be able to declare them as unconstitutional.[55] But, what is more, if we view Welsh canon law as a form of subordinate legislation, it may be subject to the jurisdiction of the ordinary courts, at least as regards its post-1920 provisions. As the Court of Appeal has recently reviewed the legislation by canon created by the Church of

---

55 However, the purposes set out in the Constitution of the Church in Wales, listing the areas of the courts' jurisdiction, do not seem to include that of reviewing the constitutionality of Governing Body laws.

England concerning the ordination of divorced persons,[56] so too might the ordinary courts be able to review the post-1920 canon law of the Church in Wales. In the event that, conceptually, the rules of Welsh canon law are a species of subordinate legislation, similar to (for example) the by-laws of a local authority, the ordinary courts might be able to control them – for instance, by invoking the concepts considered above, substantive or procedural *ultra vires* or unreasonableness, as the courts will presume that Parliament did not intend these powers to be used unreasonably by the Church in Wales. It does not seem that the pre-1920 provisions of the canon law of the Church in Wales could be so controlled as they were imposed on the Church directly by the 1914 Act (though it might be possible to argue that in so far as such provisions were made by the Church of England acting under statutory powers given to it by Parliament, pre-1920 rules too may be susceptible to the jurisdiction of the courts).

Conclusion

The status of the rules of the canon law of the Church in Wales is a difficult problem. Though these rules clearly have something in common with conventional rules, they cannot be classified as conventions – conventions are rules which are unenforceable by courts – the rules of the Church in Wales are certainly enforceable by the courts of the Church in Wales, at least. They are, therefore, in the nature of legal rules. But, what sort of legal rules? The pre-1920 English ecclesiastical law has ceased to be *law* in Wales – the 1914 Welsh Church Act says so. However, if we adopt the contract theory, the rules of the Welsh Church, pre-1920 and post-1920 still retain the status of something like law. If the rules of Welsh canon law are to be treated as the terms of a contract (though, as we have seen there is some difficulty in their ascertainability as such), then, arguably, the terms of this contract, the rules themselves, must be enforceable, not only in the courts of the Church in Wales, but also in the ordinary courts. In this sense, though they do not arise from the normal sources as orthodox legal rules (statutes, case-law) they are rules

56 *Brown and Others* v. *Runcie and Another* (1991) *Times*, 20 February 1991: see this for judicial consideration of the Clergy (Ordination and Miscellaneous Provisions) Measure 1964, the Church of England (Worship and Doctrine) Measure 1974, the Clergy (Ordination) Measure 1990 and canons made thereunder.

which are legally enforceable – plainly, legal rules in the full sense. Equally, if the post-1920 rules of Welsh canon law are treated as a species, so to speak, of delegated legislation, as they are created by a body upon which power to create rules has been conferred under a statute made by Parliament, then, again, they might be classified as legal rules, in the fullest sense, albeit legal rules of an inferior nature, controllable by the ordinary courts.

8

The Welsh Church, Canon Law and the Welsh Language

ENID PIERCE ROBERTS

In the days of the Native Welsh Church, 'Hen Eglwys y Cymry', every mother church ruled those under its authority, and the head of its ecclesiastical community, the bishop, exercised a wide range of powers over a federation of daughter churches. Bishoprics were fluid and the number of bishops could vary from generation to generation. There was no uniformity: customs, organization, even order of services, most likely differed from region to region. Although part of Latin Christendom, 'Hen Eglwys y Cymry' was far removed from the well-ordered Church envisaged by the Normans and the twelfth-century theoretical standards of reforming churchmen.

By the mid-twelfth century the four Welsh dioceses – Bangor, Llandaff, St David's and St Asaph – had been brought firmly under the institutional control of Canterbury. They accepted the general pattern and acquired cathedral chapters and dignitaries; parishes and rural deaneries were formed, synods of clergy were assembled, archdeacons held visitations, and the bishop's consistory court was (in theory) an instrument for imposing the Church's ruling. Formal and regular links with Rome were forged, papal taxes levied for crusades, and from the thirteenth century the papacy nominated bishops to Welsh dioceses.[1]

Yet, although the Welsh dioceses were subjugated to Canterbury, it is doubtful whether they ever fully conformed with the dictates of the Roman Church; as Professor Glanmor Williams

---

1 For a detailed account see R.R. Davies, *Conquest, Coexistence and Change, Wales 1063–1415* (Oxford, 1987), 172–210; and G. Williams, *The Welsh Church from Conquest to Reformation* (Cardiff, 1962), 2–32.

remarked 'the system was more easily established than its ends were attained'.[2] The Welsh clergy differed on three main particular issues down to the time of the Reformation: celibacy of the clergy, hereditary succession to ecclesiastical endowments and offices, and marriage within the prohibited degrees. Prince Owain Gwynedd had been excommunicated for the last offence, but when he died in 1170, he was buried in a place of honour within Bangor Cathedral, on the south side of the high altar, opposite the tomb of his father.

Medieval Wales had its own code of law, *Cyfraith Hywel*, reputed to have been compiled by an assembly of six men summoned by Hywel the Good (d.950) from every commote in his kingdom to the White House on the river Taf in Dyfed. The earliest Latin text dates from the last quarter of the twelfth century, and the earliest Welsh version from shortly after 1200, to be followed by several compilations, in Welsh and Latin, during the thirteenth century. All versions are a medley collection, consisting of a few customs that could have been obsolete even in Hywel's time, some tenth-century practices, matter that had accumulated during the succeeding two or three centuries, and innovations possibly from the actual date of writing. Priests were regular officers of the household, and their rights, perquisites, privileges and duties are described merely in their relation to the court and its members. However, the scribes who wrote the codices would be men in holy orders, and as the thirteenth century proceeded they became more aware of ecclesiastical law. This is particularly true of the Latin text preserved in Bodleian MS C 821, which was written around 1300, and represents the period of the final stages of the struggle for Welsh independence and the years following the Edwardian settlement. Here emphasis is laid on ecclesiastical privilege; to quote from Professor Melville Richard's English translation: 'Every sacrilegious injury which may be done to the clergy is to be repaired to them in the synod according to ecclesiastical law' – *per legem ecclesiasticam probandi in synodo* – a direct reference to canon law.[3] The writers of the later versions stated in the prologue that Hywel had undertaken the hazardous journey to Rome in order to receive the pope's confirmation and blessing, thus making, in Professor R.R. Davies's words, 'at least a nod in the

2   Ibid., 16.
3   H.D. Emanuel, 'The Latin texts of the Welsh laws', *The Welsh History Review*, Special Number (1963), 25–32. The Welsh text, *Llyfr Blegywryd*, corresponds to Bodleian Rawlinson MS C 821. *Llyfr Blegywryd* was translated into English by M. Richards, *The Laws of Hywel Dda (The Book of Blegywryd)* (Liverpool, 1954); quotation from 98, and the Latin phrase from Emanuel, op. cit., 30.

direction of *lex ecclesiastica* in the substance of their texts'.[4] Nevertheless it is doubtful what effect canon law had on the Welsh clergy, whether the church leaders ever resorted to its rulings. When Archbishop Pecham visited Wales in the summer of 1284, 'he was obviously horrified at the incontinence, drunkenness, incorrigible idleness, and general ignorance of both clergy and laity'. Nowhere had he seen such illiteracy among the clergy, and one gathers the Bishops of Bangor and St Asaph were told, in no uncertain terms, to put their houses in order.[5]

Canon law, or at least the rule of Canterbury, was enforced at the time; but how much it was respected and how often consulted are open to question. Welshmen studying canon law at the universities may well have regarded the course as a corpus of knowledge that had to be acquired in order to gain a degree; just as the Welsh poets, before they could graduate as chief poet, *Pencerdd*, had to master *y dwned*, a Welsh translation of the 'donet', the Latin grammar book of the medieval schools which, with its 'nomnadio, genedio, dadio, achwysiaid, bogaid, aplliaid. . .gerwndiau, supiniau',[6] was not the slightest help to understanding the Welsh language and mastering the twenty-four complicated metres of Welsh prosody.

Bishops nominated by the papacy were as a rule total strangers to Wales and invariably absentees. In their absence the diocese would be left mainly in the hands of the archdeacons, chosen, oftener than not, from among the prominent gentry families; for example, Trevor and Conway in St Asaph, Glyn and Bulkeley in Bangor, Morgan at Llandaff and Stradling at St David's. Their ideas and standards would be those of the gentry, and the three particular issues referred to above persisted. Sir Robert ap Rhys of Dolgynwal (d. 1534) was chaplain and cross-bearer to Cardinal Wolsey and moved in the society of bishops; yet the cardinal can hardly have been ignorant of the fact that Sir Robert had a wife and at least sixteen legitimate children at home in Dolgynwal.[7] There are instances of a son

4 Davies, *Conquest*, 194.
5 D.L. Douie, *Archbishop Pecham* (Oxford, 1952), 262–3. A copy of 'Archbishop Pecham's Directions to Bishop Anian and the Clergy of St. Asaph' may be found in Browne Willis, *Survey of St Asaph* (Wrexham, 1801), 38–45. Anian of Bangor held a general synod of the clergy of the diocese at Llanfair Garth Branan (the parochial church of Bangor) in 1291: Browne Willis, *Survey of the Cathedral Church of Bangor* (London, 1721), 69.
6 G.J. Williams ac E.J. Jones, *Gramadegau'r Penceirddiaid* (Caerdydd, 1934), section D, 'Y Dwned', 67–88.
7 Enid Roberts, 'Teulu Plas Iolyn', *Denbighshire Historical Society Transactions*, 13 (1964), 39–110; for Sir Robert ap Rhys, see 53–62.

inheriting an abbacy;[8] did Canterbury and the papacy condone such practice, or was Wales so far removed and of so little consequence as to be of no concern? When Sir Robert, as Vicar-General and Chancellor of the Diocese, presided over the episcopal courts of St Asaph, it is to be feared little justice would be administered, especially when one remembers that both he and his arch-enemy, John Salisbury of Lleweni, had their retainers, often armed, and that Sir Robert had his own prison at Dolgynwal. It may be these ills were not peculiar to Wales; they are quoted to emphasize that in pre-Reformation times neither canon law nor the pope counted for much to the majority of Welsh clerics. On the whole, parish priests in Wales suffered no pangs of conscience when subscribing to the 1534 Act of Supremacy; it did not interfere with the way they regarded their religious duties.

The Reformation period in Wales was taken up mainly with obtaining Welsh translations of the Bible and the Book of Common Prayer, with improving the education of the clergy, instructing them in the principles of the faith and the new way of preaching. While the Protestant Church of England was still in its infancy Wales became embroiled in the Puritan revolutions of the seventeenth century, bringing forth a diversity of new denominations, to be followed in the eighteenth century by the Methodist revival which lulled Wales into a religious stupor and an all but criminal indifference to the things of this world.[9] After the Napoleonic Wars the country experienced a gradual awakening, in which politics and religion became too firmly entwined, engendering hatred and bitterness which have not completely disappeared.

Wales was not a separate province; it consisted of four dioceses on the periphery of the Province of Canterbury, and the Church of England at that time had no effective legislative chamber.[10] The inevitable conclusion is that Wales, with possibly a very few exceptions among the high-ranking clergy, who had little interest in either the country or its inhabitants, was ignorant of canon law.

---

8 Thomas Pennant, Abbot of Basingwerk, handed on the abbey to his son Nicholas: G. Williams, *The Welsh Church*, 399.
9 The remarks about the Methodist Revival were heard in a lecture by Professor R.T. Jenkins, who attributed the phrase 'all but criminal indifference' to the Reverend Thomas Shankland.
10 R.L. Brown, *Lord Powis and the Extension of the Episcopate* (Tongwynlais, Cardiff, 1989), 10 and n. 2. *Editor: For the history of Convocation, see generally,* E.W. Kemp, *Counsel and Consent* (London, 1961).

The Use of Welsh in Church Services

When the Welsh Church Act was passed in 1914, the main concern of Church leaders, both clerical and lay, for the next six years, was the Constitution and the financing of the new Church in Wales; these matters occupied their attention fully, to the detriment, it is feared, of other important issues. It was decreed that the Constitution of the new Church should be published in both Welsh and English, yet it was not until 1972 that volume I of the Constitution was published in Welsh, and the Welsh version of volume II did not appear until 1980 – sixty years after disestablishment, 1920, a gap of two generations.

Before attempting to account for this delay, it will be necessary to look at the position of the Welsh language in the church services along the centuries.

From very early times the Welsh language must have been used in the churches; even if Latin was the official language of the Church and its services, in order to reach the people all the teaching and evangelizing would have to be done in the vernacular. Even the few Welsh poems that have survived from pre-Norman times bear traces of biblical phrases and teaching, proving that the authors were accustomed to hearing parts, at least, of the scriptures rendered in their own tongue. Conscientious priests would translate passages for their own use. In the late thirteenth century Archbishop Pecham decreed that every priest was to instruct his parishioners four times a year in the Ave, the Creed and the Pater Noster, and to explain the Creed, the Gospels and the Ten Commandments in the language of the people.

In cathedrals, monasteries and collegiate churches, with numerous clergy and choirs, Latin would be the language of the elaborate services. Naturally, ordinary people wished for a simpler form of service, and as devotion to the Virgin Mary increased the *Officium Parvum Beatae Mariae Virginis* became popular and by the thirteenth century was in common use. The earliest Welsh manuscript, *Gwassanaeth Meir*, dates from about 1400, but a Welsh version may have been in use considerably earlier.[11] This was used extensively in private devotion. What information we have about church services is based on records kept by the larger, important churches; we know practically nothing about the way services were conducted in remote country parishes. When we consider that many of the parish priests

11   For the Welsh version see B.F. Roberts, *Gwassanaeth Meir* (Caerdydd, 1961).

were members of the gentry or yeomen families, accustomed to
hearing *Gwassanaeth Meir* in their own homes, it is not unreasonable
to suggest it may well have been extensively used in many small
country churches.

With the Protestant Reformation the authority of the Bible took
precedence over that of the Church. Attending the services, accepting
and reverencing the Church's teaching and devotion were no longer
considered sufficient for salvation; the men of the Reformation
stressed it was faith in God's grace and that alone that can save one
from eternal damnation, and faith in God's grace can be obtained
only by reading the Word of God, the Holy Scriptures, or at least
listening to the scriptures being read.[12] The 1538 decree, that the
English Bible should be read in all churches, was in England a big
step forward; in Wales, unfortunately, it merely replaced one foreign
language by one even more foreign, Latin being at least familiar by
sound to all worshippers. When it was decreed in the time of Edward
VI, in 1549, that the Book of Common Prayer was to be used in all
churches, everyone was compelled to worship in English.

The first priority was to have the Bible and the Book of Common
Prayer translated into Welsh. But before the Prayer Book of the
established Church could be translated an Act of Parliament was
necessary. This was no simple matter. A Welsh translation of the
official Service Book of the established Church was directly opposed
to the policy of the 1536 Act of Union, which stated categorically
that only the English speech and language should be used and
exercised by all ministries and officials, in all courts of law and in all
legal documents, and in every aspect of the administration of the
realm. Yet a new statute, eventually enacted in 1563, allowed Welsh
to be the language of the established State Church in one part of the
realm. The legislation prescribed that 'from that daye forthe the
whole Dyvyne Service shall be used and sayd by the Curate and
Ministers throughout the said Dioceses where the Welshe Tongue is
commonly used in the said Britishe or Welshe Tongue'.[13] In 1585,
Bishop William Hughes of St Asaph refused to appoint a cleric to
Whittington because he was ignorant of the Welsh language.[14]

12   G. Gruffydd, *The Translating of the Bible into the Welsh Tongue* (broadcast
on Radio Wales, 6 January 1988; published Cardiff, 1988), 7–8.
13   Quoted from *The Council for Wales and Monmouthshire, Report on the
Welsh Language Today* (London, 1963), 13.
14   D.R. Thomas, *The History of the Diocese of St Asaph*, 3 vols (Oswestry,
1908–13), I, 100.

Much has been written about Roman Catholicism in Wales during the late sixteenth century: the fines imposed for non-attendance at church, the secret masses celebrated, christening and burying at night, how Welshmen were implicated in plots to dethrone Elizabeth and restore the Old Faith, giving the impression that Wales was one of the strongholds of the Roman Church.[15] Yet, as the late Archbishop David Mathew remarked, in a joint article with his brother Gervase, 'Among all the countries of Western Europe, it was in Wales that the defeat of the Catholic Church was most complete'.[16] Despite the fact that several Welshmen held prominent positions in the Catholic Church on the continent, Archbishop Mathew suggests that the Roman Church failed to understand the Welsh people, to realize that their speech, background and temper of mind divided them from non-Celtic Europe. It is only through their own culture that one can reach the people.

This is precisely what Welsh Protestant leaders realized. Through the influence of individuals like Thomas Yale (d. 1577), Chancellor and Vicar-General to the Archbishop of Canterbury, and Gabriel Goodman, Dean of Westminster 1561–1601, both natives of the old county of Denbigh, bishops were chosen who were not only Welsh-speakers, who knew the area well and had every intention of residing in the diocese, but who (as well as being highly qualified academically) were well-versed in the native literary culture. In pre-Reformation days many clerics had fostered and sponsored the Welsh poets, and several, having mastered Welsh prosody, could be

15 For a fuller discussion on the situation in North Wales, and the work of the early Protestant bishops, see E. Roberts, 'Gabriel Goodman and his native homeland', *Transactions of the Honourable Society of Cymmrodorion* (1989), 77–104.

16 D. and G. Mathew, 'The loss of Wales', *The Clergy Review*, (January–June 1932), 13–24; E.G. Jones, *Cymru a'r Hen Ffydd* (Caerdydd, 1951); G. Williams, *Reformation Essays* (Cardiff, 1967), 20–1, 172–3, 176–7; but to quote from Williams, 21: 'The relation of these vestiges to Catholic dogma was, however, very tenuous. They are far removed from the Council of Trent and the Catholic Reformation. They have almost nothing to do with papal authority or doctrinal certitude. They arise from no struggles of conscience or a painful search for salvation. What they do represent is the carry-over by an unchanging peasantry of a fixed round of custom and habit in an age of rapid, officially-enforced religious change.' For the diocese of St David's, see D. Walker, 'Religious change, 1536–1642', in *Early Modern Pembrokeshire, Pembrokeshire County History* (Haverfordwest, 1987), III, Chapter 4, in particular 111–3. *Editor: compare Mathew's view with those of modern Roman Catholic historians, such as,* J. Bossy, *The English Catholic Community: 1570–1850* (London, 1975) and H.O. Everett, *The Spirit of the Counter Reformation,* edited by J. Bossy (Cambridge, 1968).

numbered among the bardic order. Holy orders and bardism, the quintessence of native culture, were no strangers to one another. Bishops like Richard Davies (St Asaph, 1559–61, St David's, 1561–81), Nicholas Robinson (Bangor, 1566–85) and William Morgan (Llandaff, 1595–1601, St Asaph, 1601–4), while attempting to raise the academic standard of the clergy did not ignore the native tradition and learning. If we scrutinize D.R. Thomas's volumes on the diocese of St Asaph, or A.I. Pryce's volumes on the diocese of Bangor, while we cannot help being impressed by the number of graduates, what is equally important is that many of the clergy wrote, and later published, poetry, prose and works on the history of Wales and its language.[17] The link between religion and native learning was maintained and safeguarded, enabling church life in Wales to survive the infamous Restoration bishops and, later, a century and a half of non-native absentees. Clergy of this calibre had substance to impart and the understanding to present it, allowing them to become respected leaders of their communities.

One of the firm principles of the Reformation was that the services should be understood by the people. To quote Article 24 of the Articles of Religion: 'It is a thing plainly repugnant to the Word of God, and the custom of the Primitive Church, to have publick Prayer in the Church, or to minister the Sacraments in a tongue not understood of the people.' The statute of 1662 ordered the Revised Book of Common Prayer of that year to be truly and exactly translated into the Welsh tongue and used wherever the Welsh tongue is commonly used.[18]

In the nineteenth century, the developing industrial and urban areas of south and east Wales became more and more Anglicized, while the rural areas remained almost monoglot Welsh. The law relating to the use of Welsh in ecclesiastical matters was still responsive to the country's needs, for in 1838 a further statute was passed giving power to the bishops of Wales to refuse institution or licence to any clergyman unable to officiate in the Welsh language where

17 For D.R. Thomas, see n. 14 above. For Bangor, A.I. Pryce, *The Diocese of Bangor in the Sixteenth Century* (Bangor, 1923), and *The Diocese of Bangor during Three Centuries* (Cardiff, 1929); also the nine typescript volumes compiled by R.R. Hughes, *Biographical epitomes of the bishops and clergy of the Diocese of Bangor from the Reformation to the reconstruction* (1932), at UCNW Library, Bangor. For St David's, see Walker, 'Religious change', 115–6, and the list compiled by Francis Jones published in *Journal of the Historical Society of the Church in Wales*, 27 (1990).
18 C.A.H. Green, *The Setting of the Constitution of the Church in Wales* (London, 1937), 294.

proficiency in that language was in the bishop's judgment necessary.[19] When Bishop Copleston of Llandaff died in 1849, many felt
his successor should be a Welsh-speaking Welshman.[20] It was taken
for granted that the language of the Church should be that of the
community.

Unfortunately the late nineteenth and early twentieth centuries,
the period leading up to the Welsh Church Act 1914, coincided with
the heyday of the British Empire, when English was spoken in all
parts of the world and proficiency in this great universal language
opened doors to prosperity and power. It cannot be denied that many
among the middle classes betrayed their origin, not only among
Anglicans: Nonconformists were just as ready to set up 'Inglis
Cosys'.[21] There was a marked tendency in hitherto Welsh-speaking
urban and industrial areas to regard it more fashionable, a step up
the social ladder, to attend an English place of worship. In his
Memories, Archbishop A.G. Edwards relates how, as a boy, he
attended a lecture in a Methodist chapel, given to an audience of
working people, chiefly farmers and farm-servants, by a famous
Congregational minister, Dr Kilsby Jones, who ended his lecture with
the words, 'Boys, if you want to succeed in the world, learn English.
Remember, Welsh is a barley-bread language'.[22]

Bilingualism in the Welsh Church

Although the new Church in Wales was, constitutionally, a bilingual
Church, a bilingual policy was not fully implemented for many years.
At the time of disestablishment the Welsh language had no real legal
status. It would be taken for granted that all official business should
be conducted in English. Several of those who worked so hard and
diligently to draw up the Constitution and establish the new province
had no knowledge of Welsh – and, in some cases, little awareness of

19   Ibid., 295.
20   E.T. Davies, 'The Church in the Industrial Revolution', in D. Walker (ed.),
A History of the Church in Wales (Penarth, 1976, re-issued 1990), 121–43;
reference to choosing Copleston's successor, 131–3.
21   The phrase was coined by a Welsh Calvinistic Methodist minister, the
Reverend Robert Ambrose Jones ('Emrys ap Iwan', 1849–1906): see Emrys ap
Iwan, *Breuddwyd Pabydd wrth ei Ewyllys* (Wrecsam, n.d.), 18. For his tirade
against and ridicule of such practices, see also D.M. Lloyd, *Detholiad o Erthyglau
a Llythyrau Emrys ap Iwan* I (Dinbych, 1937), 51–61, and T.G. Jones, *Emrys
ap Iwan* (Argraffiad Newydd, Abertawe, 1978), gol. J.L. Williams, 71–85.
22   A.G. Edwards, *Memories* (London, 1927), 13. 'Methodist' here implies
'Calvinistic Methodist'.

the extent of its use. Church services continued as before, in the language of the community. Although duoglot Prayer Books had been available from at least 1823, it is probably correct to say that services were not conducted bilingually. Looking back, one cannot help feeling more attention was paid to maintaining the *status quo* than to envisaging the Church's role in relationship to the life of the Welsh nation.[23] It is not surprising that for more than twenty years the Church was referred to by the general public, in speech and writing, even on some official forms, as 'the Church of England in Wales', or 'the Church of England (Wales)'.[24]

The language problem had to be faced and resolved for the first time after disestablishment when electing a bishop for the new diocese of Swansea and Brecon, carved from the see of St David's. Edward Latham Bevan, Archdeacon of Brecon since 1907 and Suffragan Bishop of Swansea since 1915, much loved and esteemed, was the obvious candidate, but he had no Welsh, and, according to the 1921 Census, more than 8,500 inhabitants of the new diocese were monoglot Welsh. Since Bishop Joshua Hughes had been appointed to St Asaph in 1870, every bishop in Wales had been Welsh-speaking (it is reported that C.A.H. Green, the first bishop of the new see of Monmouth, later of Bangor and Archbishop of Wales, knew Welsh). Archbishop Edwards wanted a knowledge of Welsh to be an essential qualification. Many clergy and laity believed it would be a calamity if the new bishop was not Welsh-speaking, while others felt just as strongly that to pass over Bevan would create such bitterness as to prejudice seriously the welfare of the new diocese from the start. Frank Morgan, the first Lay Secretary of the Church in Wales, was very much opposed to compulsory Welsh. Legal advice was sought. Lord Justice Bankes suggested that to make Welsh compulsory would not be right, while Mr Justice Sankey resigned from the Electoral College because he did not wish to be involved in the controversy. Bishop Owen of St David's was in a quandary – he was probably the most thoroughly Welsh and the staunchest pro-

23 Green's *Setting* is entirely backward-looking, with very little thought for the morrow, and no conception of the Welsh as a different people with a language of its own.
24 In my secondary school and student days (1929–41) we were taught to enter 'Church of England in Wales' on forms that asked to what denomination we belonged (the question was asked in those days). Clergy whom I have questioned were of the opinion it was in the late 1940s that they became aware of the term 'Yr Eglwys yng Nghymru'. The Welsh Church Appeal, 1952–3, helped to familiarize the term.

Welsh member of the College – yet, being well aware of his suffragan's merits and of the climate of the area, he knew that not to appoint Bevan would be disastrous for the new diocese. Bevan was elected and Bishop Owen promised to see that the wants of Welsh-speakers in the new diocese were not neglected.[25]

In February 1925 the Welsh Department of the Board of Education set up a committee 'to inquire into the position occupied by Welsh (Language and Literature) in the educational system of Wales, and to advise how its study may best be promoted', under the chairmanship of Bishop Owen of St David's.[26] In a letter to Mr Justice Sankey at the end of March, the bishop commented: 'I agree with you entirely, that the future of the Church in Wales largely turns on its sympathizing frankly with all that is sound in Welsh national sentiment; and the love of the Welsh language represents loyalty to its past, the chequered and precious past, of the Welsh nation.'[27]

By this time, the language problem was obviously exercising the minds of Church leaders. The archbishop referred to the matter at the Governing Body meetings in September. There is no report of the meetings in *Y Llan*, but on 9 October, 'John Jones', in a letter to the editor, stated that, according to the press, the archbishop had said at Llandrindod: 'Nid oes un plwyf yn Esgobaeth Llanelwy lle nad oedd y gynulleidfa Saesneg yn fwy na'r gynulleidfa Gymraeg. . .Ni fuasai ei Ras yn fwriadol yn datgan yn Llandrindod yr hyn yr oedd yn wybod nad oedd yn wir. A fu i'r newyddiaduron ei gam–ddeall?'[28]

Archdeacon A.O. Evans referred to the language controversy in the Welsh Church in a sermon preached at Bangor Cathedral, 21 November 1925:

> Language was at best an accident in the life of a nation, modified by the characteristics of the land of its birth. Paul exploited expediency to secure the attention of the largest number of people. That, in the Archdeacon's opinion, was the attitude which should be adopted by the Church in Wales to-day towards those who used another language for their religious observances. More than

25 E.E. Owen, *The Later Life of Bishop Owen* (Llandysul, 1961), 489–95.
26 *Welsh in Education and Life* (London, His Majesty's Stationery Office, 1927), xviii.
27 Owen, *Later Life*, 568.
28 'There is no parish in the Diocese of St Asaph where the English congregation is not bigger than the Welsh congregation ... His Grace would not deliberately declare at Llandrindod what he knew not to be true. Did the newspapers misunderstand him?'

half the population of Wales was monoglot English.[29]

Yet, maintained Evans, we still cling to the ancient tongue of Wales.

In *Yr Haul* (January 1926), the Principal of Lampeter College, Canon Maurice Jones, in an article entitled 'Y Flwyddyn 1926 a'i Rhagolygon', writes:

> Pan yw iaith Cymru yn beth digon pwysig i Lywydd y Bwrdd Addysg, ac yntau'n Sais rhonc, benodi Pwyllgor i chwilio am y moddion goreu i'w hyrwyddo ac i'w chadw'n fyw, nid gormod fyddai disgwyl i'r Eglwys, yn anad neb, groesawu'r mudiad a rhoddi ei holl gefnogaeth iddo. Mae'n anodd gwadu iddi fod yn ddigon esgeulus a diofal yn ei hosgo tuag at yr hen iaith yn y gorffennol agos, ond gwell hwyr na hwyrach, a dyma iddi hithau gyfleustra i wneud unwaith eto yr hyn a wnaeth ganrifoedd yn ol pan waredodd y Gymraeg rhag trengi trwy osod y Beibl a'r Llyfr Gweddi yn nwylo'r werin yn ei hiaith gysefin ei hun. Dymunwn weld Eglwys y Cymry ar y blaen yn yr ymgyrch o blaid ein hiaith, sy'n ysgwyd y genedl i'w gwaelodion heddiw.[30]

In June 1926, the Archbishop 'warned the Association of Elementary Teachers that it was possible to sacrifice the higher interests of a people on the altar of sentimental devotion to a language'.[31] About the same time three representatives of the Church in Wales were giving evidence to the committee, at its last sitting: the Reverend Griffith Thomas (Vicar of Llangyfelach and Canon of Brecon Cathe-

29 Reported in *The Western Mail* and in *The Liverpool Daily Post* (23 November 1925). Archdeacon Evans compiled many large volumes of newspaper cuttings, programmes, posters, etc., that contained references to himself. These have now been deposited at the Library of UCNW, Bangor. Cuttings dealing with this period are to be found in Bangor 36415.

30 'The Year 1926 and its Prospects'. 'When the language of Wales is of sufficient importance for the President of the Board of Education, a thoroughly monoglot Englishman, to appoint a Committee to seek the best means to promote it and keep it alive, it would not be too much to expect the Church, above all others, to welcome the movement and give it her complete support. It is difficult to deny that she has been neglectful and careless enough in her attitude towards the old language in the recent past, but better late than never, and here is an opportunity for it to perform once more the service it rendered centuries ago when it saved the Welsh language from extinction by placing the Bible and Prayer Book in the hands of the people in their own native tongue. We wish to see the Church of the Welsh People to the fore in the campaign on behalf of our language, which today shakes the nation to its very foundation.'

31 *Guardian* (25 June 1926). The following day the East Glamorgan Association of Baptists responded by passing a resolution 'urging the co-operation of the Churches in emphasising the relationship between the Welsh language and religion': ibid.

dral), H.H. Richards (Professor of Welsh at Lampeter) and Archdeacon A.O. Evans. Canon Thomas pointed out that the Church in Wales was very sympathetic to the Welsh language. Professor Richards concentrated on what was being done at Lampeter, while Archdeacon Evans reminded the committee that 'the primary function of the Church is the salvation of souls and not the preservation of a language, and we would respectfully submit that our information must be within the limits of that reservation'.[32]

At the same meeting, Professor Ernest Hughes (of Swansea), and Miss Frances Rees (Headmistress of Cardiff High School for Girls), giving evidence on behalf of the Guild of Graduates of the University of Wales, stated categorically, that 'The only truly satisfactory way of raising the status of Welsh was to give it its due status, namely making it the official language of Wales'.[33]

The report of the committee's findings, *Welsh in Education and Life*, published in 1927, after listing the activities and publications of the Church in Wales, concluded that the Committee:

> ...view with some apprehension the tendency displayed in recent years to appoint monoglot English dignitaries and parish priests to positions in which a knowledge of Welsh should be regarded as indispensable. A policy of this description cannot fail to alienate from the Church in Wales the sympathies of the Welsh-speaking community, and must inevitably hasten the anglicisation of the Church herself, as well as that of the nation as a whole, a result which, in view of her history and traditions, the Church should be the first to deplore.[34]

One of the witnesses to the Nation and Prayer Book Commission, 1947–9, remarked: 'Church leaders during this century had been not so much antagonistic as indifferent to Welsh social and cultural movements.'[35] Was he/she being overgenerous?

Toward a Principle of Equal Validity

Protests regarding the lack of status of the Welsh language in law and administration had been made in the late nineteenth century and in the early years of the present century, but no definite action was taken until 1941, when a petition was presented to Parliament seek-

32 *The Western Mail* (17 June 1926); *Guardian* (25 June 1926).
33 *The Western Mail* (17 June 1926).
34 Para. 171, 146–8.
35 *Report of the Nation and Prayer Book Commission* (1949), 41.

ing 'an Act of Parliament placing the Welsh language on a footing of equality with the English language in all proceedings connected with the administration of justice and of public services in Wales'. This led to the Welsh Courts Acts of 1942 and 1943, allowing the administration of oaths and affirmations in Welsh and making the courts responsible for providing and financing a translation service.[36]

During the second quarter of this century Wales experienced a vigorous expression of its traditions in literature of all kinds, and an increasing political consciousness. Towards the end of the 1939–45 war Church leaders felt it expedient that the Church in Wales prepare for the period that would follow. Consequently, in April 1947, the Bench of Bishops appointed a commission 'to consider what reforms might be made to put the Church in a better position to take a larger part in the life of the nation'. The *Report of the Nation and Prayer Book Commission*, published in 1949, stresses that Welsh culture 'is a culture of the people. . .and it remains to-day the possession of the whole Welsh-speaking community, with its devotees drawn from all walks of life' – but adds: 'certain considerations nevertheless indicate that the Church in Wales has been for some time, and still is, though to a decreasing extent, more aloof from the nation's life than she ought to be'. One of the commission's recommendations was that a Provincial Congress be held periodically, and the Congress, held at Llandrindod in 1953, to discuss national responsibility, adopted the Reverend G.O. Williams's proposal that the Church would not become more influential until it showed greater respect for the Welsh language and culture.[37]

At the end of 1959 the Council for Wales and Monmouthshire set up, under the chairmanship of Professor R.I. Aaron, Aberystwyth, a Panel for Cultural Affairs, 'to study and report upon the situation of the Welsh language at present'.[38] The Right Reverend G.O. Williams (by then Bishop of Bangor) served on both Council and Panel. The Panel's comprehensive report was presented to Parliament in November 1963. Among its most important recommendations was 'that

36 J.A. Andrews and L.G. Henshaw, *The Welsh Language in the Courts* (Aberystwyth, 1984), 6–17. *Editor: for judicial consideration of these provisions see R v. Merthyr Tydfil Magistrates, ex parte Jenkins* [1967] 1 All ER 636, *and for a useful discussion,* S.G. Llewelyn, 'Legal status of the Welsh language – past, present and future', University of Wales LL B. Dissertation (UWC Cardiff, 1990), 2.5.

37 Quotation from 40–1 of the *Report*. I am indebted to the late Right Reverend G.O. Williams for much information and help with this section.

38 *The Council for Wales and Monmouthshire, Report on the Welsh Language Today* (1963), 5.

the Welsh language be given official status'.[39] In the same year, 1963, a committee was set up, under the chairmanship of Sir David Hughes Parry 'to clarify the legal status of the Welsh language and to consider whether any changes in the law ought to be made'. The committee considered three main principles: necessity, bilingualism and equal validity.[40] Its report on *The Legal Status of the Welsh Language*, published in 1965, clearly showed how Welsh occupied an inferior status to English in the administration of justice, and recommended adopting the principle of equal validity, that 'Any act, writing or thing done in Welsh in Wales or Monmouthshire should have the like legal force as if it had been done in English.'[41]

It was in the early 1960s that Professor Dafydd Jenkins, Aberystwyth, a barrister and the main organizer of the 1941 petition, was commissioned to translate the Constitution of the Church in Wales into Welsh. This was a mammoth task for one person, and owing to the great care needed over detail, and the pressure of academic work, it is not surprising that the Welsh version of volume I was not completed until 1972.

The Standing Committee, in March 1972, gave consideration 'to making provision for the Welsh text of the Constitution to have equal validity with the English text'.[42] A Special Meeting of the Governing Body held at Llandrindod in April recommended certain amendments to the Constitution to provide for equal validity. Judge Rowe Harding, chairman of the Drafting Committee, moved that chapter I of the Constitution be amended to include two new sub-sections to section 1: '(2) The English and Welsh versions of the Constitution shall have equal validity. (3) For the purposes of interpretation and for the resolution of any ambiguity, the English version shall be the definitive text.' Further: 'That the Welsh version of the Constitution shall be the translation approved by the Welsh Translation of the Constitution Committee appointed by the Standing Committee of the Governing Body'.[43]

39   Ibid., 145, para. 357.
40   For a 'Comprehensive Review', see Andrews and Henshaw, *Welsh Language*, 18–26.
41   *The Legal Status of the Welsh Language* (London, 1965), para. 171.
42   *Report of the Standing Committee* (March 1972), 5.
43   *Special Meeting of the Governing Body of the Church in Wales held on 12 and 13 April 1972: Summary of Business Transacted*, 'Appendix V. Welsh Version of the Constitution', 16. *Editor: Here we see something of a parallel with the Roman Catholic Code of Canon Law, revised in 1983, for which permission has been given for translation (for the first time) into the vernacular, 'subject to the understanding that the only official and binding version of the Code is the Latin text': see* Code of Canon Law (London, 1983), vii.

At the September meeting of the Governing Body, Judge Rowe Harding reported that the Drafting Committee had appointed a small subcommittee of members who were fluent in the Welsh language, in order that, in future, proposed amendments of the Constitution and bills drafted by the Drafting Committee would be submitted to the Governing Body in bilingual form.[44] Among the members co-opted was W. Beynon Davies,[45] Welsh master at Ardwyn School, Aberystwyth, one of the most successful teachers of Welsh, whose mastery of the language and meticulous care were well known and widely appreciated.

It was decided to print the Almanac for 1972/3 in bilingual form, and it was in the minutes of the Governing Body meetings held on 25 and 26 April 1973 that the Welsh version of amendments to the Constitution appeared for the first time. Two years later, in April 1975, simultaneous translation facilities were made available so that Welsh and English could be used regularly in debate in the legislature of the Church in Wales.[46] The Welsh version of volume II of the Constitution was published in 1980.

Under Welsh canon law, there are now no aspects of procedure or liturgy that must be performed in the English language. The only drawback is that not all chancellors, registrars and secretaries are bilingual, so that mandates often have to be read in English. This accounts for the fact that some documents are still not available in Welsh, but, should the need arise, there is no legal reason why a translation should not be produced and used.

Welsh in the Parishes

Since disestablishment rural areas have experienced a greater change than urban areas. The Church is becoming more urban-orientated – some will say rightly so, as that is where the bulk of the population resides and large housing estates often have serious problems. While this cannot be denied, one cannot help feeling that the rural areas are becoming more and more deprived, culturally and spiritually. Small rural schools have been closed, depriving many communities of a village schoolmaster. Parishes, often with churches several miles

44 *Meeting of the Governing Body of the Church in Wales held on 27 and 28 September: Summary of Business Transacted*, 5.
45 *Special Meeting of the Governing Body of the Church in Wales held on 12 and 13 April: Summary of Business Transacted*, 9.
46 D. Walker, 'Disestablishment and independence', in D. Walker (ed.), *A History of the Church in Wales* (Penarth, 1976, re-issued 1990), 196.

apart and with the population scattered over a wide area, are grouped, making pastoral work extremely difficult and time-consuming. There is no one left to guide and lead. All denominations are aware that rural areas – and most Welsh-speaking areas are rural – no longer produce ordinands. How can a church with no resident minister produce a lay reader, not to mention an ordinand? In urban areas one can expect to find lay intelligentsia; in rural areas the priest often stands alone, with no one to whom he can delegate responsibility.

In the last twenty years immigration has created additional difficulties. Not only are new houses, or rebuilt dwellings that had become almost derelict, springing up all over the countryside, there are numerous instances of hamlets and villages, where less than a generation ago only native Welsh-speakers lived, now taken over entirely as second homes for city-dwellers from across the border. Some of those coming into these areas are eager to learn Welsh, some wish to become part of the local community and attend places of worship.

Bilingual services, as generally conducted, are not entirely satisfactory. It is easy to reply that with a bilingual Prayer Book there is no problem; everyone can follow and understand. But are we sure the same respect is given to both languages? Is there not a tendency for the amount of Welsh to become less and less? Often, in relation to sermons, having tried a few times to say the same thing in both languages, the preacher soon opts for an all-English sermon. Much more consideration needs to be given to the form of bilingual services, thought, guidelines and practice. All who have to deliver a sermon or lecture bilingually could take Archbishop Noakes as an example. He does not repeat himself verbatim; he alternates between the two languages so frequently that monoglot English people have remarked that, though they did not understand the Welsh, they were able to follow his train of thought and argument.

Neither is trying to bypass the problem by saying that all Welsh people understand English the correct answer. Language and culture cannot be separated; culture colours the meaning of words and it is very difficult to translate culture from one language into another. We cannot affirm our faith properly in another tongue. To quote again from the *Report of the Nation and Prayer Book Commission*: 'we are not satisfied that where there are Welsh speaking Churchpeople, every opportunity is being given to minister to them in the language which makes the most direct appeal to their hearts and minds'.[47]

Priests who have learnt Welsh should be welcomed with gratitude and given every help and encouragement. But it has to be emphasized that learning the language is only the first step. More should be done to acquaint them with the religious history of Wales, our traditions and literature, even our superstitions which often influence the way we look at things. Could not this be undertaken by the lay ministry? We are a different people, and a people can be reached only through its own culture.

Problems of Translating Canon Law into Welsh

Welsh and English belong to two entirely different families of languages; there is so much difference between their syntax that they cannot possibly fit into each other's mould. Welsh has not the extensive vocabulary of the English language; on the other hand Welsh has a greater range of constructions giving a richer, more varied, often more concise means of expression. To convey the exact meaning, using the right construction can be as important as choosing the right words.

The two systems of verb conjugation, the short form and the periphrastic, give Welsh a wider range of tenses, enabling expression to be more precise. The English language cannot differentiate between two simple statements such as 'A man stood on the hill' (probably for only a few minutes), and 'A castle stood on the hill' (for centuries). The verb forms are identical in both cases, whereas in Welsh we would say 'Safodd dyn ar y bryn', but 'Safai castell ar y bryn'. When translating, one needs to be certain of the exact tense implied in the English verb form.

Much care is needed when dealing with the word 'shall', often

47 *Report of the Nation and Prayer Book Commission*, 42. *Editor: it is now common to incorporate into amendments of the Constitution of the Church in Wales provision for the use of Welsh. For example, a canon promulgated on 27 September 1979 substituted new forms of service relating to thanksgiving for the birth or adoption of a child previously contained in the Book of Common Prayer 'together with new forms of service in the Welsh language' – this is a provision frequently appearing in canonical rules relating to liturgical arrangements. Again, a canon of 17 September 1981 states that 'it shall not be unlawful to continue the use of the form of The Order for the Administration of the Lord's Supper, or Holy Communion, contained in the 1662 Book of Common Prayer and the Welsh version thereof, with such variations by the Ordinary as have been customary in the Church in Wales'.*

incorporated by legislators into the structure of rules. In chapter XI, section 7 of the Constitution of the Church in Wales, a rule is expressed, in English, in this form: 'The Bishop of each diocese shall. . .appoint a fit and proper person to be Chancellor of the diocese.' This, rendered in Welsh, is 'Bydd Esgob pob esgobaeth. . .yn penodi person cymwys a phriodol yn Ganghellor yr esgobaeth', taking 'shall' to indicate futurity. The Welsh form 'bydd' conveys the future meaning, and can also convey the present habitual tense. But in this instance, in the English, 'shall' denotes obligation or necessity – this is what renders the rule a command; in which case 'Bydd *i* Esgob pob esgobaeth. . .benodi. . .' would be a more accurate translation. This would clearly express the notion of command fundamental to the structure of the canonical rule. One needs to be absolutely certain of the exact meaning of the English version. Regrettably, there are several such instances in the Constitution. 'May' is another difficult word: it can imply sanction or permission to do something, imply possibility, or convey the subjunctive mood.

The preposition, probably the most idiomatic part of speech in any language, the correct use of which proves above all else one's mastery of a language, needs special care in translating. In English one prays *for* clergy and people, *for* peace and *for* rain, irrespective of the fact that where people are concerned we are praying on their behalf, whereas we are asking for peace and rain. The Welsh language differentiates: 'gweddïo *dros* esgobaeth, dros glerigion a phobl', but 'gweddïo *am* heddwch, *am* law'. Using a different preposition with the verb-noun can change the meaning of a periphrastic verb form: *i* implies obligation, *am* intention, *ar* on the point of, while *wedi* conveys the perfect tense and *heb* perfect and negative. Several Welsh verbs are followed by certain prepositions, and as some prepositions have personal forms the construction of a sentence can often differ from that of the English counterpart.

Some subordinate or dependent affirmative clauses, in particular oblique relative clauses (in whom, of which, on account of which, etc.) can pose a real problem. The sentence can, at times, sound stiff and unnatural in English; to try to translate it as it stands would produce a completely un-Welsh sentence. It is advisable to convert such expressions into co-ordinate clauses; fortunately Welsh does not condemn the too frequent use of the conjunction 'and'. To give a simple example, in chapter II, section 49 of the Constitution, in relation to the Governing Body, 'One hundred shall be a quorum. . .in which number there shall be no less than one Diocesan Bishop', expressed in Welsh, 'Cant fydd corwm y Corff Llywodraethol, ac ymhlith y rheini bydd o leiaf un Esgob Cadeiriol.' On other occasions a paragraph has to be rearranged (as in the case of chapter II, section 52).

According to the rules of modern Welsh grammar, when the relative pronoun is the subject of an affirmative dependent clause, the verb following should be in the third person singular, irrespective of the person and number of its antecedent. For example, 'Yr ydym *ni* (first person plural) a gly*wodd* (third person singular) y cais yn cytuno'; 'Agorodd y sêr-ddewiniadd (plural noun), a *ddaeth* (third person singular) i weld Iesu, eu trysorau.' However, as *a* can stand for both 'who' and 'whom', this can lead to ambiguity. In the earlier version of chapter VII, section 36 of the Constitution, 'the right of nomination. . .shall. . .be exercised. . .by the Board or Patron whose first nomination has been rejected' was translated, 'gellir arfer yr hawl i enwi. . .gan y Bwrdd neu'r Noddwr a enwodd y sawl a wrthodwyd'. This could be taken to mean 'by the Board or Patron who nominated the person who was rejected', or, equally correctly, 'by the Board or Patron whom the rejected person nominated'. Here, the canonical rule would have been quite unclear. Although common sense should dictate the correct meaning in this case, to remove any doubt, the new version reads, 'gan y Bwrdd neu'r Noddwr a oedd wedi enwi'r sawl a wrthodwyd'.

This problem had to be faced by those responsible for the new Book of Common Prayer, containing the law of worship of the Church in Wales. By adhering strictly to modern grammatical rules, the Welsh version of the Collect for Epiphany would read, 'O Dduw, a roddodd dy unig-anedig Fab i fod yn oleuni i'r holl genhedloedd. . .', and that for Palm Sunday, 'Hollalluog a thragwyddol Dduw, a anfonodd dy Fab. . .i gymryd ein cnawd. . .' In these forms the first could be taken to mean, 'God *who* didst give thy only begotten Son . . .' and also 'God *whom* thy only begotten Son gave. . .'; and the second 'God *who* hast sent thy Son. . .' and also 'God *whom* thy Son sent. . .', creating not only ambiguity but, with the second alternatives, the possibility of heresy. There was no option but to disregard modern Welsh grammatical rules and revert to the older practice of making the verb in the relative clause agree with its antecedent. The Collects now read: 'O Dduw, a roddaist dy unig-anedig Fab. . .', and 'Hollalluog a thragwyddol Dduw, a anfonaist dy Fab. . .'

Syntax and mutations make listing subsections in the Constitution difficult. When subsections depend on 'if' at the end of the preamble, in Welsh, for syntactical reasons, 'if' has to be transferred to each

subsection (as in VI,2(b)). The preposition *yn* takes the nasal mutation, and as it is not possible to begin a sentence with a mutated form
(with the exception of occasionally the soft mutation), it would have
been more accurate in chapter I, section 1 of the Constitution to have
transferred *yn* to the subsections. The same applied to *am* – as in
XI,18(e); in the new edition *am* has been replaced by *oherwydd*
which is followed by the radical consonant. Mutations can cause
many problems: for example, it is not always possible to avoid using
a mutated form when titles are printed in bold lettering or initials
only are used; his/her/their are more troublesome in Welsh as *ei* (his)
is followed by the soft mutation, *ei* (her) by the aspirate mutation
and takes an *h* before vowels, while *eu* (their) is followed by the
radical consonant but takes an *h* before vowels. Again, it is usual for
clauses in bills to begin with the word WHEREAS. The Welsh equivalent is not so simple, and can appear as GAN FOD, GAN Y BYDD, and
GAN MAI, depending on the tense of the verb and the construction of
the sentence.

Lastly, the problem of vocabulary. Culture colours vocabulary,
and usage can limit or change the meaning of a word. An English–
Welsh dictionary, quite correctly, gives *cymanfa* for the word
'assembly'; but in Wales, for more than a century, usage has confined
cymanfa to a Nonconformist hymn-singing or preaching festival.
Such an ordinary everyday word as 'person' can create ambiguity as
the Welsh *person*, in mid and north Wales, is the usual word for a
parish priest, the parson. If possible it is advisable to use an indefinite
pronoun, such as *un, rhywun, y sawl*, to convey the English 'person'.
Similarly, *dwyn* is the word used for 'to steal' in mid and north Wales:
dod â would be a safer translation for 'to bring' in the Rules of the
Provincial Court, and has been corrected in the new edition.[48]

'Dictionary translation', unfortunately, is far too common today;
the translator looks up a word in a dictionary, finds a word he/she
likes, and down it goes, without further consideration and no regard
for usage. There are obvious mistakes of this kind in the second
volume of the Constitution. In the previous edition of the Rules of
the Provincial Court (para. 44), 'Notice of Withdrawal' was translated as 'Hysbysiad Encilio' – *encilio* being the word for 'withdraw'
in the sense of 'to retreat'; 'Hysbysiad Tynnu'n Ôl' is the phrase
needed here, and has been corrected in the new edition (para. 45).
Similarly 'Chancellor's Order' was translated 'Archeb y Canghellor'
in the previous edition (p. 53), but *archeb* means 'order' in the sense

48 'Rheolau Llysoedd yr Eglwys yng Nghymru, yr Atodlen Gyntaf, Ffurf 11'.

of 'direct to supply'; this has been corrected to 'Gorchymyn y Canghellor' in the new edition (see instances in 'Yr Atodlen Gyntaf, Ffurf 9, Ffurf 10,). A dictionary gives *rhyw* as one of the meanings of 'any'; but 'any church' should be translated 'unrhyw eglwys'; 'rhyw eglwys' implies 'a certain church' or 'some church', according to the context.

It is difficult to determine what exactly is implied by the term 'school house' (III,26(a)). If it refers to the house pertaining to a school for the use of the schoolmaster, then *tŷ ysgol* would be the correct translation; *ysgoldy*, plural *ysgoldai*, in mid and north Wales is the term used for 'schoolroom', *ysgoldy capel* being in common use for 'chapel schoolroom or vestry'.

Another troublesome word is *negesau* for 'affairs', as translated from s.13(1) of the Welsh Church Act 1914 (the Church in Wales can create canon law for 'the property and affairs thereof '). It also appears in II,33(1), IV,22, and V,15. In medieval Welsh law *neges* was used for 'business, affairs, matters'. It was used occasionally in religious texts in the sixteenth and seventeenth centuries, the last recorded instance on the slips for *Geiriadur Prifysgol Cymru* comes from *Drych yr Amseroedd*, 1820. This meaning is now obsolete – *materion* would be a better choice for today.

Conclusion

The two essential requirements for translation are a good dictionary of the English language, and a thorough knowledge of Welsh grammar, syntax and usage. When a word is unfamiliar or difficult to translate, it is always advisable to consult an English dictionary rather than an English–Welsh lexicon; then, having ascertained its meaning in its present context, consider how best to convey that meaning in Welsh. In order to be accurate and easily understood it might be necessary to reconstruct the whole sentence, or even the paragraph. After all, for purposes of interpretation and construction, the intention of the legislator must be accurately expressed in the linguistic formulation of the canonical rule. Unless the average Welsh-speaker finds the Welsh version more easy to understand than the English version, the translation is a failure. Andrews and Henshaw state categorically that 'the principal aim of legal documents is to produce clarity of meaning rather than elegant prose'.[49]

49 J.A. Andrews and L.G. Henshaw, *Welsh Language*, 40.

Inelegant prose does little to help clarity of meaning. The real test, and one the applicability of which is particularly relevant in the bilingual Welsh system of canon law, is to be able to convey the exact meaning of a word, rule or idea in a simple, direct style, which makes for easy reading. By so doing, the cultural value expressed in the principle of equal validity, a fundamental of the bilingual Welsh canon law, is afforded its proper worth.

9

The Case for Constitutional Renewal in the Church in Wales

ANTONY T. LEWIS

That canon law has been of great benefit to the Church over the centuries is beyond doubt. In this essay I want to look at canon law as it is enshrined in the Constitution of the Church in Wales,[1] to look at the social and ecclesiastical context in which it was first written, at the present-day Church in Wales and the contemporary society in which it now exists. I want to ask whether the law that we have inherited and made our own provides the best framework within which to proclaim the Gospel in the modern world. There has been some talk in recent years of the Church in Wales being a *Celtic* Church, suggesting a nature somehow distinct from the *Anglo-Saxon* Church of England, and also a particular relationship with Churches in other Celtic nations. I want to examine the validity and implications of this idea, and to ask whether it affords an alternative model to that within which we presently organize ourselves and take decisions as a Church. Finally, I want to look more closely at some aspects of the Constitution and, as the new 'ecumenical instruments' take shape in Britain, to ask to what extent it is conducive to ecumenism becoming normative rather than exceptional, and to what extent it facilitates members of the Church in Wales working together with those of other Churches within and beyond the boundaries of Wales without perpetuating a sense of rivalry and vulnerability.

---

1 The Constitution of the Church in Wales is privately printed by the Representative Body of the Church in Wales, 39 Cathedral Road, Cardiff, CF1 9XF

The Evolution of Law in the Church

The earliest recorded occasion demanding authoritative decision-making within the Church appears to have been in AD 48, within twenty years of the crucifixion of Jesus. The issue concerned the circumcision of pagan converts and, according to Henry Chadwick, 'the cleavage between conservatives and universalists led to an acute and at times passionate controversy'.[2] The conservative camp was led by James, the brother of Jesus, and Peter, representing the Church in Jerusalem, while the universalists were represented by Paul and the Church at Antioch. It seems that Paul exercised his superior powers of advocacy and the universalists won the day.[3] Other disputes obviously arose as the influence of the Church spread, and Paul's Epistles record him as appealing to tradition and custom, where possible, as the basis of authority.[4] Then, at the end of the first century, as the ministry of apostles, prophets and teachers gave way to that of bishops, presbyters and deacons,[5] tradition and custom came under the protection of bishops. Gradually, the organization of the Church was strengthened by the institution of at first informal, and later formal, councils and synods, and collegiate authority to legislate began to be exercised.[6]

Thus the Church developed in the context of a body of laws; and over the centuries this legal framework has evolved and expanded, and has inevitably and rightly given rise to questions about the relationship between law and the Church.[7]

Here, we immediately find contradictions. Law has been defined as a process for the resolution of disputes as to a person's rights or duties;[8] whereas the Church is about building relationships, about preaching the Gospel and witnessing to the Gospel. Law is based upon the principle of fairness; but the teaching of Jesus, upon which the Church is founded, is based upon the principle of love, which

2 H. Chadwick, *The Early Church* (London, 1967), 19.
3 W.H.C. Frend, *The Rise of Christianity* (London, 1984), 92.
4 1 Cor. 11:16; 2 Thess. 2:15.
5 B. Ramsey, *Beginning to Read the Fathers* (London, 1986), 109.
6 W.H.C. Frend, *The Rise of Christianity*, 398.
7 Space does not permit a discussion of the history of ecclesiastical law. See, however, F.W. Maitland, *Roman Canon Law in the Church of England* (London, 1898); H.L. Clark, *Constitutional Church Government* (London, 1924); Moore and Briden, *Introduction*, 1–17; G.W.O Addleshaw, 'The study of canon law', in H.S. Box (ed.), *The Priest as Student* (London, 1936); and W.J. Hankey, 'Canon law', in S. Sykes and J. Booty (eds.), *The Study of Anglicanism* (London, 1988).
8 A. Watson, *The Nature of Law* (Edinburgh, 1977).

transcends law.[9] The aim of law is the inhibition of unregulated conduct;[10] but the aim of the Church is nothing less than the transformation of the whole world.[11] So, whereas both Church and law are certainly dynamic, in all other respects they are starkly contrasting and it is remarkable that they have existed together, albeit in an atmosphere of some mutual suspicion, for so long.

In her book *Law and Love*, Helen Oppenheimer suggests an analogy which offers a useful explanation of this coexistence, namely the relationship between the Church and the human family.[12] Just as the human family exists for the sake of relationships and is both a personal and a legal reality, so it is with the Church. Rules exist within a family, and their enforcement is sometimes necessary, for example, for the bringing up and protection of children.[13] Family rules are conducive to an ordered life within the family and are a good guide to conduct. And it is in the framework of these rules that loving family relationships, which entirely transcend the legal relationships, have a chance to develop and prosper. Just as with the family there is a certain continuity of relationship and affection through the generations, so it is with the Church. But within the context of this continuity, just as the family in each generation can choose the extent to which it will be governed by rules, and the nature of those rules, so the Church must, in each generation, address itself to the rules that govern it, asking whether they are appropriate to that age. As Helen Oppenheimer says, 'it is as easy for the church as for human parents to over-emphasize law, to treat grown-ups or adolescents as children, to become devoted to rules which were once simply meant to be useful, to confuse means with ends'.[14]

So what, then, was the social and ecclesiastical context at the time the Constitution of the Church in Wales was first written? Looking back at the conception, birth and early years of the independent Church in Wales (for an extensive discussion see chapters 2 and 3), which extended over a long period from the middle of the nineteenth

9   For example, Matt. 5:39–40; Mark 3:1–6; 7:1–23.
10   H.L.A. Hart, *The Concept of Law* (Oxford, 1961), 97–107.
11   Matt. 28:19.
12   H. Oppenheimer, *Law and Love* (London, 1962).
13   Both the family and the Church are, of course, also subject to external rules, such as in relation to marriage and divorce. As we have seen in chapter 3, C.A.H. Green was alert to this (*The Setting of the Constitution of the Church in Wales* (London, 1937), 296–318). Indeed, this fact is now commonly woven into definitions of ecclesiastical law: see, for example, Q. Edwards, 'The canon law of the Church of England', *Ecclesiastical Law Journal*, 1 (3) (1988), 18.
14   Oppenheimer, *Law and Love*, 59.

century through to the 1920s, two remarkable phenomena stand out. The first is the coincidence during much of the period of another issue of much greater political and nationalist importance, that of Irish Home Rule. The two issues, although greatly contrasting in effect, both involved the principle of devolution of power, and so came to be linked in the political mind. The Irish question tended to overshadow and to diminish the significance of Welsh disestablishment and, in the event, with the outbreak of the First World War, legislation was hurriedly passed by Parliament giving effect to both causes. Although Asquith, the Prime Minister, was understandably anxious to dispose of all business which might intrude upon the parliamentary time needed to consider issues relating to the war, the haste with which the Welsh Church Act 1914 eventually passed through all its stages in Parliament, after many years of campaigning and debate in the country, led to a sense of outrage and betrayal in the minds of supporters of the Welsh Church.[15]

The other phenomenon is the extraordinary fact that the Welsh bishops had to proceed with detailed plans for an independent Church while at least ambivalent towards and in some cases opposed to the principle of independence. The Bishops of St David's and St Asaph appear to have been ready to discuss the future of the new Province, while the Bishop of Bangor remained implacably opposed to it, refusing to cooperate. Eluned Owen vividly describes the tensions between the bishops and the strong desire and conviction of some of them, even as late as 1917, that the Act of 1914 would be repealed and the Church in Wales be restored to its former position as part of the Church of England.[16] Certainly, the whole situation engendered a painful atmosphere of mistrust, resentment and bewilderment. Indeed, it is hard to imagine an atmosphere less conducive to intelligent and creative planning for a new Anglican province.

However, to the great credit of the more pragmatic church leaders, particularly Bishops Owen of St David's and Edwards of St Asaph, plans were laid for a new province. At the outbreak of the war, Parliament had enacted a short Act postponing the date of disestablishment for twelve months or until the end of the war, and, ironically, the prolonging of the duration of the war gave time for extensive work on the Constitution of the new province.[17] In the

15 E.E. Owen, *The Later Life of Bishop Owen* (Llandysul, 1961), 220–40.
16 Ibid., 285–317.
17 Suspensory Act 1914, s.1(1).

event, once the war was over an additional Act was passed postponing further the date of disestablishment until 31 March 1920.[18] It is remarkable that in those critical early days, despite all the tensions and uncertainties, the Church in Wales was able to rely upon the active support of leading parliamentarians, industrialists and other leaders of society in Wales.[19] It was able to call upon the services of three distinguished judges, two from the High Court and one from the Court of Appeal, to undertake the work of drafting the new Constitution. It was able in 1919 to raise £680,000 (£13,872,000 in 1990 terms) in a public appeal to compensate for endowments lost by legislation.[20] All of this is evidence that in its moment of vulnerability, and despite continuing mistrust and hostility within its own ranks,[21] the Church was able to rely upon a very broad basis of support in Welsh society.

The leading part in drafting the Constitution was taken by Mr Justice Sankey. Provision for the Representative and Governing Bodies had been made in the 1914 Act,[22] but the detailed constitutional structures of the Church in Wales were drafted by Sankey on the basis of ideas submitted to him by Bishop Owen and Frank Morgan, a don at Keble College, Oxford, who subsequently became the first Secretary of the Representative Body.[23] Although he did not take part in the original drafting, the leading authority and commentator on the Constitution in its early form was C.A.H. Green. His book, *The Setting of the Constitution of the Church in Wales*, published in 1937, sets the Constitution in its historical and traditional context.[24] However, from the standpoint of the present-day Church, not to speak of that of the Gospel, this book makes extraordinary reading, with its thirty-six appendices of declarations, decrees, commissions, citations, regulations and forms, mostly written by Green himself. The book gives an impression of a monarchical and legalistic Church, fiercely anti-ecumenical and bereft of the qualities that we associate with the person of Jesus Christ. Perhaps in the early years of the Church in Wales, an emphasis on discipline was appropriate, but it is unfortunate that the influence of Green's book remains strong and that no modern author has attempted a

18 Welsh Church (Temporalities) Act 1919.
19 Owen, *Later Life*, 353.
20 Ibid., 432.
21 Ibid., 496.
22 Welsh Church Act 1914, s.13.
23 Owen, *Later Life*, 306.
24 For a discussion of C.A.H. Green's *Setting*, see above, chapter 3.

comprehensive examination of the Constitution in the context of the
present age. A gradual revision of the Constitution has certainly been
carried out over the years by the Governing Body, but its essential
structure and ethos remain as they were when it was first written, in
times which have long since passed away, and for a Church which
has changed dramatically.

In the 1950s and 1960s Western society entered a period of rapid
change in which much that had previously been accepted as conducive to good order was questioned and often rejected, especially by
the young. Lesslie Newbigin describes this as the death of a culture,
the final passing from the age of Enlightenment into the post-
Enlightenment era.[25] For many people, this has meant a detachment
from traditional institutions such as the Church, and a new determination to assume more control over their own destinies.[26] This goes
some way to explain the remarkable decline in the membership of
the main Churches, including the Church in Wales, in the years since
the Second World War.[27] One consequence of this withdrawal of
loyalty from the Church, and this is beginning to be felt quite
markedly in the Church in Wales, is the sharp reduction in the
number of lay people, particularly younger lay people, who are
prepared to commit themselves to serve within the complex structure
of committees which remain a central feature of most Church
institutions. Such committee structures are perceived as being man-
ifestations of the old order, and lacking in relevance to the new more
direct and personal approach to Christianity. No longer, as it did in
the 1930s, does the Church in Wales enjoy the service on its
Governing Body of 'at least six barons, ten baronets, five knights,
eleven titled ladies, three sons of peers, two generals, one vice-
admiral, one brigadier-general and sixteen colonels', as D. Parry-
Jones described in his book *A Welsh Country Parson*.[28] So much the
better, it may be claimed; such people did not represent the true
membership of the Church in Wales. Probably they did not, but the
withdrawal of commitment of many people whose loyal service the

25 L. Newbigin, *The Other Side of 1984: Questions for the Churches* (Geneva,
1983).
26 We can see evidence of the same forces of change at work in other areas,
notably in the scientific field and in health care. This is evidenced in numerous
works: see, for example, F. Capra, *The Turning Point: Science, Society and the
Rising Culture* (London, 1982).
27 The number of Easter Communicants in the Church in Wales fell from
197,032 in 1939 to 107,854 in 1989.
28 D. Parry-Jones, *A Welsh Country Parson* (London, 1975), 109.

Church in Wales could count upon for the smooth functioning of its complicated committee structure has taken its toll and left the Constitution looking somewhat vulnerable.

The Celtic Church

One interesting way of contemplating the Church in Wales is as a Celtic Church. This idea, which has been evolving over a number of years, offers the possibility of extracting the Church from the age of Enlightenment and investing it with traditions and structures associated with the early Celtic Fathers. It also frees the Church from its perceived association with the Church of England and offers the possibility of new links with Churches in other Celtic nations. So, what is distinctive about a Celtic model of the Church and what would be the practical implications of adopting it?

Historians depict the early Celtic Church as being based upon small, vulnerable, ascetic and sometimes itinerant communities, often focused on a particular holy man or 'saint', and dedicated to mission.[29] From the fourth century, some of the saints became bishops, and the fledgling communities became monasteries, which, by the end of the sixth century were often powerful and substantial institutions.[30] Not much is known of how decisions were taken in the early Celtic Church, but the famous story of the meeting between Augustine and Welsh bishops in 603 gives us a certain insight.

Bishop A.G. Edwards tells in his book *Landmarks in the History of the Welsh Church* how, before the bishops were due to meet with Augustine, they consulted a 'certain holy and discreet man' as to how they should respond to him.[31] They were advised that the test should be whether Augustine was 'meek and lowly of heart, and had taken upon him the yoke of Christ'. This was to be evidenced by whether or not Augustine rose from his seat to receive them on their arrival. The bishops accepted the validity of this test and Augustine received them sitting in his chair.

Another feature which seems to characterize the Celtic Church is

29 E.J. Newell, *A History of the Welsh Church* (London, 1895), 1–66; see further M.W. Barley and R.P.C. Hanson, *Christianity in Britain: 300–700* (Leicester, 1968) and N.K. Chadwick, *The Age of Saints in the Early Celtic Church* (Oxford, 1961).
30 R.W.D. Fenn, 'The age of the saints', in D. Walker (ed.), *A History of the Church in Wales* (Penarth, 1976, re–issued 1990), 1.
31 A.G. Edwards, *Landmarks in the History of the Welsh Church* (London, 1912), 42; see also Fenn, 'The age of the saints', 5.

its readiness to disregard the rules laid down in Rome. One of the questions that Augustine wanted to discuss with the Celtic bishops was the acceptance of the Roman method of calculating the date of Easter; but this was not finally accepted in Wales until 777.[32] And, what is more, the Roman canon law prohibiting the ordination of married priests was disregarded in Wales so widely that, according to Edwards, there was 'a considerable danger of the formation of an hereditary clerical caste'.[33] This scepticism for the rules appears to have been a feature of the Welsh Church until its independence was finally surrendered to the see of Canterbury in the twelfth century.[34]

With a history of independence over some nine centuries, and with seventy years now having elapsed since its links were severed with Canterbury, it is not surprising that a distinct Celtic identity is once again being canvassed for the Church in Wales. And this revival of interest has undoubtedly been sustained by the publication in recent years of a number of books of inspiring Celtic prose and poetry.[35]

The notion of a distinctive present-day Celtic Church in Wales is perceived as having four particular attractions. First, it is seen as offering an alternative to the Nonconformist Churches as a basis upon which a Welsh culture can be built. Secondly, it offers the prospect of a special relationship with the Church of Ireland, the Episcopal Church of Scotland and, perhaps, also Churches in Cornwall and Brittany. Thirdly, it diminishes the emphasis on links with the Church of England, which, even after seventy years, still result in the Church in Wales being known in parts of Welsh-speaking Wales as 'the State Church'. Fourthly, and paradoxically, it may reduce tensions over the Welsh language, since Welsh would be seen as one amongst several Celtic languages and not so isolated and vulnerable in opposition to English.

But whether or not these are seen as advantages (and certainly closer links with other Churches whether Celtic or not must be an advantage), the fact remains that in the Celtic model of the Church, we have a model that existed without a written constitution at all, and with only a primitive organizational basis. So while reverting

32 Ibid., 85.
33 Ibid.
34 Ibid., 86.
35 For example, see J.P. Mackey, *An Introduction to Celtic Christianity* (Edinburgh, 1989); C. Bamford and W.P. Marsh (eds.), *Celtic Christianity, Ecology and Holiness* (Edinburgh, 1986); A.M. Allchin and E. de Waal (eds.), *Threshold of Light: Prayers and Praises from the Celtic Tradition* (London, 1986); E. de Waal (ed.), *The Celtic Vision* (London, 1988); and A.M. Allchin, *Praise Above All: Discovering the Welsh Tradition* (Cardiff, 1991).

entirely to that model would be so radical a step as to be unacceptable to most people (and anyway a step unlikely to diminish denominational divisions), it is certainly not inappropriate, as we contemplate the future of the written constitution of the Church in Wales, to keep in mind some of the more attractive aspects of the Celtic Church, particularly the emphasis on local community and local leadership.

Constitutional Renewal

If the Church in Wales is not to abandon altogether its written constitution, then, what should be the way forward? The basis of the present document is now more than seventy years old, and it is rooted in an age from which society at large has moved on. Ironically, as in the early Celtic Church, there is evidence at different levels within the Church of the Constitution being disregarded,[36] which inevitably brings the whole idea of constitutional regulation into disrepute, and which, in turn, fuels further infringement. Piecemeal amendment, which has been the practice over the years since disestablishment, often gives rise to inconsistencies in style and inhibits the abandonment of outmoded language.[37] There must, therefore, be a strong case for a complete rewriting of the Constitution.

A new constitution should contain all that is essential for the effective mission and ministry of the Church in Wales as we prepare to enter the next millennium. It should contain a clear statement of its aim and objectives as a Church and be couched in language which is inclusive of both genders, is without legal jargon and may be readily understood by ordinary people. The adoption of a new constitution would help to ease the transition of the Church in Wales into the 'post-Enlightenment age'; it would offer the opportunity of a document which would speak to and be felt to be relevant by people at all levels within the Church, and in all parts of Wales. It should need, therefore, in Helen Oppenheimer's words, 'to be a framework out of which loving relationships can grow',[38] relationships not just within the Church in Wales, but between Churches and beyond Churches, in commitment to the principle of interrelatedness and

---

36 For example, in the regularity of meetings and functions of the Ruridecanal Conference (Constitution, V,13 and 15), in the display of the electoral roll at vestry meetings (VI,2(3)) and near the principal door of the parish church (VI,2(9)); in the regularity and functions of PCC meetings (VI,22(1) and (3)).
37 For example, sometimes the masculine includes the feminine (Constitution, I,4), sometimes the masculine and the feminine are both provided for (III,8).
38 Oppenheimer, *Law and Love*.

interdependence. Especially it should build on the achievements of the constitutions of the new ecumenical instruments,[39] and commit the Church in Wales to sharing its not inconsiderable resources not only with other less well-resourced Churches, but also with the poor.[40] But, above all, it would need to be an effective springboard for mission and evangelism.

The Constitution of the Church in Wales

Against the background of this prospect, in the remaining section of this essay, I want to examine the present Constitution of the Church in Wales, and identify several passages which, in my judgment, fall short of conforming to the vision I have outlined. The Constitution is divided into two volumes, the first containing provisions for the administration of the Church, and the second containing canons passed by the Governing Body and certain additional rules and regulations, including the extensive Rules for the Courts of the Church in Wales.

The first major omission from the present document is any reference to what the Church in Wales purports to be, what it is committed to, what its vision is or what its objects are. There is no mention of God, of worship or service, of evangelism or mission (except in two fleeting references amongst the many matters to be considered at the Annual Vestry Meeting of parishes and at meetings of the Parochial Church Council).[41] These matters go to the heart of the whole purpose of the Church and it is extraordinary that they receive no mention at all, or are dealt with in only a cursory way. Then the whole document is punctuated with language and with concepts which are anti-ecumenical, exclusive, discriminatory, arbitrary, obscure or simply outmoded.

For example, there is no provision for representatives from, or for sharing with persons from, other Churches in any of the assemblies of the Church in Wales,[42] and throughout the Constitution, it is

39   The Council of Churches for Britain and Ireland and Churches Together in Wales (usually known as CYTUN) were launched in 1990 as a new commitment to Christian unity.
40   The Church in Wales would be precluded (without further Act of Parliament) from giving away capital or income for purposes inconsistent with the terms of the Welsh Church Acts 1914 and 1919, or such other purposes for which money was given to the Representative Body. But this need not preclude a sharing of staff and plant, or the giving of money expressly raised for the purpose of such giving.
41   Constitution, VI,15(1)(a)(i) and VI,22(3)(a).
42   There is ecumenical representation on certain committees of the Board of Mission, but this is not directly provided for in the Constitution.

provided that membership of a 'religious body not in communion with the Church in Wales' is a disqualification.[43] The use of such language on so many occasions not only emphasizes the exclusiveness of the Church in Wales, but it is insensitive to our fellow Christians and must call into question for them the commitment of our Church to ecumenism.

The provision that, in the case of lay persons, the masculine includes the feminine,[44] although a common drafting technique amongst lawyers, must surely be out of place in the Constitution of a Church, and it is good to see in some later amendments that the notion has been abandoned.[45] But in the provision of the date for their retirement, there remains clear discrimination between male and female clerics.[46]

Many of the concepts that feature in the Constitution belong to a bygone age. The reference to 'precedence' amongst bishops is a case in point;[47] although, in some places, the more up-to-date phrase 'order of seniority' is employed.[48] Likewise, the phrases 'order of bishops', 'order of clergy' and 'order of laity' are not only outmoded, but also divisive, although widely used.[49] It would be quite possible to refer simply to 'bishops, clergy and laity'. And in a recent amendment, the divisive word 'classes' (of membership) has been introduced,[50] which, as is demonstrated elsewhere, is entirely unnecessary.[51] Other words which seem out of place in today's world are 'dignity' and 'preferment', both used to describe particular forms of employment within the Church.[52] The phrase 'religious body', as well as being objectionable on ecumenical grounds, is so imprecise as to be almost meaningless.[53]

Some of the procedures and practices laid down in the Constitution are out of place in a modern Church. Meetings of the Governing Body must be convened by the delivery of a 'mandate' to the secretaries, who then have to summon the Governing Body by

43 For example, Constitution, II,11; II,14; III,7; III,9; IV,13; VI,2; XI,5; XI,13; XI,19; XI,24.
44 Ibid., I,4.
45 Ibid., III,8; VII,27; XI,1(2)(b).
46 Ibid., XII,1.
47 Ibid., II,3; II,19; IV,4; IX,6; IX,27.
48 Ibid., VI,42; VIII,30.
49 Ibid., II,1f.; IV,32 and 33; VIII,18; IX,13.
50 Ibid., III,1.
51 Ibid., IV,5.
52 Ibid., II,10; III,6.
53 For the usage of this phrase, see note 41 above.

'citation'. And at the opening session of the meeting, the secretaries 'certify the due execution of the mandate'.[54] How much more appropriate to send a simple 'notice of meeting'. Then, there are some remarkable and sometimes apparently arbitrary powers of expulsion and exclusion bestowed by the Constitution. The Governing Body can remove any of its own number, or of the Representative Body, for any unspecified reason which it deems 'sufficient'.[55] And a Diocesan Conference can exclude the representatives of any 'district or area' who default over any 'engagement' or payment.[56] Such powers hardly seem consistent with the compassion and conciliation that may be expected from an assembly of Christians.

The supervisory powers that are laid down are also exceptionally strict. The Governing Body has power to 'control, alter, repeal or supersede any regulation made by a Diocesan Conference',[57] and a Diocesan Conference has the same powers over regulations made by a Ruridecanal Conference, a Vestry Meeting and a Parochial Church Council.[58] In both cases it is provided that the superior body shall be the final judge of what is necessary. Once again, how far this all seems from an approach of love and mutual understanding.

In the context of the parish, the same atmosphere prevails. Disputes relating to the electoral roll, to the parish inventory and as to who can or cannot attend a Vestry Meeting are all designed to be dealt with in a quasi-judicial manner, with no provision at all for conciliation or counselling.[59] And the application form for entry on the electoral roll is not only baffling to many people, but also strongly anti-ecumenical.[60] However, it is very much to be hoped that a new form proposed by the Board of Mission Sector for Ecumenical Affairs will shortly be accepted in its place.

The whole complex system of declarations (some of them solemn declarations) that office-holders must make affords an example of a further anomaly. Declarations are presumably designed to test the office-holder's qualifications and commitment for the job. As already observed, the reference in most of them to the phrase 'religious body not in communion with the Church in Wales' makes them inappro-

---

54 Constitution, II, 18,; II, 52.
55 Ibid., II,56; and III, 17.
56 Ibid., IV, 12.
57 Ibid., II, 57.
58 Ibid., IV, 44.
59 Ibid., VI, 4; VI, 8; VI, 21(10); VI, 14.
60 Ibid., VI, 2.

priate for use at a time when we are trying to break down barriers with other Churches. Furthermore, although it is intended that they shall be made before the office-holder acts in that capacity, there is evidence of disregard of this requirement, particularly in the case of membership of the Ruridecanal Conference, the Parochial Church Council and the office of churchwarden.[61] This perceived disregard brings the process of declarations into disrepute. Furthermore, why the declarations of the parochial church councillor and churchwarden should not be *solemn*, while those of every other office-holder should be *solemn* is unclear. In all the circumstances, the office-holder's preparedness to take up office is sufficient evidence of his or her commitment to the Church in Wales. And as to his or her qualifications for the office, if there is doubt, these can be checked by the chairperson or secretary of the appropriate body. This is how it would be done in any other context, and it is unfortunate that the Church in Wales continues to use an outdated method which in many cases is not taken seriously.

Perhaps the most spectacular anomaly in the Constitution is the existence of no less than five tiers of Church court. It must seem inconceivable to all but the most hardened ecclesiastical lawyer that a Church that has contracted to such a small size as has the Church in Wales, and that (notwithstanding any impression gained from the Constitution to the contrary) really is committed to loving one's neighbour and building up the Kingdom, should need the services of an Archdeacon's Court, a Diocesan Court, a Provincial Court, a Special Provincial Court and a Supreme Court.

The Constitution assigns to each court its jurisdiction over a great variety of disputes and grievances ranging from appeals by persons whose names have been expunged from a parish electoral roll, to complaints by the Bench of Bishops that the archbishop has become incapacitated.[62] In his life of Archbishop Green, A.J. Edwards describes the proceedings in the Provincial Court in a case brought by a Monmouthshire vicar, Edmund Macnaghten, against the Bishop of Monmouth in 1941.[63] This bizarre story graphically shows how

61 Ibid., V,12; VI,26; VI,18.
62 Ibid., VI,7; VIII,32. *Editor: for the judicial system in the Church of England, see* Moore and Briden, *Introduction*, 130–53, *now governed by the* Ecclesiastical Jurisdiction Measure (No.1) 1963 *and the* Ecclesiastical Jurisdiction (Amendment) Measure (No.2) 1974. (*For general government see the* Synodical Government Measure (No.2) 1969.)
63 A.J. Edwards, *Archbishop Green: His Life and Opinions* (Llandysul, 1986).

a court presided over by four judges, including a Lord Justice of
Appeal, is totally inappropriate to deal with a dispute which essentially concerned the refusal of an eccentric vicar to attend his
archdeacon's visitation. It is hardly surprising that, according to
Arthur Edwards, the final judgment (which ran to eleven pages)
'brought credit to no-one', and 'illustrates the weakness of legalism
and litigation' in resolving Church disputes. How much better to deal
with such disputes and misunderstandings as inevitably arise with a
provision for counselling and reconciliation.

Other miscellaneous features of the Constitution which seem
anomalous in the modern age include the widespread provision of
the chairperson's casting vote at meetings,[64] the use (albeit occasional) of the Latin language and obsolete English words,[65] a ban on
investment in Ireland but not in South Africa,[66] and the continuance
of provision for private patronage to 'a newly-created cure'.[67] Most
people believe that private patronage was abolished in Wales at the
time of disestablishment.

A new Constitution, then, would need to resolve these anomalies.
It would need to give recognition to the fact that Wales, albeit a small
nation, is a very diverse nation. This diversity should be reflected in
the provisions of different patterns of ministry, particularly including
non-parochial ministry.[68] The proven impossibility of affording a
single model of parish administration that is equally appropriate to
the busy urban parish and to the remote rural parish, strongly
suggests the wisdom of consigning much of the chapter on parochial
administration to a code of practice which would contain more
flexible provisions to suit the variety of circumstances in parish life
in Wales.[69] Likewise, the detailed parsonage regulations seem out of
place in the main body of the Constitution and would be better
reproduced elsewhere.

---

[64] This is afforded to rural deans at Ruridecanal Conferences (Constitution,
V,3), to incumbents at Vestry Meetings (VI,12(5)), to bishops at Diocesan
Conferences (IV,3) and Patronage Boards (VII,14), and to chairpersons of
Diocesan Parsonage Boards (X,4), but expressly denied to the president of the
Electoral College (VIII,19 and IX,13).

[65] For Latin see ibid., IV,40 and X,8; for English see II,71 and 78 (muniment
room).

[66] Ibid, III,23(1)(d).

[67] Ibid., VII,8.

[68] A small recognition of the existence of 'extra-parochial' ministry already
exists: ibid., VII,76.

[69] For parochial administration see ibid., VI.

Conclusion

A constitution is rather like a suit of clothes.[70] In the case of the Church in Wales, the clothes give an impression of having been handed down from an earlier generation, from a more prosperous but now bygone age. Obviously intended for a body of greater stature, the clothes are now somewhat faded and worn out. Although in places patched up with new cloth, the result is not always a good match.[71] The Church moves awkwardly in these ill-fitting clothes. What is needed is an entirely new suit, made to measure by a competent modern tailor; a suit that fits perfectly and is comfortable, in which the Church can move with freedom as it undertakes its mission; a suit which does not clash with the clothes worn by other Churches, one in which the Church can feel at ease and relaxed in their company. For although now a small Church in comparison with that which was disestablished in 1920, the Church in Wales is in good heart, and, for the most part, of willing spirit. Constitutional renewal, then, should be made a priority if the Church in Wales is to be ready for the challenges of the twenty-first century.

70 W. Bagehot, *The English Constitution* (1867), with Introduction by R.H.S. Crossman (Glasgow, 1963), 59.
71 Matt. 9:16; Mark 2:21; Luke 5:36.

10

Some Reflections on Welsh Canon Law

RIGHT REVEREND R.T. DAVIES, BISHOP OF LLANDAFF

To many within the Church in Wales the Constitution is a necessary 'evil'. When amendments are required or additions made, such people at the Governing Body tend to withdraw mentally, thinking it is for the legal experts to sort things out. The Constitution for such people represents what is laborious in the running of the Church and, also, a likely stumbling-block when change is deemed desirable. For that kind of mentality the cold hand of canon law is what will quench the warmth and spontaneity of zeal and renewal.

What has just been written is a parody but nevertheless it is close enough to the truth to explain the reluctance to 'tamper' with the Constitution. Making things possible without resort to bill procedure is preferred to the legislative grind. Jeffrey Gainer's essay poses a challenge to this mentality. He argues that the bishop's *jus liturgicum* is adversely affected both by the vagueness as to pre-1920 canon law and its application in the Church in Wales and by the 'evasiveness', as he perceives it, in the issuing of Bishops' Statements on Intercommunion, whereas he insists that bill procedure should have been pursued because matters of faith and order are involved. Whether he finds agreement or not in any particular case it must be admitted that 'the failure of the Church in Wales to revise its canons and clarify the precise nature and scope of the bishop's *jus liturgicum*' leads to confusion not only for the bishop and his understanding of his rights in liturgical worship but also for the 'difficult problem' of the status of the canon law of the Church in Wales, which is examined by David Lambert and Norman Doe.

Whatever stance the authors in this book take, as each tackles a particular theme, there is no one who is dismissive of canon law. These authors take canon law seriously because they take the Church seriously. They all agree on the positive nature of the Church's law and the need for it. Disagreement emerges over canon law as it now pertains in the Church in Wales supremely in its Constitution.

The 'tolerant' (if they can be described as such) do not see a great deal wrong with the Constitution, claiming for it theological as well as legal integrity. Its concern for 'order' is for positive reasons. Norman Doe argues that canon law is facilitative, not fundamentally coercive and duty-imposing. Its intention is not to limit the freedom of the Church of Christ. The Church is the Body of Christ needing encouragement and restriction if all its members are to fit in and grow together.

To turn to the 'less tolerant', it has already been noted that they agree with the need for law but are finding that law, as at present expressed, unduly restrictive with the emphasis on coercion. The vagueness with regard to English ecclesiastical law prior to disestablishment has already been referred to with the implications for status and applicability. The one whose tolerance is strained to the limit is Antony Lewis who pleads for the complete rewriting of the Constitution so as to be expressive of the Church's mission today. It is because of what he believes the Church is and ought to be that he wants its canon law to facilitate the expression of its faith and life in a way that will accord with the reality of its calling to be the People of God. For that reason the 'damper' image must go, giving way to a Constitution that will enable the Church to move with freedom and feel relaxed in the company of other Churches. He is radical in his ecumenical approach, but not only in that. The ecumenism forcefully argued for stands in stark contrast with the Constitution when written and with Archbishop Green's *Setting of the Constitution*, published in 1937. When surrounded by those who questioned its claims and strove successfully for its disestablishment and disendowment, the Church in Wales had to be fiercely assertive about the integrity of its own position – and that in days when ecumenism was nothing like what it is today. To be 'fiercely anti-ecumenical' in 1920, or indeed 1940, would have a different meaning from the sort of situation to which those words would apply in 1991.

Antony Lewis is also radical in his approach to the 'monarchical' and 'legalistic' in the Constitution and in Green, and indeed must be if he is to argue for an ecumenical canon law. The monarchical model, constitutionally limited, as Arthur Edwards recalls, is what was ensured in the independent province. Bishops seem to be the problem, not least in dealings with Churches who do not have them. What the Constitution of the Church in Wales does, and what the re-written Constitution (if it comes to be) must also do, is to ensure that the role of the bishops as guardians of the faith is preserved. Ecumenical conversations come to grief on this very point. Too much is conceded, or not enough, depending on the tradition of the ecumenical partner. The prerogative of the bishops to initiate legislation affecting faith and order, and their ability to exercise a veto when the voting is by houses, secures for them a position of great strength, albeit within constitutional limitations. Clerics and laity have an important and necessary role in the government of the Church in Wales, but not at the expense of the episcopal principle. Not to preserve the 'substance' in the ecumenical quest would be to fall foul of faith and order. The challenge of an ecumenical canon law is not only radical but chastening as the incidental is sifted from what is basic.

Antony Lewis's complaint against the 'legalistic' could also have significant consequences. By legalistic he is taken to mean the legal language in which the Constitution is couched, which makes it forbidding in tone and rarefied in expression, hence his plea that a completely rewritten Constitution should have no 'legal jargon', so that it can be understood by ordinary people. No longer would it be regarded as forbidden territory except for experts if, along with its clarity of expression, it contained a clear statement of aims and objectives. A translator is a good judge of success in this regard. Enid Roberts, who writes about the translator's experience with the present Constitution, would be a good catalyst in that she knows from experience what it is like to seek to express accurately the intention of the legislator and convey his exact meaning in a simple and direct style. Antony Lewis, the most critical of the essayists, is also the one who is boldest in his justification for constitutional renewal. It should be a priority, says he, if the Church in Wales is to be ready to face the challenges of the twenty-first century.

A model for a (rewritten and ecumenical) canon law is to hand, Antony Lewis suggests, in the new Ecumenical Instruments. The ecumenical arrangements in Britain and Ireland are very new indeed and, consequently, untried. Furthermore ecumenical bodies are not Churches and they do not legislate for the Churches that belong to them. The Church in Wales whilst making provision for ecumenical growth cannot in the meantime forgo its responsibility to govern itself without prejudice to its conviction about itself within the One Holy Catholic and Apostolic Church. As with the episcopate, the tension between opening up to other Churches and remaining faithful to what is essential in one's own is an exciting aspect (if frightening for timid souls) of the radicalism of his approach.

Roman Catholic canon law, revised in 1983, receives more than one complimentary mention in the course of these essays. John Griffiths, for example, with the mentally handicapped in mind, states that it 'provides as contemporary and comprehensive an instrument as one might hope to find' with regard to their needs. A far cry from the image of coercion and the nuts and bolts of Church government from the Parochial Church Council upwards (necessary as these are). A salutary reminder also that a Church that has not become radical in its ecclesiology is not thereby reactionary when it comes to meeting the needs and challenges of pastoral and sacramental situations today. The Church in Wales can look to Rome with benefit if and when it rewrites its Constitution. Neither should it forget the Church of England, drawing already as it does on its experience and legislative provision for such developments as local ecumenical projects. David Lambert and Norman Doe's claim that a formal and comprehensive publication of predisestablishment canon law is needed will dispel any idea that the task is quickly if thoroughly done. Will it be done? The publication of these essays makes it more likely that the answer will be in the affirmative.

Subscribers

The following have associated themselves with the publication of this volume through subscription:

R. H. Arden, Liverpool
Kenneth J. Auty, Abergavenny
J. H. Baker, St Catharine's College, Cambridge
Margaret R. Barlow, Sheffield
Brian Barnes, Llandaff
Stuart Batcup, (Morgan Bruce), Swansea
Revd D. G. Belcher, Margam
Revd and Mrs Paul J. Bennett, Rhondda
Revd R. A. Bird, Llanymynech
Canon P. H. Boulton, Southwell
The Very Revd Lawrence Bowen, Fishguard
Revd and Mrs A. R. Boyd-Williams, Parish of Treharris
    with Bedlinog
The Rt. Revd D. M. Bridges, Brecon
Malcolm Brothers, Newport
Revd and Mrs R. L. Brown, Tongwynlais
Canon T. Kenneth Brunsdon, Swansea
Chancellor the Revd R. D. H. Bursell QC, Winscombe, Avon
Revd George R. Bush, St John's College, Cambridge
Canon J. C. Buttimore, Cardiff
G. Campbell, London
D. N. Cheetham, St Albans
Revd Malcolm L. Chiplin, Pontypridd
Revd H. A. Chiplin, Ysbyty Cynfyn, Dyfed
O. W. H. Clark, Hampton
Revd Arthur Clark, Haverfordwest
T. S. H. Collins, Nefyn, Gwynedd
Mr and Mrs Raymond Cory, Llanblethian, Cowbridge
Canon Allan Craven, Haverfordwest

Revd P. A. Crockett, Penarth
Canon John Dale, Hallow, Worcester
Parch. F. J. Saunders Davies, Eglwys Dewi Sant, Caerdydd
Fr. Roy Gabe Davies, Lakenheath
The Very Revd A. R. Davies, Dean of Llandaff
Revd Robert Donkin, Aberaman
Revd David J. Dredge, Llanllechid, Bangor
Revd Martin R. Dudley, Owlsmoor, Berkshire
Revd J. S. Dunn, British Steel PLC, Port Talbot
C. Edwards, Cwmbrân
Canon E. Ll. Edwards, New Quay, Dyfed
The Very Revd Erwyd Edwards, Bangor
The Venerable Geoffrey B. Evans, Archdeacon of the Aegean
    and the Danube
Canon T. R. Evans, Lampeter
Canon J. Wyn Evans FSA, Trinity College Carmarthen
Canon Conrad Evans, Carmarthen
Morton Evans, Denbigh
Roger Evans, London
Revd D. R. Felix, Runcorn
Gareth Foster, Llandaff
Anne Fothergill, St Mary's Church, Dolgellau
His Honour Judge Norman Francis, Cardiff
Revd Dr Leslie J. Francis, Trinity College, Carmarthen
Sir William Gladstone Bt., Hawarden
Revd Michael Gollop, Cardiff
Revd Joseph W. Griffin, Llanrhidian, Gower
Revd Brian Vann Griffith, Aberystwyth
His Honour Bruce Griffiths QC, Cardiff
Revd David Griffiths, Gresford, Wrexham
The Venerable Dr David N. Griffiths, Lincoln
K. F. W. Gumbley, Isle of Man
Revd Richard Hanford, Ewell, Surrey
John M. Hanks, Pusey House, Oxford
Brian Hanson, Registrar and Legal Adviser to the General Synod
    of the Church of England
Revd R. Harper, Haverfordwest
Canon and Mrs Leslie O. Harris, Kessingland, Suffolk
Revd Jonathan Redvers Harris, London
Richard Hawkins, Twickenham
N. Mark Hill, Temple, London

Canon Michael Hodge, Bidborough, Kent
Brian Hodges, Gilfach Goch
David J. Hooson, St Asaph
John Vivian Hughes, Port Talbot
Revd J. T. Hughes, Wrexham
Canon John Humphreys OBE, Estoril, Portugal
Revd Godfrey W. James, Kenfig Hill
Canon D. T. I. Jenkins, Carlisle
Revd H. M. Jenkins, Ogmore Vale
William H. John, Cardiff
M. A. H. Johns, Malpas, Newport
Revd Bernard T. Johns, Wenvoe, Cardiff
M. S. Johnson, Hawkshaw, Bury
Jasper Salisbury Jones, Castletown, Isle of Man
Canon William Jones, Llanystumdwy
Canon Bryan M. Jones, Brecon
Canon and Mrs Brian Howell Jones, Swansea
Gareth Jones, Colwinston
The Most Revd Alwyn Rice Jones, St Asaph
Revd Roger Jones, Wiston, Haverfordwest
Revd Charles Eurwyn Jones, Nottingham
Revd Andrew Collins Jones, Llangefni
Revd T. J. Rhidian Jones, Llanpumsaint
The Revd Prebendary T. Peter Jones, Stratford-upon-Avon
The Venerable T. Hughie Jones, Archdeacon of Loughborough
Revd Graeme Knowles, Portsmouth
D. G. Lambert, Llandaff
Dalby Landen, Reading
David S. Lee, Nelson, Mid Glamorgan
David Leonard, London
Canon Don and Revd Ann Lewis, Swansea Saint Mary
The Very Revd Bertie Lewis, Dean of St Davids
Revd Stewart Lisk, Cardiff
Revd Dr Graham D. Loveluck, Marianglas, Gwynedd
Revd Michael J. F. Mannall, Kingston upon Thames
Revd J. W. Masding, Hamstead, Birmingham
Fr. Philip Masson, Porthcawl
Alan K. McAllester, Chester
James F. W. McConnell, Monmouth
The Rt. Revd J. C. Mears, Bangor
Canon S. H. Mogford, Cardiff

Revd Enid R. Morgan, Llanafan, Aberystwyth
Revd Simon Morgan, Dowlais, Merthyr Tydfil
The Venerable Dr Barry Morgan, Cricieth
Revd David J. Mortimore, Pembroke
Revd Frederick Mudge, Penarth
Charles Mynors, London
Sir John Owen, Idlicote, Warwickshire
Revd W. D. Parry, Aberystwyth
T. G. Penny, Bevan Ashford, Cardiff and Tiverton
D. A. Phillips, Chester
Graham Phillips, Diocese of Winchester
M. J. S. Preece, Bangor
Revd and Mrs M. R. Preece, Penarth
Canon D. T. W. Price, Lampeter
Canon W. Kenneth Price, Neath
Canon Norman H. Price, Monmouth
Philip Price QC, Cardiff
The Venerable T. W. Pritchard, Archdeacon of Montgomery
Thomas J. Prichard, Llangwnnadl, Llŷn
Canon D. G. Prosser, Hamburg
Revd A. Pryse-Hawkins, St Benet, London
David Harding Rees, Felinfoel
The Right Revd J. Ivor Rees, Abergwili
The Venerable J. Wynford Rees, Llanyre
B. L. V. Richards, Carmarthen
Revd G. W. Rimell, Bridgend
Canon Arthur C. Roberts, Shotton, Clwyd
E. ap Nefydd Roberts, United Theological College, Aberystwyth
Elwyn Roberts, Bangor
Enid Roberts, Bangor
The Right Revd Eric Roberts, Penarth
Parch. Tegid Roberts, Llanrug, Caernarfon
Revd Christopher C. Robins, Kingsbridge, Devon
John Rogers QC, Rhuthun
Canon J. H. L. and Mrs Rowlands, Llandaff
Revd Frank S. Saint Amour III, Dunkirk, New York
Pastor Raymund Schwingel, Walkenried, Harz, Germany
Revd D. J. Sherwood, Hullbridge, Essex
Canon Michael Short, Caerphilly
Ingrid Slaughter, London
The Venerable Donald Smith, Stretton-on-Fosse, Gloucestershire

Revd S. J. Stephens, Caldicot
Nicholas D. W. Thomas, Bebington, Wirral
P. Ungoed Thomas, Llanelli
Revd David Thomas, Newton, Swansea
Revd Dr Patrick Thomas, Brechfa
The Venerable C. E. Thomas, Archdeacon of Wells
Vernon Thomas, Leeds
Dewi W. Tomos, Rhydaman
Revd Stephen Trott, Boughton, Northampton
Revd A. J. Turner, Bridgend
Revd A. Tweed, Llandrindod
The Venerable Keith Tyte, Archdeacon of Monmouth
Hans Van de Wouw, University of Leyden
Revd Michael Vasey, Durham
Canon G. J. Vaughan-Jones, Mallwyd, Powys
Revd G. J. Waggett, Port Talbot
Alan Walker, Polytechnic of Central London
Michael and Gwyneth Watkins, Capel Bangor
Revd Wilfred R. J. Watts, Cheltenham
Derek M. Wellman, Lincoln
Revd C. P. Wells CF, Bagshot, Surrey
William Todd West, Bridlington
Revd and Mrs C. J. Wilcox, Rectoral Benefice of Llanmartin
Revd D. R. Wilkinson, Swansea
Canon David Williams, Pendoylan
Canon G. K. Williams, Aberystwyth
Canon Robert Williams, Aberdaron
Cyril G. Williams, Coleg Prifysgol Dewi Sant, Llanbedr Pont
    Steffan
N. C. Williams, Newport
Revd Gwilym E. Williams, Llanblethian, Cowbridge
Revd J. Glyn Williams, Bridgend
Revd M. I. Williams, Cardiff
David Willink, Magdalene College, Cambridge
Messrs Winckworth & Pemberton, Oxford
Revd David Yeoman, Mountain Ash
Revd Roger Young, Peterston-super-Ely

St Deiniol's Library, Hawarden
Ecclesiastical Law Society
The Librarian, St John's College, Durham
Lincoln Theological College
The Dean and Chapter of Llandaff Cathedral
The Library, St Michael's Theological College, Llandaff
Trinity College, Carmarthen
The Library, United Theological College, Aberystwyth

Index

Aaron, R. I., 164
Albany, William, 8, 9
Alesandro, John, 72, 78, 84
Anglican Communion, 1, 3, 27, 39, 43,
    45, 55, 60, 111 n.1, 119
Apostles, the, 45, 51, 80, 94, 176
Aquinas, Thomas (1225?–1274), 91, 93
    n.24
archdeacons, *see also* Church in Wales,
    Church of England, 10, 11, 17, 32,
    40, 153
Arches, Court of, 9, 10
Asquith, H. (Prime Minister), 178
Augustine of Canterbury, St, 181–2
Augustine of Hippo, St (354–430), 93

Bagshaw, John, 8, 9
Bankes, John, Mr Justice (later Lord
    Justice), 64, 160
Baptism, *see also* Church in Wales *and*
    Roman Catholic Church, 35, 36, 93,
    101, 102f., 107
Bevan, E.L. (Bishop of Swansea and
    Brecon), 160–1
bishops, *see also* Church in Wales *and*
    Roman Catholic Church, 50–2, 94,
    103
    dispensation, power of, 126–8
    jus liturgicum, see Jus liturgicum
    marriage and, 36 n.13
    presentation and, 8–24
Bowles, Thomas, 9–12
Box, H., 77f.
Brooke, Z.N., 53f., 56
Bruce, H.A., 15
Burgess, T. (Bishop of St David's,
    1804–25), 12
burial, 36f., 41, 124, 141 n.29

Campbell (Bishop of Bangor, 1859–90),
    23
canon law,
    coercive, 66, 69f., 192

concept of family and, 177
convention, as, 133f.
custom and, *see* custom
discipline and, 32, 34, 59f., 78–9
duty-imposing, 70f.
ecclesiastical law and, 4, 30–1, 44,
    177 n.13
ecclesiology and, 1–5, 30–1, 101, 120,
    177
enforcement, 134f., 183 n.36
evolution of, 176–81
facilitative nature, 69–88, 192
forgiveness and, 69–70, 83–8
justification, need for, 1–5, 56–7, 69f.
love and, 176–7, 183
medieval, 47, 52–5, 57, 115, 151–3
mental handicap and, 2, 89f., 99–109
pastoral need, and, 2, 7–24, 72
sanctions, 69–88
responsibilities, 70f., 101
scriptural basis, 69 n.1, 77f.
theology and, 2f., 45–6, 192
Welsh language and, 7–24, 119 n.23,
    151–73
Canterbury, Archbishop of, 8, 14, 17f.,
    21, 35, 39, 114 n.10, 121 n.29, 124,
    157
Canterbury, Province of, 10, 25, 53, 61,
    117, 152, 153, 154
cathedrals, 19f., 32, 38, 39, 40, 49, 59,
    67
Celtic Church, 175, 181–3
Chadwick, Henry, 176
Christ, 3, 45, 46, 51, 59–60, 70 n.2, 73 n.12,
    77–8, 80f., 87, 92, 98, 101, 102f., 107,
    113, 132, 170, 176, 179, 181, 192
Church courts, *see* Church in Wales,
    Church of England *and* Roman
    Catholic Church
Church in Wales, 1, 2, 5
    archbishop, 35 n.11, 40, 41, 72, 76, 123
    archdeacons, 32, 40, 42, 134–5, 153, 187
    Baptism, 93 n.27, *see also* Baptism